# She Comes to Take Her Rights

# She Comes to Take Her Rights

## Indian Women, Property, and Propriety

**Srimati Basu**

*State University of New York Press*

Production by Ruth Fisher
Marketing by Nancy Farrell

Published by
State University of New York Press, Albany

For information, address the State University of New York Press,
State University Plaza, Albany, NY 12246

**Library of Congress Cataloging-in-Publication Data**

Basu, Srimati.
    She comes to take her rights : Indian women, property, and
propriety / Srimati Basu.
        p.   cm.
    Includes bibliographical references and index.
    ISBN 0-7914-4095-8 (hardcover : alk. paper). — ISBN 0-7914-4096-6
(pbk. : alk. paper)
        1. Women's rights—India.   2. Women—Legal status, laws, etc.
(Hindu law)   3. Sex role—India.   4. Property (Hindu law)   5. Women—
India—Social conditions.   6. Women—India—Economic conditions.
I. Title.
HQ1236.5.I4B375   1999
305.42′0954—dc21                                                    98-25982
                                                                              CIP

10  9  8  7  6  5  4  3  2  1

# Contents

# List of Illustrations

# List of Tables

# Acknowledgments

Some of the most valuable parts of the process of research and writing that have gone into the making of this book have been making friends in various parts of the world, engaging in wonderful conversations and arguments, and recognizing the fundamentally collaborative nature of all research projects. In the following list of significant players, I have not even begun to account for an immensely long list of organizations, friends, and even many strangers, without whose generous help and spontaneous warmth this project could not have taken off.

I am deeply indebted to the residents of the New Delhi neighborhoods where I sought interviews, for all that they taught me with such affection, and the patience they showed with my endless questions, strange forms, and malfunctioning tape recorder. Jaya Shrivastava, Purabi Roychowdhury, Shashi Gupta, Shashi Chauhan, Urmil Sharma, Kanta Devi, Gita Devi, Rimmy Taneja, Angana Chatterji, Meenakshi Ganguly, and Anuradha Paul were invaluably helpful with information and contacts in Delhi; I treasure their love and friendship. Thanks also to the staff at the libraries of the Indian Law Institute and the Center for Women's Development Studies for their help.

I am very grateful to Marlene Longenecker and Judith Mayne, and especially to Claire Robertson, for the time and effort they have put into reading drafts, for the detailed comments and the reenvisioning they suggested, for putting research in its political context, and most of all, for being unfailing sources of encouragement and support. Thanks to the Ford Foundation for the Woodrow Wilson Research Grant in Women's Studies, and to Ohio State University for the Presidential Fellowship which partially funded my research. Thanks also to The Women's Studies Program at Southern Illinois University for housing me as Visiting Scholar during the writing of the book. A very special thank you to Deb Morrow, without whose expertise formatting would have been a nightmarish fishing expedition.

A big thank you to all those who have generously read and commented on drafts, or offered professional advice: Mrinalini Sinha, Clem Hawes, Annelies Moors, Rajeswari Sunder Rajan, Ravina Aggarwal, Kathy Ward, Jane Adams, Tom Alexander, Gloria Raheja, and especially Geraldine Forbes. I am very grateful to Zina Lawrence, Ruth Fisher, and the editorial staff at the State University of New York Press for their help with details, for their flexibility and good humor. Thanks to Jan Best and Nanny de Vries at *Thamyris* for permission to reprint parts of my article appearing in volume 4.1 of the journal.

Most of all, I cannot thank enough my family and friends who have kept me going over the years of research and writing, and have enthusiastically joined in everything from scouting interview locales and scrutinizing statistics to extensive help with making research contacts. In particular, I would like to thank Dipali, Biren, and Abhijit De and Aditi Sengupta De for sharing their Delhi home with me with such love. Anubha Chatterji and Ashok Ravat, thanks for looking out for people and issues that interest me and unfailingly answering the weirdest requests for information. Thank you to Audrey Light, Rini Das, and Lisa Maatz for all the help in Columbus, from mathematical puzzles to bureaucratic problems and of course, lots of fun. My parents, Sujata and Tapas Basu, have also been drawn into these nebulous searches for people and places and sources of information, but have been most important for having inspired habits of intellectual inquiry and questioning received ideologies, and as sources of love and encouragement. With Tiku Ravat, who has been called upon to do everything from managing my life in the United States while I was doing fieldwork, editing proposals, pondering the design of statistical instruments for qualitative data, computer troubleshooting, and especially questioning and working through all sorts of half-formed and convoluted thoughts with me, and who claims to have broken a tooth or two in brave attempts to persist with deciphering the manuscript as a scientist, I can only begin to express my love and thanks by sharing this book.

# 1

## Women, Law, and Property in India

O
ne mild autumn day in December 1991, my routine door-to-door visits in a middle-class neighborhood in South Delhi, collecting demographic data from households to construct a neighborhood census, were interrupted by a furtive moment of conspiracy. Seeing me on the path between buildings, the retired army colonel opened the door of his apartment slightly and gestured to me secretively to come in; he and his wife wanted to consult me about something that had been worrying them since their youngest son's death several months ago. How, they wanted to know, could they make sure that their widowed daughter-in-law (and her children) got access to a substantial portion of their cash and land assets? Of course they could make wills to that effect, and also make their intentions verbally clear, but how could they ensure that their eldest son would not coerce her into relinquishing her portion by convincing her that the "family" would prefer her to rely on her wage income?

Nearly a year later, Vidhu, a community worker in a squatter colony in New Delhi, posed a different version of the dilemma to me, bringing up her own brothers' attitudes. She had been divorced for a few years, and was now living with her parents and her two brothers and their families; her sisters had married into households that were financially comfortable. Vidhu was the only daughter who insisted that she would claim her inheritance share of her parents' house, believing that this was particularly important to her because she had no marital or affinal property to rely on. Even though she tried to balance this claim by undertaking the responsibilities allegedly accompanying property ownership, such as contributing regularly to family expenses including weddings (despite

1

her relatively low income), her brothers were furious with her because of her direct and open intentions of claiming property. Aware of her intention to adopt a child, they had lately been suggesting that she adopt one of their children, and immediately draw up a legal document transferring her inheritance to the adopted child. What security, she worried, could this arrangement possibly ensure her? What strategies would be effective for claiming the legal share she needed without forfeiting all support from her brothers?

These moments of anxiety consistently interrupted my planned schedule for conducting interviews about property with women in certain Delhi neighborhoods. Knowing me to be someone who had an interest in women and property, people sought me out with their numerous worries related to property distribution, and particularly women's troubled status as putative property owners. They expressed concern over a range of issues: a middle-class woman who had just retired from her job wanted to know how she could keep her perpetually unemployed and gambling-prone husband from getting his hands on her savings; a wealthy man worried about legal recourse against his nephew who had formally ousted him and his wife from the family home in order to build a high-rise apartment in its place; a new mother in the squatter colony who had been widowed while pregnant sought advice about reckoning with her in-laws, who were pressuring her to forfeit the government job that she would get in lieu of her husband's job in favor of her husband's brother. These situations revealed property issues as a prime site of cultural discord, a space where the conflict between "modern" legal guidelines and customary notions of family and entitlement was laid bare. This highly unstable space of property relations in contemporary India is the subject of this book.

This book explores women's feelings about and actions with respect to family property through the voices of particular Indian women: they are women I talked with in New Delhi between October 1991 and February 1993, a sample consisting of equal numbers of middle-class and poor women of various ages and ethnicities, residents of New Delhi both rural and urban in upbringing. They appear in the context of talking about the most mundane and yet fundamental concerns of their lives: the business of weddings, family relationships, the distribution of property and access to wealth, daily problems and dreamed-of solutions. The focus of these interview-conversations is the issue of property, the distribution of family assets and related gender-specific roles and class-differentiated interests. Both the legal and sociocultural operations of property are examined, with analysis of recent legal cases supplementing information gleaned from the interviews.

In post-Independence India, property issues—and particularly the gendered division of property—have centrally marked the conflict between the perpetuation of older systems of privilege and the establishment of a "modern" new nation founded on principles of individual rights and liberties. At the heart of this conflict is the Hindu Code Bill, visualized by Law Minister Ambedkar and Prime Minister Nehru as the flagship of modernization and a radical revision of Hindu law. Although this optimistic code met with strong opposition from legislators and was finally incorporated in a much-tempered form as a set of four acts, it is widely regarded as dramatic benchmark legislation giving Hindu women equitable if not superior entitlements as legal subjects.

Equity by gender in Hindu property law lies within a very narrow compass. Under the Hindu Succession Act (1956), Hindu women theoretically acquired equal rights to the "self-acquired" property of their parents in cases of intestate succession only; that is, they could be disinherited through wills, and got at best minimal portions and usually nothing of ancestral family land under Mitakshara succession. In addition, the act gave Hindu widows absolute (as opposed to usufructuary) rights over affinal property they had received in lieu of maintenance—that is, the power to sell or gift property—whereas family property remained largely inalienable for male heirs. These narrow provisions continue to be hailed by judges and legislators as triumphs of postcolonial jurisprudence, and tokens of the superiority of "reformed" Hindu law over the personal laws of other religious communities. They were perceived as radical experiments at the time they were drafted, and brought widespread predictions of doom from legislators: Pandit Thakur Das contended that "the purity of family life, the great ideal of chastity and the great ideal of Indian womanhood" were at stake in this example of "equality run mad" (Kapur and Cossman 1996, 56), and M. A. Ayyangar responded to the provision of women having rights to family property with the fervent prayer, "May God save us from . . . having an army of unmarried women" (Agarwal 1994, 198). A Resolution of the All-India Anti-Hindu Code Convention stated that the change would "seriously and inevitably undermine the foundations of the Hindu religion, Hindu culture and Hindu social structure," and lead to "fractionization and the disruption of the Hindu family system which has throughout the ages acted as a cooperative institution for the preservation of family ties" (R. Kumar 1993, 98).

And yet, not only have these catastrophes not come to pass, but even the narrow provisions for women's inheritance are seldom utilized, and Hindu inheritance practices remain remarkably unaffected by legislative change. Most Hindu women are not given shares of natal family property, or appear to refuse their own inheritances.[1] This nonevent of the passing of the Hindu Succession Act is the central absent presence in this book, which explores the basic question: why have laws of equal inheritance not worked for Indian women in over four postindependence decades?

Answers to this question cover a range of political, cultural, and economic issues, indicating how property transmission reproduces hegemonic space. The role of law needs to be considered from diverse angles: the functions of the cultural imaginary created through state legislation, the cultural mechanisms that inhibit legal reform, and the ambivalence of turning to the law for women's empowerment. The reinvention of systems of kinship, processes of class formation in the postcolonial nation-state, and the articulation of gender hierarchies with class and kinship are also crucial components. A particularly strong emphasis is laid in this book on examining notions of agency and choice: if Indian laws of inheritance have not been availed of by women who "chose" to refuse their natal property shares, what factors governed their decisions? Were they random or misguided assertions of agency? Were these women indeed acting contrary to their material interests? Were they resisting or reformulating cultural prescriptions? How did these decisions depend on and affect other aspects of their lives, and were they optimal choices in retrospect?

The focus of the book is on ideological mechanisms through which systems of property transmission are perpetuated. One of the modes of reinscribing socioeconomic hegemonies in changing political contexts that is crucial here is the invention of a pastiche of traditions, the transformation of the past to serve contemporary ends, what Jameson calls "the simulacra of what, in the postmodern present, are imagined to be those older folkways" (1995, 96). Such reinvention of "ancient traditions" in late capitalist, postcolonial contexts often serves a contemporary political economy, naturalizing preexistent privileges in the new nation.[2] Property transmission is an optimal topic for studying how such myths of tradition are put to use, because of the ways in which bequeathal of property marks certain family members with particular rights and privileges, and confers economic entitlement and social status. Furthermore, issues of class formation that complicate gender hierarchies are also crystallized in property transmission.

As the title of this book indicates, one of the central tropes that codes Indian women's disentitlement to property on the grounds of customs and ancient loyalties is the specter of the uncaring and greedy sister who claims family property. She is an overreaching woman grabbing at undeserved resources, so intent on pursuing the privileges enshrined in the letter of the law that she ignores emotional ties and destroys family harmony. This trope is not only reiterated in various forms by women explaining their voluntary forfeiture of family property in this and other studies, but also appears in other contexts such as in legal judgments or in marital negotiations.

The power and danger underlying such images of the property-owning Indian woman were vividly brought home to me early in the interviewing process, in the highly charged reaction from one of the respondents, Kamla, a fifty-nine-year-old retired schoolteacher originally from ex-West Pakistan.[3] Even before I had unpacked my gear, while we were still conversing casually about who I was and what I was doing there, Kamla said vehemently as soon as she heard of my interest in property issues:

Women should not have any property in their name, or own their home, or maintain very close connections with their natal family. Otherwise, women are too eager to go back to their own parents; as soon as there is any trouble they want to put on their slippers and leave, and that is very hard on the children. So, if there is anything to own, it should be in the man's name first and after him in the children's [meaning sons'?] names. The woman should just take care of her own home. The only thing is that the husband should not be bad (bura). As a result of making laws [about women getting property], all that happens is that quarrels and disputes increase.

Kamla herself had no property; her husband owned the "middle-income group" flat they lived in, and her brothers shared her natal family house in Delhi, from which she had received no share. Her delineation of women's property rights iterated a particular self-abnegating discourse of femininity, often used to deny women's property entitlements. But it also typified fears about profound social transformation resulting from women's equal access to material resources, which could fundamentally alter the perpetuation of a patriarchal system.

An abundance of property-owning women would affect not just formal ownership patterns, but would also be likely to change existent notions of family relations, domestic work, marital success, and most of all, "feminine" acquiescence based on economic subservience. In Kamla's family, for instance, her two sons, who were much older than her daughter, had ostensibly decided to remain bachelors until their sister was married, so that their wives would not lay jealous claim to wedding gifts for their sister purchased by their parents; after she was out of their lives, they said, the wives could "have" everything through their husbands. In place of this alleged gesture of fondness and generosity that naturalized male entitlement to property and women's dependence, a radical reconceptualization of property relations would mean not just changing wills and adjusting dowry, but finding new scripts for love and duty, indeed for the simplest of social gestures.

## Women and Property

It is hardly possible to venture on an exploration of contemporary women's relationship to property without contending with one of the most famous of feminist[4] ghosts: Virginia Woolf, particularly her musings on "a room of one's own" (1929). Her luminous metaphor for female self-determination, a prototypical feminist symbol, simultaneously reveals the enormous power and limitation of the very concept of property. On the one hand, the trope is a symbol of economic and cultural empowerment based on Enlightenment paradigms of individual liberty and equality, holding out for women the desirable vision of having one's own space, one's own property, and enough economic resources to be able to be immersed in creative self-development. And yet, if it is read against global statistics such as that from the 1970 UN Report on Women—that women constitute half the world's population, perform two-thirds of the world's work hours, earn one-tenths of the world's income and own one-hundredths of the world's property[5]—it is impossible to miss the ease underlying Woolf's vision, or to ignore her assumption that the fruits of capitalism and colonialism would bring freedom from patriarchal pressures and heterosexual mandates. Woolf's seemingly radical proposition is written over the silences of voices too subaltern[6] to speak within this discourse: such as slave women, who could not even "own" themselves or their wombs or choose to create homes; refugee and immigrant women who have been forced to relearn home, kinship, and images of self; or indigenous/"tribal" women who have lost communal rights to land and livelihood as a result of "development" policies.

These shadows present within Woolf's trope can also be seen in continuing conflicts within feminism—for instance the debate between approaches based on integrating women into existing structures based on their equality, and those which deconstruct the terms of equality-based rhetoric and emphasize differences between women. They centrally mark feminist explorations of property like this book as well, where the idea of women's property is always immensely empowering and yet fundamentally complicated. While access to property may be an impossible notion for some women, the lasting power of Engels's contention in *The Origin of the Family, Private Property and the State* ([1940] 1985) (that women's subordination is connected to men's accumulation of private property at the cost of women's labor, and that the solution lies in women accumulating resources with exchange value) cannot be disputed. In the contemporary world where few people live outside capitalist relations, women have a lot to gain if they control their own labor and own or have access to financial resources on par with other family members (Agarwal 1994). Thus the trope of room of one's own, reflecting notions of both private/personal space and the economic resources/opportunities to acquire that space (a duality redolent in Woolf's metaphor), weaves through this book both as an embarrassingly nearsighted and as a profoundly visionary trope.

Scholarship on property, and particularly gender and property, attests to the nebulous and complex meanings of property. Numerous scholars contend that the significance of wealth and resources can only be revealed through an understanding of concepts of persons, things, and valuables within specific cultural systems, what Moors calls "the situated nature of property" (1995, 5). Moors's study of contemporary property relations among Palestinian women, *Women, Property and Islam*, echoes in this aspect the arguments made in the 1984 volume *Women and Property, Women As Property* edited by Renee Hirschon (notably Strathern and Whitehead's essays), that analyses of property should not be circumscribed by narrow definitions of capitalism and commodity, but should consider specific ideas of kinship and ideologies of personhood. As others have argued, the relative value of different assets may make apparently bilateral divisions of property inequitable,[7] or security of tenure over state-owned land may have more economic importance for women than formal ownership.[8] Control over the products of labor (wages) or reproduction (children),[9] "whiteness" in a society privileging that "color" (Harris 1993), marriage (Ocko 1991), or "honor" for women[10] can also be designated as property in a broad framework.

Women's access to property is thus best appreciated by considering various kinds of resources cumulatively. Moors's work examines inheritance, dower, wages, and other income; Morris and Nott's study, *All My Worldly Goods: A Feminist Perspective on the Legal Regulation of Wealth* (1995), explores family wealth, income, effects of divorce, taxes and benefits, and resources available through the state, as well as the history of property law. The present volume, similarly, deals with dimensions of property that were significant for the women interviewed: natal inheritance, affinal wealth, dowry, potential for education, and employment. While the primary focus is on inheritance, other sources of obtaining resources such as dowry or eldercare are also evaluated.

In addition, the ideological significance of property is central, and much of the emphasis in this book is on ways in which property functions metonymically to satisfy yearnings about kinship, intimacy, or empowerment. Refusing legal shares of property is therefore as important in revealing the meanings of self and community as attempts to acquire property would be. As Moors, whose sample also includes numerous women who did not initiate property claims, contends, "[w]hile inheriting property is not always an indication of gendered power, neither is refraining from taking one's share necessarily an expression of total subordination" (1995, 76). The portrait of property relations presented in the following chapters is thus not so much a dirge as an investigation of multiple negotiations.

The outline of property relations developed here adds to the growing body of work on Indian women and property. An early example that continues to be influential is Ursula Sharma's *Women, Work and Property in North-West India* (1980), an ethnographic study of two villages that examines women's access to property in the context of agricultural and domestic labor, marriage and dowry, and social relations with other men and women. More recently, other scholars have confirmed Indian women's marginality in land ownership by way of research on widows and poverty (Gulati and Gulati 1993; Chen and Dreze 1992), and accounts of women's struggles to get land in tribal and Christian communities (Vishwanathan 1989; Kishwar 1987). Perhaps the greatest visibility has been brought to the issue with the publication of Bina Agarwal's *A Field of One's Own: Gender and Land Rights in South Asia* (1994), a near-encyclopedic volume using economic, legal, and anthropological analyses. These works have all consistently underlined the need for women to get land or property, and the ways in which notions of "family" and "tradition" are used to deprive them of it.

Even though the focus of this book is on the legal provisions for Indian Hindu women to obtain family property (and the reasons they do not avail themselves of these), it is important to place these limited provisions in the context of inheritance provisions for Indian women as a whole. Within "family law," including marriage, adoption, guardianship, custody and inheritance, Indian women have different legal rights and access to different remedies depending on their religion. Existent property rights reveal the political influence of groups such as large landowners and religious leaders on laws that define women in terms of dependent and circumscribed roles within the family. Agarwal's telling example of a comment from an official source responsible for reform vividly shows the intransigent domination maintained through unequal property laws, and the fear of altering fundamental power relations through change; as she narrates, the Indian Minister of Agriculture said to her at an Indian Planning Commission seminar on law reform, "Are you suggesting that women be given rights in land? What do women want? To break up the family?" (1994, 53).

Hindu women's rights to property have been worked over most extensively, largely because Hindu family law has been "reformed" most extensively by legislators. While all property is alienable and wills or gifts can easily be made to deprive female heirs, and while daughters can receive only minuscule shares of "ancestral" property compared to sons under the Mitakshara system, in case of intestate succession women are equal heirs of self-acquired property.[11] Some states such as Andhra Pradesh and Maharashtra have passed or are planning laws giving women equal shares of all property. These are the pockets of equity that have seldom been utilized by Hindu women.

However, there are some crucial corollaries that limit these rights. Tenancy rights to agricultural land are exempt from the Hindu Succession Act (1956) and legislated by individual states. In most North Indian states this means that daughters are either excluded as heirs or are very low on the list of heirs (Agarwal 1994, 216–18).[12] Moreover, in most states, when land ceilings are determined to limit individual ownership, extra portions may be retained for adult sons but not for adult daughters. Worst of all, ceiling laws are included in a special category of legislation that is exempt from challenges on constitutional grounds such as sex discrimination (Agarwal 1994, 218–23). Thus, even the best-case scenario for Hindu women is marred by many legal barriers, especially for rural women, and it is quite easy to disinherit daughters entirely.

Under Muslim personal law, not all land can be alienated, and heirs including daughters must be given shares. But inequality is entrenched in the general rule that daughters receive half-shares compared to sons, and many shares that are allegedly given as inheritance continue to stay within the undivided natal family land (Agarwal 1994, 227–36). Inheritance for Parsis (Zoroastrians), Christians, Jews (and others married under the nonreligious Special Marriage Act [1955]) is generally governed by the Indian Succession Act (1925), which makes no distinction between sons' and daughters' shares (Agarwal 1994, 223–26). Parsis now have complete gender parity in inheritance following a 1991 Amendment. Some Christian communities (the Syrian Christians of Kerala being the most notorious example), are governed by inequitable regional laws of inheritance, although these have been the subject of recent legal challenges. Tenancy and ceiling exemptions do apply for all communities, to the detriment of women. There are also numerous other ethnic groups, the so-called scheduled tribes, plus matrilineal Hindu and Muslim communities, who continue to be governed by exception clauses and customary law.

## The Power of Law on Women and in the "New" Nations

By looking at the workings of property law, this book asks the questions: How do cultural factors affect the outcome of laws intended to bring about social reform? Can social change be precipitated by legal reform? The answers lie in the very meaning and authority of law, in the overdetermination of law as an ideological apparatus. As Rosen suggests, a legal system rests upon the "paradox" that it seems "central to the imposition of decisive pronouncements aimed at the very structure of social relationships" while being "dependent on forces beyond its direct control for the acceptance and implementation of these strictures" (1978, 3).

Overreliance on law for bringing about change is thus fundamentally problematic. If, as numerous scholars suggest,[13] new laws are most effective when they legitimize changes that are socially amenable, and legal transformation is a better reflector than initiator of political or economic change, then laws established in the interest of greater redistributive justice are unlikely to be successful. Moreover, law itself may be resistant to radical change, and may incorporate superficial changes only to reinforce hegemonic principles, as feminist legal theorists have frequently pointed out.[14] Carol Smart argues that law can "be understood as a mode of reproduction of the existing patriarchal order, minimizing social change but avoiding the problems of overt conflict" (1984, 21–22). Others contend that law is one of the primary cultural sites where gender identity is constituted, a crucial space where notions of gender are created and reinforced through judgments relating to subjects such as family or sexual violence.[15]

In the life of postcolonial states like India, in the development of "imagined communities" as Anderson (1983) terms them, "progressive" social legislation may be largely symbolic, especially when it comes to altering roles and entitlement patterns within the family. Rosen's important essay on this subject, "Law and Social Change in the New Nations" (1978), contends that newly established nation-states used agrarian reform and industrial policies to try to achieve a change in class relations, and structures like a constitution or an independent judiciary were created to check a state's absolute control, but that the transformation of "social relations" through legal reform was far less successful. He points to effective change in inheritance practices as one of the areas most resistant to reform, because women may have to trade off new legal rights in order "to retain the broader social support of their male kinsmen" (1978, 23).

However, law is not only a space where the nation is imagined, but a site that has multiple significations depending on the locations of persons who use the law. The legal apparatus works at multiple levels to serve various purposes;[16] it is not, Smart contends, "a unitary category which serves the interest of men" (1995, 124). As much recent anthropological research shows,[17] the micropolitics of various environments and people's complex motivations in reading and using the law determine how particular laws are played out. For example, women's use of courts are tied to notions of obtaining financial redress as well as to kinship-based constructs of justice in some cases, and women have been able to launch successful campaigns for legal reform by invoking appropriate tropes within a particular social-political discourse (Toungara 1994; Lazarus-Black 1991, 1992).

In this book, law is regarded as heterogenous, and as an ambivalent source of social change. The legal cases are examined for signatures of authority and constructions of gendered issues. They show that judgments do not simply echo the laws but are mediated by the cultural perceptions of judges and lawyers, by acts of legal translation that revise and recreate gender and can profoundly affect the originary intent of legislation. The interviews, on the other hand, reveal the decoding of laws in different social contexts. Marking the circumstances in which people turn to or threaten to use the law, they point to cultural transgressions meriting legal redress, and common paths of circumventing formal law and resolving conflict. Together, these perspectives help to evaluate the impact of Indian laws of inheritance, and indicate reasons for their widespread receptivity or rejection.

### Nominating Agents, Marking Resistance

In the following chapters, property relations are studied as a site of intense cultural contestation, and law is read in terms of its heterogenous manifestations in the modern state. The focus is on ways in which individuals negotiate between dominant discourses of family, nation, and tradition, and make optimal personal choices given socioeconomic and ideological constraints. One of the central issues is thus the question of agency, of who acts and to what purpose, who refrains from acting and why, and whether actions replicate or modify dominant cultural ideologies. This exploration of subject positions allows for a critical evaluation of the notion of resistance being ubiquitously celebrated among cultural studies scholars.

Gramscian concepts of the struggle for hegemony (1971), Foucauldian notions of microprocesses of workings of power (1980), and James Scott's model of "hidden transcripts" which concretely demonstrates oppositional actions and thoughts beneath the surface of compliance (1990) have become popular tools for reading the motivations of groups and individuals. These approaches, which indicate that ideological power is not absolute but is constantly reconstituted, have perhaps been particularly important for validating the contention that lack of rebellion and overt protest do not necessarily signify mute acceptance or submission. Rather, the social fabric is seen to be seething with small acts of nay-saying. As Gordon in his explication of Foucault puts it, "[t]he existence of those who seem not to rebel is a warren of minute, individual, autonomous tactics and strategies which counter and inflect the visible facts of overall domination (Foucault 1980, 257). Thus, "[p]ower is depicted . . . as constantly being fractured by the struggles of the subordinate. Social structure, rather than being a monolithic, autonomous entity . . . appears more commonly as a constellation of contradictory and contestatory processes" (Haynes and Prakash 1991, 2). Numerous explications of such processes have come from feminist scholars showing the ways in which women appropriate, resist, reformulate (and also perpetuate) dominant discourses according to their positions within a socioeconomic matrix, rather than passively replicating social expectations.[18]

However, the temptation is to valorize resistance too enthusiastically, and to underemphasize the limitations of the structures of power within which resistance is framed. "The romance of resistance," Abu-Lughod contends, often leads to "read[ing] all forms of resistance as signs of the ineffectiveness of systems of power and the resilience and creativity of the human spirit, thereby foreclosing questions about the workings of power" (1993, 102). She advocates using the concept of resistance "as a diagnostic of power," echoing others such as Haynes and Prakash (1991) and Sangari (1993) who emphasize the need to focus on the totality of the interaction between domination and resistance. While resistance provides a way to understand the complexity of human actions, it should not be overused to underestimate power.

As Adas points out, South Asia is an appropriate arena for applying covert notions of resistance given its recent history of nonviolent struggle and its characterization as an area of passive and apolitical people by Marx (1991, 291). Among numerous works analyzing resistance to colonial domination and textual resistance, several analyses of South Asian women's worlds and their redefinition of seemingly oppressive socioeconomic circumstances have demonstrated the richly textured use of the concept of resistance.[19] The study of property issues in this volume, concentrating on women's refusals of resources and decisions that seem contrary to material self-interest, fits particularly well within this mode of looking beyond compliance and examining subversion. However, the focus on cultural sensemaking is always inflected by a consciousness of the ultimate effects of property decisions on the consolidation of resources, the transformation of kinship ideologies and the "reconstitution of patriarchies" (Sangari 1993),[20] in the particular context of contemporary India and a capitalist world system.

## Camouflaging the Self:
## Methodological Choices and Other Fieldwork Angst

I had long been interested in working on a project involving Indian women and law, hoping to examine the reimagination of laws in everyday discourse and to analyze the efficacy of legal solutions for feminist reform. Family law, having been the site of intense national debate in the wake of the Shah Bano case,[21] seemed to be a rich site for inquiry, where there was an abundance of political rhetoric but the need for much more information about cultural negotiations of legal rhetoric. Within family law, I finally decided to concentrate on property because it illumined both socioeconomic and ideological processes in the workings of the modern state.

Given the overdetermining quality of social class in shaping lives and determining priorities in the postcolonial Indian context of vast economic disparities and effectively nonexistent class mobility (Patnaik 1992, Omvedt 1992), and keeping in mind the diverse signifiers of gender connected with diverse cultural locations and practices (Alcoff 1988, 431–35), seeking a cross-class sample was an important focus of this project.[22] In Marxist feminist analyses,[23] property issues are often assumed to be most relevant for wealthy women,[24] but property relations are also salient for the middle and lower classes, especially for women (Agarwal 1994, 27–44). To get a feel for how property transmission affected women in various classes, I planned to divide the interviews equally between women from middle-income and low-income neighborhoods.[25]

Women's lives take very different forms depending on their household's access to material resources, but the question remains whether or not women as individuals occupy the same class positions as men in their households/families, who may own far more property or make far more money in wages.[26] In this study, women are assigned "class criteria" according to the neighborhoods they live in; that is, their class interests and needs are presumed to be related to their household income, family property, and residential circumstances. However, just as households in general assumed a class character by being in a neighborhood, so too individual women's circumstances were sometimes atypical of the general area. For instance, one widow in the middle-class area barely made a living by running a tiny makeshift store, while some married women in the poorer area benefited from having husbands running informal sector businesses with substantial cash incomes. In general, women materially benefitted from the wealth or resources of their families and could justifiably be said to share in the household's class status. Women's jobs/wages were also distinctly different according to "class," and helped to reproduce class relations. For example, middle-class women were able to acquire educational and employment resources that gave them individual advantages over poorer men. However, within each stratum women did have markedly different access to formal property compared to their husbands or brothers, and thus were inevitably a subclass dependent on the resources of males in that class (Robertson 1984).

New Delhi was my chosen fieldwork site for various practical reasons. As a multiethnic conglomerate drawing middle- and low-income migrants from various other parts of the country (and from surrounding countries), it also allowed me to examine heterogeneous forms of property transmission and their potential transformation in the urban context. But finding neighborhoods appropriately stratified by "class" (in terms of an income-status complex) proved to be a challenging task. Government standards for income levels (middle income being Rs. 2500–3500/month) were clearly outdated, considering that mid-level government or teaching jobs often paid about Rs. 6000 in 1991, and some middle-class office jobs paid in the low five figures. Moreover, an enormously wealthy business class existed in Delhi, as well as an upper middle class with high levels of conspicuous consumption working in the private sector and for multinational corporations; thus, notions of middle-level income had been transformed greatly.

In search of a representative "average" middle-class area, I eliminated as being distinctly upper middle class many neighborhoods where two cars with chauffeurs were a frequent sight, and finally picked two areas that represented a range of middle-class living by talking to rental agencies and shopkeepers in the areas: one a middle middle class area of "middle-income group" (MIG) flats largely occupied by people in mid-level government and private jobs, and the other a lower middle class area where residents had small shops or businesses or were in somewhat lower ranked government jobs, which had originally been a resettlement colony for refugees from Pakistan. While there were some differences in living standards between the neighborhoods, people in those areas clearly identified themselves as being neither very wealthy nor poor. For the low-income area, my choice was one of Delhi's numerous squatter colonies; the neighborhood I finally chose was determined by ease of access to the community through liaisons with an appropriate social service organization.

The plan was to draw interview households by random sampling from demographic surveys I had conducted in residential areas of about one hundred units each. Every third household where the demographic questionnaire had been administered was marked as a potential interview household, and included subject to the consent of the household's women. Fewer women consented to interviews than I had anticipated, necessitating a second round of requests based on selecting every sixth household among the remaining ones. Finally, there were thirty interviewees each from the middle-class and poor neighborhoods. One woman per household was asked to participate, with a preference being expressed for particular women in the households chosen, based on the goal of having the total sample contain variation in ages, marital statuses, and employment situations. If that was not agreeable, I opted to talk to any other woman in that residence, thus adhering to the households picked by random sampling.[27] I did interviews and surveys in the middle-income areas between November 1991 and April 1992, and in the low-income area between September 1992 and January 1993.

My gender, class, ethnicity, and religion obviously affected the interview process in complex ways.[28] Was I going to be "out" as a feminist? How much could I challenge dominant constructions of gender roles? In what ways would my predominantly Hindu cultural upbringing impinge upon the research process, despite my self-proclaimed status as a card-carrying atheist? How were caste privileges encoded into my decision to study class rather than caste as the primary variable in the study? How would being a Bengali influence the rapport with those from similar and different ethnic groups? Perhaps most difficult of all was the resilience of class boundaries; was it at all possible to find an uncorrupted space for conversation where my middle/upper middle-class status could be "invisible" for research purposes?

My daily travel, baggage, and costume regimen provides a telling portrait of negotiating worlds. While in Delhi, I lived quite literally in a "postmodern" house designed by an architect friend. Most mornings I left this markedly unique home armed with tape recorder, tapes, a flask of chilled boiled water (from fear of hepatitis, typhoid, etc., something I have been doing since high school), papers and files, a separate money purse (to be guarded more closely from pickpockets on buses); not a researcher who was traveling light or who would seamlessly become part of the "field"! I either walked about five blocks or took a three-wheeler for about six km. to reach the relevant neighborhoods in the first half of the project (working in middle-class areas), while in the second half I needed to travel about twenty-five km. by bus, by changing several buses, or by a combination of bus and three-wheeler depending on daily availability. Although the families I visited were aware of where I was living, the distances meant that some of the women (in this case the most prosperous ones) could easily check this out by taking a slight detour from the market, whereas to the others my residential origins remained much more nebulous, an unequal access to information tied to relations of class/power.

In both the middle-income areas, I simply showed up on doorsteps talking about my project and seeking demographic information, and later returned to some houses asking for interviews. Thorne narrates that during her study of the Draft Resistance movement she was often the object of suspicion, the target of the ever-present fear that strangers in that group were Feds/informants (1983, 227–30); given the spate of burglaries in areas close to where I was working, I fervently hoped my visits with questions about income and people's professions (and hence schedules) would not be followed by burglaries there, because I fully expected to be a logical choice for "suspicious nosy stranger in neighborhood"! Every morning when I dressed up more formally than I normally would, under the impression that this would create a trustworthy first impression, I could not help reflecting ironically on the class-based assumptions about crime and decency this action perpetuated. The hollow justification that I was doing this for the crucial reason of gaining access to respondents underlined for me the researcher's methodological passivity of being unable to challenge the structures under examination, especially under financial and time constraints.

However, various social paradigms could become the basis of rapport: my age, my living in the United States for those who had children or siblings there, my Hindu cultural legacy, or my Bengali ethnicity all created intimacy in different milieus. Most people believed me to be single (though I would talk about my partner if this came up in the conversations), and I felt that this nonmarital appellation articulated with my age and my being a student often made me an easy object of affection and candor, someone to whom the facts of life could be explained elaborately. There was a very strong rapport with younger single participants because of the perceived commonality of our education and upbringing, while young married women living with their in-laws appeared most guarded. Some people did refuse to begin or continue conversations, but on the whole I was astounded by the way I appeared as a complete stranger and was taken into people's homes, fed, introduced to others, made privy to family dynamics, and even sought out repeatedly for information on legal rules or reproductive health facilities.

If appearing on doorsteps in middle-income areas had the potential to raise suspicion in those residents, this was nothing compared to the discomfort and fear that I could have caused by appearing with self-identified credentials and machines and forms in a squatter colony, where people are frequently subjected to questioning by the myriad development and demographic organizations studying "the Indian poor," and where residents live in daily fear of being persecuted by the police or other state agencies on the basis of information that they have unknowingly given out. Thus in this case, I decided to seek entree by working with one of the grassroots community development organizations that had established relations of trust in such communities. I contacted an organization that works for education and political and social mobilization of communities through centers in numerous squatter colonies, and is primarily staffed by grassroots workers drawn from those areas. They agreed to help me, and requested that for a few weeks I go along with the community workers, on daily visits to people seeking their help or for reenrolling class dropouts. When I started doing surveys and then interviews, a junior staff member would often come along, ostensibly to learn the research methods; because she also lived in that neighborhood, I was very fortunate in being able to piggyback on her community relations.

In this area, I was usually dressed in my working attire (usually quite low-key), but it was embarrassingly obvious that markers of class were not simply translatable into clothing. There was no way to "blend"; women would drag out special chairs or mats for me to sit on despite my fervent protests and feed me *lassi* or tea or *parathas*. Yet this was also the same kind of hospitality as was extended to the community workers whom I had originally accompanied, so the treatment was not necessarily all class related. Perhaps because both middle-class and working-class women worked together at this community organization, women in the area were already fairly used to talking about their problems with middle-class women, and thus I benefited immensely from my association with the group.

I appear from traces in the interviews with the latter group to have been positioned as a Bengali, an urbanite, an unmarried woman; these paradigms were used by people who were both insiders and outsiders to those categories. The women I talked with generally treated me with great warmth and intimacy, many being far more open and affectionate than women I encountered in the previous neighborhoods, who were supposedly closer to me in terms of social class. I was alarmed to find myself nominated as expert advice-giver on everything from divorce and dowry recovery procedures to death and disability benefits to medicine labels and indeterminate pills and most of all, problems with contraception, being only academically aware of court procedures and completely out of my depth in doing medical guesswork. Yet this appearance of possessing information somewhat useful for the residents mediated the potentially insurmountable distance between our social locations, giving me a limited usefulness in being there and perhaps setting me apart from other information-mining strangers.

As Clifford's remark prefacing Sanchez-Eppler's essay on Freyre and Hurston's experiences of fieldwork in their home communities—"Perhaps there's no return for anyone to a native land—only field notes for its reinvention" (Sanchez-Eppler 1992, 464)—suggests, fieldwork is often marked by the profound ambivalence of trying to reconstruct one's familiar culture as a describable Other, while also confronting the impossibility of returning as an untouched "native" self (Narayan 1993). Even for those who may not have lived away from the field, there *is* no absolute self that can be an insider across social classes, ethnicities, religions, and many other microcategories. The narrative of fieldwork thus cannot but be a story of passing, of creating selves from residual fragments in multiple situations.

### The Three Delhi Neighborhoods

With a 1991 population of 9.37 million (7.18 million being officially urban or part of the Delhi Municipal Corporation), the Union Territory of Delhi is home to 1.11 percent of the Indian population, and with a population density of 6,319 people/sq. km. ranks first among states and Union Territories in order of density (Census of India [Delhi] 1991, 13; Bose 1991, 57–58, 433). The 1991 sex ratio of 830 females to 1000 males (the highest among all decades since 1901) is the second lowest in the country but probably reflects skewed migration patterns (Bose 1991, 433). Eighty-four percent of Delhi's population are Hindus, 7 percent Sikhs and 7 percent Muslims (Grolier 1993).[29]

While modern Delhi started out as a city carefully planned by Lutyens and Baker and continued with a "master plan" of urban development to be materialized by the Delhi Development Authority starting in 1957, unexpected political and economic pressures foiled this careful planning (Pugh 1991). Two of the most significant pressures have come from Independence and Partition resulting in a huge flow of Pakistani and later Bangladeshi refugees, and from rural poverty resulting in hundreds of thousands of laborers coming to the capital city for the poorest of service and labor jobs, which make more than sharecropping wages (Fernandes 1990; Datta 1986). The first of these is related to the history of the two middle-class neighborhoods I studied, the second to the composition of the squatter colony.

It is impossible for me to claim that the experiences of women portrayed in this book are representative of the "Indian" situation or are even typical of Delhi. The sample is too small and idiosyncratic for that, and the immense heterogeneity of national or even state demographics can only be accidentally captured in a small sample of qualitative data. However, the demographic profile of the survey neighborhoods did mirror the larger Indian situation (Mullatti 1995; Grolier 1993; Bose 1991) in some aspects: 81.7 percent of total households surveyed were Hindu (Table 1.3); the predominant urban family form was nuclear (Table 1.1); at least 33.4 percent women had less than a Grade III education (Table 1.5); and a total of 75.9 percent women overall did not report any paid employment (Table 1.7). But the differences between the neighborhoods revealed socioeconomic disparities concealed by the above aggregate figures.

The first area selected, which I shall be referring to as Kailash Enclave or KE, was part of a larger South Delhi neighborhood containing some wealthy and upper middle-class areas in addition to a lot of middle-class housing and a few areas with huts. The part I worked in consisted of a few rows of so-called middle-income group (MIG) two- or three-bedroom flats sold by the Delhi Development Authority in the late 1960s. The flats were all painted in uniform colors; the streets were fairly broad and clean; and economy- or medium-priced cars were typically parked in front. The area was quite well connected by public transport while not being too close to any congested areas. A small shopping complex of about twenty-five to thirty shops served this area, including vegetable stalls, a

**Table 1.1** Household Structures in KE/KC/SN (in Percentages)

| HOUSEHOLD TYPE[a] | KE<br>N=47 | KC<br>N=56 | SN<br>N=94 | TOTAL<br>N=197 |
|---|---|---|---|---|
| Nuclear | 55.3 | 41 | 52.1 | 49.7 |
| Nuclear + H's parent | 6.4 | 14.3 | 1.06 | 6.1 |
| Nuclear + H's parent + sibling/s | 2.1 | 0 | 4.3 | 2.5 |
| Nuclear + H's siblings/nephews | 0 | 1.8 | 10.6 | 5.6 |
| Nuclear + W's siblings/nephews | 0 | 1.8 | 6.4 | 3.6 |
| Joint | 17 | 32.1 | 4.2 | 15.2 |
| Couple | 10.6 | 3.6 | 3.2 | 5.1 |
| Couple + grandchildren | 0 | 0 | 3.2 | 1.5 |
| Couple + H's sibling/s | 0 | 0 | 2.1 | 1.02 |
| Couple + W's siblings | 0 | 0 | 2.1 | 1.02 |
| Woman + children | 2.1 | 3.6 | 1.06 | 2.03 |
| Woman + brother-in-law + children | 0 | 0 | 1.06 | 0.05 |
| Woman | 4.3 | 1.8 | 2.1 | 2.5 |
| Men (Kin) | 0 | 0 | 3.2 | 1.5 |
| Men (Non-Kin) | 2.1 | 0 | 3.2 | 2.03 |
| Total | 100 | 100 | 100 | 100 |

[a]"Nuclear" refers to families consisting of married couples plus children; "joint" refers to families of married brothers, their wives, children, and parents (or some married brothers, etc., plus unmarried brothers and sisters); "couple" refers to married heterosexual couple.

**Table 1.2** Household Incomes in KE/KC/SN (in Percentages)

| TOTAL HOUSEHOLD INCOME (RS.) | KE<br>N=47 | KC<br>N=56 | SN<br>N=94 | TOTAL<br>N=197 |
|---|---|---|---|---|
| < 1500 | 2.1 | 8.9 | 34 | 19.3 |
| 1500–2500 | 4.3 | 12.5 | 34 | 20.8 |
| 2501–3500 | 8.5 | 21.4 | 18 | 16.8 |
| 3501–4500 | 12.8 | 21.4 | 7.4 | 12.7 |
| 4501–5500 | 8.5 | 5.4 | 4.3 | 5.6 |
| 5501–6500 | 8.5 | 8.9 | 1.06 | 5.1 |
| 6501–7500 | 10.6 | 5.4 | 1.06 | 4.6 |
| 7501–8500 | 10.6 | 3.6 | 0 | 3.6 |
| 8501–10,000 | 6.4 | 3.6 | 0 | 2.5 |
| > 10,000 | 19.1 | 3.6 | 0 | 5.6 |
| Unknown | 8.5 | 5.4 | 0 | 3.6 |
| Total | 100 | 100 | 100 | 100 |

**Table 1.3** Religion of Households in KE/KC/SN (in Percentages)

| RELIGION | KE<br>N=47 | KC<br>N=56 | SN<br>N=94 | TOTAL<br>N=197 |
|---|---|---|---|---|
| Hindu | 74.5 | 64.3 | 95.7 | 81.7 |
| Sikh | 8.5 | 28.6 | 0 | 10.2 |
| Muslim | 0 | 1.8 | 4.3 | 2.5 |
| Sindhi | 4.3 | 3.6 | 0 | 2.03 |
| Jain | 2.1 | 0 | 0 | 0.5 |
| Unknown, None | 10.6 | 1.8 | 0 | 3 |
| Total | 100 | 100 | 100 | 100 |

**Table 1.4** Ethnic/State Origins of Households in KE/KC/SN (in Percentages)

| ETHNICITY/<br>STATE OF ORIGIN | KE<br>N=47 | KC<br>N=56 | SN<br>N=94 | TOTAL<br>N=197 |
|---|---|---|---|---|
| Uttar Pradesh | 14.9 | 3.6 | 71.3 | 38.6 |
| Ex-West Pakistan | 27.7 | 44.6 | 0 | 19.2 |
| Bihar | 2.1 | 0 | 14.9 | 7.6 |
| Punjab | 10.6 | 8.9 | 0 | 5.1 |
| Delhi | 4.3 | 8.9 | 0 | 3.6 |
| Haryana | 6.4 | 5.4 | 0 | 3 |
| Tamil Nadu | 12.8 | 0 | 0 | 3 |
| West Bengal | 2.1 | 3.6 | 1.06 | 2.03 |
| Gujarat | 0 | 1.8 | 0 | 0.5 |
| Himachal Pradesh | 2.1 | 0 | 0 | 0.5 |
| Kashmir | 2.1 | 0 | 0 | 0.5 |
| Nepal | 0 | 0 | 1.06 | 0.5 |
| Orissa | 2.1 | 0 | 0 | 0.5 |
| Rajasthan | 2.1 | 0 | 0 | 0.5 |
| More than one state/<br>    Ethnicity | 10.6 | 23.2 | 11.7 | 14.7 |
| Total | 100 | 100 | 100 | 100 |

**Table 1.5** Education of Women in KE/KC/SN (in Percentages)

| LEVEL OF EDUCATION | KE<br>N=74 | KC<br>N=107 | SN<br>N=101 | TOTAL<br>N=282 |
|---|---|---|---|---|
| Nonliterate | 0 | 7.5 | 73.3 | 29.1 |
| 1–3 years school | 0 | 0 | 11.9 | 4.3 |
| Grades 3–10 | 8.1 | 13.1 | 11.9 | 11.3 |
| School Leaving Exam (Matriculation) | 8.1 | 23.4 | 0.99 | 11.3 |
| Higher Secondary Grade 12 | 8.1 | 6.5 | 0 | 4.6 |
| Postsecondary Diploma | 6.6 | 1.9 | 0 | 2.5 |
| Bachelor's Degree | 32.4 | 38.3 | 0 | 23 |
| Master's Degree/B.A.B.Ed. | 18.9 | 5.6 | 0 | 7.1 |
| Master's Plus | 10.8 | 0.93 | 0 | 3.2 |
| Professional (Law/M.B.A./ Medicine/Engineering) | 5.4 | 0.93 | 0 | 1.8 |
| Unknown | 1.4 | 1.9 | 1.98 | 1.8 |
| Total | 100 | 100 | 100 | 100 |

**Table 1.6** Age of Women in KE/KC/SN (in Percentages)

| AGE (WOMEN'S) | KE<br>N=74 | KC<br>N=107 | SN<br>N=101 | TOTAL<br>N=282 |
|---|---|---|---|---|
| <21 | 5.4 | 9.3 | 17.8 | 11.3 |
| 21–25 | 14.7 | 18.7 | 19.8 | 18.1 |
| 26–30 | 14.7 | 14 | 20.8 | 16.7 |
| 31–35 | 8.1 | 9.3 | 17.8 | 12.1 |
| 36–40 | 8.1 | 7.5 | 5.9 | 7.1 |
| 41–45 | 8.1 | 6.5 | 5.9 | 6.8 |
| 46–50 | 6.6 | 9.3 | 3.96 | 6.8 |
| 51–55 | 16.2 | 7.5 | 2.97 | 8.2 |
| 56–60 | 8.1 | 7.5 | 2.97 | 6 |
| 61–65 | 5.4 | 2.8 | 0 | 2.5 |
| 66–70 | 2.7 | 4.7 | 0.99 | 2.8 |
| >70 | 1.4 | 2.8 | 0.99 | 1.8 |
| Total | 100 | 100 | 100 | 100 |

**Table 1.7**  Past and Present Paid Work Status of Women in KE/KC/SN (in Percentages)

| EMPLOYMENT SITUATION | KE N=74 | KC N=107 | SN N=101 | TOTAL N=282 |
|---|---|---|---|---|
| Employed/Self-Employed | 35.1 | 17.8 | 11.9 | 20.2 |
| Retired | 4 | 1.9 | 0.99 | 2.1 |
| Previously Employed | 2.7 | 1.9 | 0 | 1.4 |
| Agriculture | 0 | 0 | 0.99 | 0.4 |
| No Paying Work Reported | 58.1 | 78.5 | 86.1 | 75.9 |
| Total | 100 | 100 | 100 | 100 |

flower stall, grocers, sweet shops, book and video lending libraries, a stationery and card store, a pharmacy, a post office, tailoring and dry-cleaning stores, even a government liquor store. A wholesale vegetable market was close by, although one had to go some distance to get fish or meat.

The men in this area worked in fairly senior government jobs— for example, as undersecretaries, in private companies and banks, as owners of small shops or businesses, or as lawyers, doctors, or chartered accountants. Employed women were mostly teachers, with some working in government and private offices and research labs. Among women, there was also a doctor, a fashion designer, a journalist, and a lawyer. Several of the women who had no outside employment tutored school students at home. As shown in Table 1.2, 19.1 percent households had incomes over Rs. 10,000, placing them at the higher end of their neighborhoods. Women's comparatively high rate of paid employment from this neighborhood (35.1 percent, Table 1.7) was no coincidence in this respect; rather, most houses were at the wealthier end of the spectrum because of multiple income earners, often including women. Women's far higher levels of education and training in this area (Table 1.5) was thus a valuable asset, often used to get a good job and enhance the family's standard of living.

The second area, called Kalka Colony or KC in this study, is a so-called WPRC, or West Pakistani Resettlement Colony, where the Government built inexpensive housing in the early 1960s for Pakistani Hindu and Sikh refugees. Many of the residents told me that the flats were hurriedly built and allotted because squatter units had been rapidly spreading in the area. Though the original structures had two or three small rooms with kitchen and bathroom, many people had added on rooms, and spread out, taken in tenants or started shops in this extra space. Depending on their later prosperity, some people had redone the facades, so the total effect appeared much less uniform than KE. Most people owned two-wheeler scooters and only a few owned cars. This area was in a prized urban spot, being close to one of Delhi's newly developed office complexes, and just a few streets away from the facilities of wealthy south Delhi localities. While there were only a couple of small general stores selling bread, milk, biscuits, soft drinks, eggs, soap, and the like, in the immediate area, there were several large markets nearby, with easy access to a much greater variety of goods than KE due to the location. Within KC itself, there was a beauty parlor, a textile shop, an electronic goods repair store, a car parts store and a travel agency, all small businesses run by the owners in extensions of their houses.

In this area, the men also worked in government and private offices, though often at lower ranks. A large number of families owned small shops or businesses. There were a few teachers, a couple of factory workers, and a little overlap with the third area in jobs like vending vegetables from carts and driving three-wheelers. As Table 1.2 shows, 42.8 percent households had incomes of less than Rs. 3500 as opposed to only 14.9 percent from KE in the same category; however, compared to the poorer area where 86 percent of households earned less than Rs. 3500, KC was much better off. While few households here earned over Rs. 10,000, 25.1 percent homes had incomes over Rs. 5500,[30] whereas only a negligible number of households from the third area did so. Among the employed women, there were several stenographers or typists, a few teachers, and many women managing small businesses (many others who did not report working also said later that they helped out in the businesses); less than 20 percent of women were in formal jobs (Table 1.7) and were also markedly less educated than in KE (Table 1.5).

Many sociocultural studies of Delhi have concentrated on squatter colonies. In 1990, 32.85 percent of Delhi's population lived in such colonies or "slums," most of which had electricity but few had clean water or adequate sanitation. Studies show that residents came from the lowest sectors of the rural population in terms of caste and class, and primarily worked in the informal sector (Fernandes 1990, 11, 16, 53–54). The third area, here called Siddharth Nagar (SN), also lacked electrical connections or a plumbing system, but it was atypical in some ways. For one, it was almost semirural. It stood on the bank of a heavily polluted river; until 1991, people had extensive farmland next to the river. Under a sudden "environmental" scheme initiated by the government, the lands along the river were seized to create a Green Belt, though there had been little visible improvement. According to residents' accounts, this was rural farmland till the 1950s, and some of the original families continued to live there. One of the major waves of migration was around 1958, when there was a demand for labor to build and develop a power plant, a flyover, and a major office center nearby. A second large wave was around 1980 when a stadium was built nearby prior to the Asian Games. In between, a steady stream of both seasonal migration and relocation near relatives continued and was still going on at the time of the interviews.

The current area occupied by SN had been progressively diminished since the 1950s, as Delhi authorities chose the locale for various "development" projects. Like the other alleged "urban renewal" projects in slums described by Fernandes (1990), there were at least three episodes when the huts were violently destroyed and people were given alternative housing in planned low-income housing areas: when the stadium was built; when railway tracks were laid for coal wagons to go up to the power plant behind SN; and during the "environmental initiative." Particularly egregious is a twenty-one-story empty structure that was built to be a hotel for the Asian Games in 1982 but never took off, and may ultimately be sold to a group that provides medical facilities for the ultrarich. SN thus became a narrow strip scrunched between the train tracks, the power plant, the river, and the highway, all sources of extremely high pollution and a profusion of respiratory illnesses.

Still, as the director of the community organization pointed out,[31] SN had an advantage over many other squatter colonies in being relatively elevated and thus free of backed-up dirty water. The proximity to government offices, shops, and construction projects as well as excellent transport connections also made it attractive. Even with the successive constrictions, people still got more space than in low-income housing projects to keep livestock or grow vegetables. Hence, a large number of families who had been "relocated" to other housing had either sold their allotment or moved part of their families back to SN.

Although most dwellings here were temporary, with mud walls and tin roofs and no running water, electricity, or sanitation, each hut had small enclosed areas for urination and bathing, and a few of the more prosperous families had built cement structures. A couple of groundwater wells provided relatively clean water. A tea shop, a vegetable vending stall, and a very small general store were run by some residents. "Ownership" of the huts or *jhuggis* was supposed to inhere in "jhuggi cards" issued by the municipal district, but these have little legal value and are tokens of political panacea.[32] As in many other squatter colonies, certain individuals with political connections often used violent extortion on vulnerable people like new migrants.

A majority of men in this area were self-employed. This included those who drove three-wheelers and rickshaws and those who sold vegetables, utensils, or cheap clothing from temporary shops or carts. A large number of men in this group sold *chhole* (a snack of spiced gram). A few who had businesses were better off financially (Table 1.2 shows 6.4 percent households earned over Rs. 4500, with the highest earners being those with businesses), but for most the earnings varied with the location. Many also worked in government jobs prized for their permanence and benefits, and some in private offices, mostly as guards, sweepers, or general helpers. The lowest wages were earned by those who worked as daily hired labor for construction projects or who were subcontracted for skills like polishing floors or operating specific machines.

The women in paid work had either taken on government jobs previously held by their husbands, or worked in their shops, or as daily laborers or vendors, with one woman being a teacher in the community school. The smaller number of women in paid employment (11.9 percent, Table 1.7) reflected not only the low level of literacy in this area and hence the lack of good employment opportunities, but also stricter community norms about seclusion of women.[33] Gambling and drinking by men and boys was rampant in the area, connected to much domestic violence and also a dearth of living expenses for women and children. Many women resorted to informal sector work like home-based sewing, but most prevalent in this area was the atypical "business" of garnering coal from railway wagons for sale and consumption. Children were involved in getting the coal and this also led to widespread absenteeism from school.

The average family size in this area was 5.17, as compared to 3.98 in KE and 5.25 in KC. The residential pattern, with a predominance of nuclear families and an occasional presence of brothers/brothers-in-law (as shown in Table 1.1), was related to male migration during "off" season as well as the fact that many apparently nuclear households in SN were within family "compounds," with relatives living in adjacent jhuggis. Most families here had much more ongoing financial and social dealings with rural areas than in KE and KC, and some women shifted between urban and rural living. Women living here were predominantly in their twenties and thirties (Table 1.6), but because they were often married in their teens (women in the middle-class areas were usually married in their twenties), there was a life-cycle asymmetry with the women from the other areas even within similar age groups.

The status-gap between the three neighborhoods was more than a matter of income difference; there were different standards of living in evidence. In KC, as compared to KE, there was a distinctly different occupational profile, less prestigious (and expensive) schools and colleges were attended by children, housing was less spacious and more poorly built, and there was a predominance of three-wheelers as opposed to cars, dingier shops, and fewer homes with air conditioners and washing machines. Notably, the wealthier people in KC had remedied the difference in shabbier housing, cars, or appliances. Yet, even most homes in KC had refrigerators and telephones and air coolers and hired domestic employees and private tutors, representing a substantially different standard of living from the third area, SN, where electricity was "stolen" from city lines, bathrooms were al fresco by the river or in a public toilet, water came from a communal tap, and houses had mud or brick walls.

KE and KC differed from SN in several obvious aspects: the ethnic constituencies of the former were predominantly Punjabi as opposed to the Uttar Pradesh majority in the latter (Table 1.4); there were few joint families[34] in SN given the system of residence in individual huts (Table 1.1); and women in KE and KC had a far lower fertility rate. The lives of young women from KE and SN occupied different registers of possibility: in SN, women/girls would typically be married by their late teens; have several children by their early twenties; and only a few would go to high school and work at "unskilled" office jobs; whereas in KE, most women got married after graduating from college; delayed and spaced childbearing; and many worked in high-paying professional jobs. In fact, household income was higher in a few SN households compared to some KE and KC households, and women in all three neighborhoods frequently earned income within the "informal sector." However, the concrete conditions of SN women's lives, including defecating by riverbanks, extreme difficulty in urban mobility given the inability to read bus numbers or street markers, markedly different health care, such as an abundance of fake gynecologists, and even the quality of food and clothing available, framed a substantially different world.

As shown in Tables 1.8 through 1.15, the sample of sixty women broadly reflected the aggregate characteristics of the population

**Table 1.8**  Household Positions of Interview Respondents (in Percentages)

| HOUSEHOLD POSITION | KE N=14 | KC N=16 | SN N=30 | TOTAL N=60 |
|---|---|---|---|---|
| Sole Married Adult Woman | 50 | 43.8 | 76.7 | 61.7 |
| Woman Head of Household | 7.1 | 6.2 | 6.7 | 6.7 |
| Senior Married Woman (M-i-l) | 14.3 | 18.8 | 3.3 | 10 |
| Junior Married Woman (D-i-l) | 7.1 | 25 | 10 | 13.3 |
| Single Woman | 21.4 | 6.2 | 3.3 | 8.3 |
| Total | 100 | 100 | 100 | 100 |

**Table 1.9**  Household Structures of Interview Respondents (in Percentages)

| HOUSEHOLD TYPE | KE N=14 | KC N=16 | SN N=30 | TOTAL N=60 |
|---|---|---|---|---|
| Nuclear | 57.1 | 43.8 | 60 | 55 |
| Nuclear + H/W's parent/sibling | 7.1 | 25 | 23.3 | 20 |
| Joint | 21.4 | 25 | 10 | 16.7 |
| Woman Headed | 14.3 | 6.25 | 6.7 | 8.3 |
| Total | 100 | 100 | 100 | 100 |

**Figure 1.** View of the neighborhood near KE. Each unit of houses is set off from others by brick fences. Cars are parked on-street.

**Figure 2.** Neighborhood market near KE. This view includes two "general stores," a snack shop, a tailoring shop, and a dry cleaning shop.

31

**Figure 3.** View of the neighborhood near KC. Apartments are smaller and crammed much closer together than in KE. The original living space has been extended in many cases by adding a third story or a room with a corrugated tin roof in front (many of these are used as shops). Exterior space is often used for doing domestic chores or repair work, or for socializing.

**Figure 4.** A "general store" within the KC neighborhood. Note also that two-wheeler "scooters" are more common than cars in KC.

32

**Figure 5.** View of numerous *Jhuggi* or squatter colonies including SN, with the smoke stack of the power plant in the background. Most jhuggis are temporary structures, but a few are constructed of cement and some are two-storied.

**Figure 6.** Approach road to several colonies including SN. Exterior space is used even more extensively than in KC, for performing chores including washing dishes, as well as bathing and sometimes even cooking. Gender- and age-segregated groups work and talk together outside in various spots, and groups of children are supervised simultaneously by numerous neighbors and relatives.

**Figure 7.** Neighborhood market near SN, including wares sold from hand carts as well as from shops. The tall building in the background, whose construction constricted the area of the squatter colonies further, was built to be a hotel but stands empty for over a decade. Bicycles, as shown in the picture, are a common mode of family transportation in SN.

**Figure 8.** The river forms the boundary of several colonies including SN. The land slopes down to the river. While no crops grow on the riverbank any longer, and the water is very polluted, the river bank is still used for defecation and other waste disposal.

**Table 1.10** Household Incomes of Interview Respondents (in Percentages)

| TOTAL HOUSEHOLD INCOME (RS.) | KE N=14 | KC N=16 | SN N=30 | TOTAL N=60 |
|---|---|---|---|---|
| <1500 | 0 | 12.5 | 40 | 23.3 |
| 1501–2500 | 7.1 | 12.5 | 30 | 20 |
| 2501–3500 | 7.1 | 18.8 | 30 | 21.7 |
| 3501–4500 | 21.4 | 12.5 | 0 | 8.3 |
| 4501–5500 | 7.1 | 18.8 | 0 | 6.7 |
| 5501–6500 | 7.1 | 12.5 | 0 | 5 |
| 6501–7500 | 0 | 0 | 0 | 0 |
| 7501–8500 | 7.1 | 0 | 0 | 1.7 |
| >8501 | 42.9 | 12.5 | 0 | 13.3 |
| Total | 100 | 100 | 100 | 100 |

**Table 1.11** Ethnic/State Origins of Interview Respondents (in Percentages)

| ETHNICITY/STATE OF ORIGIN | KE N=14 | KC N=16 | SN N=30 | TOTAL N=60 |
|---|---|---|---|---|
| Uttar Pradesh | 21.4 | 6.3 | 46.7 | 30 |
| Bihar | 7.1 | 0 | 33.3 | 18.3 |
| Punjab | 21.4 | 31.3 | 3.3 | 15 |
| Ex-West Pakistan | 14.3 | 31.3 | 0 | 11.7 |
| West Bengal | 7.1 | 12.5 | 10 | 10 |
| Delhi | 0 | 12.5 | 3.3 | 5 |
| Haryana | 7.1 | 6.3 | 0 | 3.3 |
| Himachal Pradesh | 7.1 | 0 | 0 | 1.7 |
| Madhya Pradesh | 7.1 | 0 | 0 | 1.7 |
| Nepal | 0 | 0 | 3.3 | 1.7 |
| Tamil Nadu | 7.1 | 0 | 0 | 1.7 |
| Total | 100 | 100 | 100 | 100 |

**Table 1.12** Religion of Interview Respondents (in Percentages)

| RELIGION | KE N=14 | KC N=16 | SN N=30 | TOTAL N=60 |
|---|---|---|---|---|
| Hindu | 92.9 | 62.5 | 93.3 | 85 |
| Sikh | 7.1 | 31.2 | 0 | 10 |
| Muslim | 0 | 6.3 | 6.7 | 5 |
| Total | 100 | 100 | 100 | 100 |

**Table 1.13** Education of Interview Respondents (in Percentages)

| LEVEL OF EDUCATION | KE N=14 | KC N=16 | SN N=30 | TOTAL N=60 |
|---|---|---|---|---|
| Nonliterate | 0 | 12.5 | 53.3 | 30 |
| 1–3 years school | 7.1 | 0 | 13.3 | 8.3 |
| Grades 3–10 | 0 | 0 | 30 | 15 |
| School Leaving Exam/ Matriculation | 7.1 | 25 | 3.3 | 10 |
| Higher Secondary/ Grade 12 | 0 | 12.5 | 0 | 3.3 |
| Bachelor's Degree | 42.9 | 43.8 | 0 | 21.7 |
| Master's Degree/ B.A.B.Ed. | 14.3 | 0 | 0 | 3.3 |
| Master's Plus | 21.4 | 6.3 | 0 | 6.7 |
| Professional (Law) | 7.1 | 0 | 0 | 1.7 |
| Total | 100 | 100 | 100 | 100 |

**Table 1.14** Age of Interview Respondents (in Percentages)

| AGE | KE N=14 | KC N=16 | SN N=30 | TOTAL N=60 |
|---|---|---|---|---|
| <21 | 0 | 6.3 | 16.7 | 10 |
| 21–25 | 14.3 | 12.5 | 20 | 16.7 |
| 26–30 | 35.7 | 6.3 | 30 | 25 |
| 31–35 | 7.1 | 18.8 | 20 | 16.7 |
| 36–40 | 7.1 | 6.3 | 3.3 | 5 |
| 41–45 | 7.1 | 12.5 | 6.7 | 8.3 |
| 46–50 | 7.1 | 6.3 | 3.3 | 5 |
| 51–55 | 7.1 | 25 | 0 | 8.3 |
| 56–60 | 7.1 | 0 | 0 | 1.7 |
| 61–65 | 0 | 0 | 0 | 0 |
| 66–70 | 7.1 | 0 | 0 | 1.7 |
| >70 | 0 | 6.3 | 0 | 1.7 |
| Total | 100 | 100 | 100 | 100 |

**Table 1.15**  Past and Present Paid Work Status of Interview Respondents
(in Percentages)

| EMPLOYMENT SITUATION | KE N=14 | KC N=16 | SN N=30 | TOTAL N=60 |
|---|---|---|---|---|
| Employed/Self-Employed | 57.1 | 31.3 | 30 | 36.7 |
| Previously Employed | 7.1 | 18.8 | 0 | 6.7 |
| Retired | 14.3 | 0 | 3.3 | 5 |
| No Paying Work Reported | 21.4 | 50 | 66.7 | 51.7 |
| Total | 100 | 100 | 100 | 100 |

from the three neighborhoods in certain aspects: the number of nuclear households (Table 1.1 and 1.9), the predominance of respondents from Uttar Pradesh, Bihar, and Punjab/Pakistan (Table 1.4 and 1.11), the breakdown by religion (Table 1.3 and 1.12), the levels of education (Table 1.5 and 1.13), and the age cohorts (Table 1.6 and 1.14, although the sample is biased toward younger women, particularly from SN). Even income corresponds at the lowest levels, although there is some discrepancy at the higher end (Table 1.2 and 1.10). The substantially higher number of employed women in the sample as opposed to the population (Table 1.7 and 1.15) is perhaps an indication that these women felt more confident in granting interviews, confirming my experience of numerous refusals from women saying they would not grant interviews because they did not "know" anything and had nothing to say.

Each of the interview respondents is referred to by the same name throughout the book. While brief life histories of some of them are provided in several chapters, the focus of this work is on aggregate responses and so the majority of respondents have not been fleshed out as fully as I would have liked. I have tried to remedy this to a small extent by providing demographic data and information on property ownership for each respondent in Appendix A. While this list does not provide a sense of their personalities or goals, I hope that readers curious about a particular individual can at least get a fuller sense of her identity. A related cautionary note: demographic variables such as age, ethnicity, or marital status are often foregrounded in brief descriptions of the respondents (e.g. X, a single Punjabi woman of fifty-six, said Y), but these are likely to be overdetermined parameters. That is, while a majority of responses that correlate with age or economic situation may indicate that these factors influence the beliefs, and while experiences are likely to play a constitutive role in constructing worldviews, an individual woman does not inevitably "speak from" a gender-, class-, or age-related "standpoint" (Kapadia 1995, 6; Hawkesworth 1989, 537).[35]

## Looking Ahead

The focus of this book is on the myths and practices surrounding property transmission in India—that is, some of the material and ideological structures through which the current distribution of property is maintained. To this end, each of the chapters explores some of the myths within the discourse on property, showing their lack of substance but also their resilience.

Chapters 2 to 5 provide a critical analysis of the myths of property and wealth, including property transmitted both as marriage prestations and as inheritance. Chapter 2 sets the stage by describing the facts of property ownership. It provides information about amounts of property and property divisions in the respondents' families, showing prevalent modes of inheritance and the consolidation of wealth. It profiles both women as property owners and women who are deliberately deprived of family property, thereby revealing the discursive limits within which women's property ownership is coded. It also demonstrates how gender privileges complement or contradict privileges of class or age.

Wedding costs were often invoked by women in explaining their disenfranchisement from property. Chapter 3 deals primarily with property exchanges surrounding marriage, focusing on the economics of weddings. The meanings and purposes of wedding gifts and wedding-related expenses, the equivalence between women's versus men's weddings, and contributions to wedding expenses are analyzed. These paradigms illumine contemporary constructions of kinship and alliance, and show how myths of marriage are articulated with systems of property transmission.

Chapter 4 focuses directly on the ideologies used to rationalize women's alienation from family property. The various myths invoked by women in explaining their attitudes toward accepting or rejecting natal property are presented in order of prevalence, and deconstructed to show their symbolic implications, usually affirming male entitlements to property. Some of these rationales that confirm male inheritance are eldercare, sonlessness, long-term help to women from natal families, and women's severance from their natal homes upon marriage.

Chapter 5 evaluates myths of wealth and considers how they affect social change and influence women's priorities. It lays out the financial resources preferred by women and the principal social problems experienced by them, showing that women often define their needs and analyze their lives in ways that are dissonant with dominant ideologies of gender but also adapt and acquiesce to existent systems given the absence of realistic alternatives. The ultimate significance of property for women and the advantages of using the law are also explored, adding to the picture of sociocultural transformations envisaged by women.

In chapter 6, the focus shifts from analyses of women's perspectives to representations of women's entitlements in legal texts. While women often have favorable outcomes in property cases, these tend to be influenced by certain narrow constructions of femininity, responsibility, dependence, and autonomy, as well as constricted definitions of family and religious identity. These tropes retread the ground covered in postindependence debates about women's rights. They also demonstrate how prevalent myths encoding women's entitlement to property seep into legal judgments.

Chapter 7, the conclusion, pulls together some of the principal questions concerning the power of ideology in maintaining property relations discussed in the preceding chapters: the myths and realities of the equation drawn between property, family responsibilities, and dowry; the ways in which dependence within marriage determines women's entitlements; the effect of social class on women's attitudes and options; and the importance of legal solutions for social change. By foregrounding women's delineations of problems, needs, and preferred wealth, both the gaps in ideology visible from subaltern social positions and the significance of resistant and critical gestures can be evaluated.

# 2

## Women and Property Inheritance

### Scant and Slippery Footholds

How much property do Indian women really own? And how well does actual ownership of land or housing correspond with the legal possibilities envisaged for women? This chapter evaluates the significance of women's property by focusing on these questions, foregrounding women as owners of land and housing and examining the discourse surrounding women's property ownership. By looking at circumstances in which interview respondents formally owned property and those in which they were deprived of it, it constructs a map of property ownership which also reveals the relationships between gender and class, and property and cultural entitlements.

Gender is a significant parameter for differences in inheritance in this sample. The amount of property owned by women is much less than what is owned by their male counterparts, viz. husbands or brothers. This is often culturally justified by the claim that women "get" property through husbands and affinal families while men directly inherit from their natal families, but the data shows that, while men routinely inherit family property, women do not always succeed to their husbands'/in-laws' property either formally or informally. The disinheritance of women from natal family property is ubiquitous, and extreme family wrath comes down upon women asserting any claims to natal property.

Disenfranchisement by gender is complicated by issues of class. Women's relative "class" in the urban setting is a significant determinant of the form of property they might own; whereas many older women in middle-class areas owned family residences that were steadily increasing in value, married women among the urban poor rarely got any shares of their families' substantial rural land, although they had the dubious privilege of owning informal dwellings. Women's best chances of owning property were as owners of the flat/hut the nuclear household lived in or as widows, and in much more unusual circumstances, in sonless families or as rewards for eldercare.

In the following sections, the total family resources of the sample households are tabulated by putting together the various sources from which property may potentially come: the assets of the nuclear unit, possible inheritances from the husbands' and wives' families, and resources from children or other relatives or nonrelatives. Since few women inherit property from their natal families, their natal family's wealth usually affects their household's resource base less directly than marital or affinal resources, but it is necessary to tabulate the resources owned by the natal families to understand what women forfeit by not having access to that wealth. Women's in-laws' property is more directly relevant because couples typically get a share from that if there is anything to divide, and along with the resources the couple themselves may have saved, this makes up the major property fund for the nuclear family.

These patterns of property ownership in the families surveyed show some mechanisms of property transmission among contemporary North Indian communities, but are also important for conceptualizing the complex relationship between gender and property in general. For example, what material goods and social capital should be designated as property? Are women's claims to property better protected within joint families and kinship networks, or formal jural systems? The findings from this sample indicate that in the contemporary political economy, property resources are important for women of all socioeconomic classes, and thus the widespread dissociation of women from property enhances their socioeconomic vulnerability and dependence on male protection.

### Property Values

One of the main reasons that data on property is sparse, even more so in the Indian context, is the fluid and unfixable value of land and housing. Value depends not only upon region and locality, but is also affected by the formal or informal channels through which property is acquired, the potential development prospects of the area, and the economic benefits directly deriving from the land or house, such as crops or access to good jobs. I was made keenly aware of these complexities in meanings of property as I set out to compare the amounts of property owned by the interview households. It was impossible to get a sense of patterns of property ownership without laying out some broad categories, and yet the parameters chosen did not seem reflective enough of complex differences.

For example, I differentiate urban and rural property because they typically have significantly different values, but the variations *within* those categories are likely to be just as large. One of the biggest variations is in the value of residential versus commercial property in both rural and urban areas. In the city, the proportionate value (residential:commercial) in some instances is around 1:4, but the cost of land per bigha,[1] or square foot, varies further depending on the social class and facilities associated with the neighborhood. As cities expand, property in "remote" suburbs typically explodes in value. In rural areas too, there is an immense difference between the cost of swampy land, cultivable fields, residential plots, forest areas, orchards, and commercialized strips. Orchards and shops (especially those close to highways and railway stations) are regarded as prime areas, and fields where cash crops are grown are more prized than land where food crops are typically cultivated. In terms of profitability, an urban apartment in a middle-class area bought long ago by a retired couple now living on their pension yields no additional financial benefits per se, but has a far higher monetary value than rural land which provides its owners with direct economic advantages.

Furthermore, some of the urban land tabulated here is squatter land, that is, it may have been obtained "free" or with a small bribe to the community leaders. Such "property" has potential economic value because it provides access to urban jobs for rural migrants and can also be sold to others or traded for better housing, depending on the development of the area. But because residents hold no formal legal titles to the land and huts, this form of property is also particularly vulnerable to loss without compensation.

Nonetheless, the following estimated costs of residential property for the interview respondents provide a general idea of the property values at issue.[2] For KE, most of the apartments were bought in the late 1960s. For instance, Rani and her husband got their flat in 1969 and paid about Rs. 20,000 in all, in installments over a period of five years. They had been told that a conservative current value in 1991 would be Rs. 1,000,000.[3] In KC, the "lottery" for the flats was held in the early 1960s; the total cost for the flats was between Rs. 3200 and 4000, and Seema and her husband got their flat in 1964 and paid off their debt, Rs. 3600, in about three years. In 1991, each flat was valued between Rs. 400,000 and 500,000.[4] In SN, when extensive migration started in the late fifties, families had settled free on both residential and agricultural land, but now there was no longer any cultivable land in SN and buying a readymade jhuggi/hut or getting one made could cost between Rs. 5,000 and 10,000. Jaya got hers for a "discounted" price of Rs. 1500 because her brother was well acquainted with the people who took this money, but others who had set up huts without bribing the self-designated community collectors or the police had been subjected to harassment and even violence.[5]

### The Significance of Class and Residence

The kinds and amounts of property owned by the women's in-laws and parents, as shown in Table 2.1, illustrate the different ways in which urban and rural wealth are consolidated. While most middle-class urban settlers tended to invest in urban housing, families with a rural base placed a high value on land per se, concentrating on cultivable rural land and regarding urban housing (such as squatter land in this case) as more informal and temporary. As Moors contends, property in the urban context can often be more of a *consumptive* resource, a conduit for having access to amenities like education and proximity to employment, rather than the *productive* resource that cultivable rural land stands for; for many families, wage labor and education could be the most important property fund (1995, 45–48).

The families of KE and KC women had little rural property: only 13.3 percent women from the middle-income group reported their in-laws having some ancestral rural land or houses (i.e., these had been inherited and no assets had been put into acquiring them), and the parents of only 20 percent women from the middle-income

**Table 2.1** Property Ownership by Women's In-laws and Parents (in Percentages)

| PROPERTY OWNED[1] | KE/N=14 IN-LAWS | KE/N=14 PARENTS | KC/N=16 IN-LAWS | KC/N=16 PARENTS | SN/N=30 IN-LAWS | SN/N=30 PARENTS |
|---|---|---|---|---|---|---|
| **Urban** | | | | | | |
| LIG flat | 0 | 0 | 43.8 | 0 | 3.3 | 0 |
| MIG flat | 21.4 | 7.1 | 6.3 | 6.3 | 0 | 0 |
| House | 7.1 | 64.3 | 25 | 68.8 | 0 | 3.3 |
| 1 jhuggi | 0 | 0 | 0 | 0 | 0 | 3.3 |
| >1 jhuggi | 0 | 0 | 0 | 0 | 13.3 | 3.3 |
| <1 bigha[2] land | 0 | 0 | 0 | 0 | 3.3 | 0 |
| >1–5 bighas | 0 | 0 | 0 | 0 | 3.3 | 3.3 |
| >5–10 bighas | 0 | 0 | 0 | 0 | 0 | 0 |
| >10 bighas | 0 | 0 | 0 | 0 | 6.7 | 0 |
| Unspecified land | 21.4 | 28.6 | 6.3 | 12.5 | 0 | 6.7 |
| Business/ Shop | 0 | 21.4 | 0 | 25.1 | 0 | 0 |
| Makeshift Shop | 0 | 0 | 0 | 12.5 | 0 | 0 |
| **Rural** | | | | | | |
| House | 0 | 7.1 | 12.5 | 0 | 10 | 20 |
| <1 bigha land | 0 | 0 | 0 | 0 | 0 | 6.7 |
| >1–5 bighas | 0 | 0 | 0 | 0 | 16.7 | 10 |
| >5–10 bighas | 0 | 0 | 0 | 0 | 13.3 | 3.3 |
| >10–50 bighas | 0 | 0 | 0 | 0 | 20 | 16.7 |
| >50–100 bighas | 0 | 0 | 0 | 0 | 6.7 | 0 |
| >100 bighas | 0 | 0 | 0 | 0 | 3.3 | 10 |
| Unspecified land | 14.3 | 21.4 | 6.3 | 25 | 23.3 | 13.3 |
| Shop | 0 | 0 | 0 | 0 | 3.3 | 0 |
| **None** | 28.6 | 0 | 18.8 | 0 | 3.3 | 16.7 |

[1]Amounts of property were calculated per family, viz. 21.4 percent KE women said their in-laws owned one MIG flat each; some women gave multiple responses. 8.3 percent responses were coded as "not applicable" for in-laws' property.

[2]1 bigha = approx. ¹/₃ acre = approx. 1613 sq. yds.

group had any rural family land. Mostly, these families owned only the houses or apartments they currently resided in, and a few also owned additional urban property: 14.3 percent KE women's in-laws had land in addition to a flat or house, and 31.3 percent of the KC women's in-laws owned two or three flats, houses, or land. This indicates that extended property acquired in urban areas was also directed toward housing, in forms that could be distributed between multiple heirs in the next generation.

In contrast, the affinal families of SN women focused more on rural and cultivable property resources but less on formal acquisition of residences. The in-laws of 13.3 percent of the SN women who had moved to the city had acquired multiple jhuggis for living in, thus spreading out their living quarters with no formal acquisition of property, while also holding on to varying amounts of rural land and even suburban land in one case. 6.7 percent SN women reported a substantial amount of land in the SN area also being taken over by their in-laws, largely for agricultural purposes. Only 6.7 percent SN women reported their parents having jhuggis and urban land in settlement colonies; however, this number reflected the virilocal and neolocal residence norms,[6] i.e. few women's parents lived in SN.

A tabulation of the marital (as opposed to affinal or natal) property owned by the respondents and their husbands (Table 2.2) also shows a similar pattern for the acquisition of rural and urban property. In addition, marital property ownership provides a convenient lens for examining the importance of age or life-cycle stage, indicating the ways in which changing market values and accumulation of resources had made acquisition of property possible. For example, while the older generation in KE and KC had been able to acquire property for the nuclear household quite early in their lifetimes, younger couples were unable to afford buying property given the huge rise in value and higher standards of living, and depended far more on inheritance or possibly buying property much later in their lives.

In KE, many of the flats were still owned by those who had bought them immediately following the original allotment in the 1970s, when they were still quite affordable for young couples starting families: 21.4 percent of sample KE households consisted of couples who had bought the original flats and were now forty-one or older. In addition, two other widowed women (14.3 percent of KE women sampled) in this age group also owned flats, one having

**Table 2.2**   Couples' Marital Property Ownership (in Percentages)

| COUPLES' PROPERTY[1] | KE N=9 | KC N=13 | SN N=27 | TOTAL N=49 |
|---|---|---|---|---|
| **Urban** | | | | |
| LIG flat | 0 | 69.2 | 7.4 | 22.4 |
| MIG flat | 66.7 | 0 | 0 | 12.2 |
| House | 0 | 0 | 7.4 | 4.1 |
| 1 jhuggi | 0 | 0 | 77.8 | 42.9 |
| <1 jhuggis | 0 | 0 | 11.1 | 6.1 |
| <1 bigha land | 0 | 15.4 | 3.7 | 6.1 |
| Business/Shop | 0 | 38.5 | 0 | 10.2 |
| Makeshift Shop | 0 | 15.4 | 14.8 | 12.2 |
| **Rural** | | | | |
| >1–5 bighas | 0 | 0 | 22.2 | 2 |
| >5–10 bighas | 0 | 0 | 3.7 | 2 |
| **Shares in H's family reckoned** | 22.2 | 30.8 | 33.3 | 32.7 |
| **None** | 22.2 | 30.8 | 7.4 | 16.3 |

[1]Amounts of property were calculated per couple, viz. 66.7 percent married KE respondents said that they and their husbands owned one MIG flat each; some women had multiple responses. Widows' property was not counted as being part of the couples' share, but property in married women's names was counted as joint. 22.4 percent of responses were coded as "not applicable"; 1 percent as unknown.

bought the flat during the original allotment using her late husband's insurance and provident fund money, and the other having got the flat in her name about seven years ago (thus at a higher price) with resources including her sons' contributions, her own jewelry, and her late husband's savings. Similarly, from KC, 37.5 percent of the women related that they (along with their husbands) had purchased flats during the original allotment at the very low price, as well as two widows (12.5 percent) who had been married at the time. One couple in the older age group had bought the flat eight or nine years ago at a much higher price, but they had sold their property elsewhere to buy this. Thus, either the age-related opportunity to buy in cheaper times or the accumulation of resources with age were related to the acquisition of property.

Among the 22.7 percent of twenty-two middle-class couples who owned flats at a younger age, 18.2 percent had got the residences through the husbands' inheritance upon their parents' deaths, and in one instance (4.5%) a flat had been given by a KE woman's father to the couple as a wedding gift. Only 15.4 percent married women from KC described their husbands having other land or houses in addition to the flat, although 53.9 percent did report having businesses or shops. In other words, people in KE tended to be professionals or high-level waged employees, and couples appeared to have no investments in businesses or shops. While urban housing was the focus of acquisition, it had become increasingly difficult to acquire, and most younger couples relied on inheritance of portions of the man's family residence as the sole path to property.

Age was obviously a far less significant factor in SN, where it was possible for migrants of all age groups to acquire some property because minimal capital outlay was required in most cases.[7] In all, 77.8 percent of 27 SN couples either had formal jhuggi cards or had laid informal claim to squatter land. Only 33.3 percent of the couples reported *buying* any other property, including 22.2 percent who had claims over squatter land, and 3.7 percent who had some family land additionally inherited from the husbands' side plus the jhuggi. Some couples had acquired LIG flats or small houses when the government had offered these in exchange for jhuggis (and had subsequently returned to SN, profiting from the deal). On the whole, the jhuggis were the main property owned by the couple, and these were highly unreliable as a property fund. The history of settlement at SN showed that state recognition of squatter huts as property was highly arbitrary; although claims had been recognized and equivalent housing provided when huts were destroyed for some municipal projects, there were also numerous instances of families losing large amounts of crop land when informal claims over land in the form of jhuggi cards were not recognized for compensation purposes—for example, after floods in the late 1980s or in 1991 following an alleged environmental initiative.

Given the unreliable status of the jhuggis as property, couples looked to other sources; getting property through the husbands' families was thus crucial for many (only 22.2 percent of SN couples had already inherited land or other assets). In contrast with KE and KC couples, SN couples were far more interested in buying rural land with their savings. However, because even relatively cheaper rural property could only be bought in very small amounts from wages after other urban expenses, inheritance was extremely important for providing core support.

In general, the residential history of SN indicated that families with rural origins used the initial toehold of huts in squatter areas to take advantage of economic benefits like jobs or businesses in the city in succeeding generations, and some families also sold or exchanged these huts later to gain urban property. Yet, unlike the families of the KE and KC women where most property assets appeared to be acquired with the aim of living and working in the city (there being few directly profitable or productive uses of flats and houses not rented out or used as shops), the apparent urbanization of the families of the SN women was almost always accompanied by efforts to retain and extend rural, especially cultivable, land. Acquiring or expanding existent rural property was seen as being a long-term, stable economic asset, as opposed to buying urban residences which could be easily obtained or even free, or urban property with high potential value but little direct productive return.

This two-pronged process of resource acquisition among the families of the urban poor illumines not just the complex dynamics behind urbanization/modernization, but also shows the difficulties of delineating the class positions of rural landowners and urban wage earners in terms of ownership of productive assets. When property assets are considered, the families of the urban poor owned *far* more land than that of the urban middle class, and the total value of such rural property could be greater even after considering the higher value of urban land. Yet despite access to such capital, they lived in the worst conditions and often worked in the lowest-paying jobs in the city, a situation they were rarely able to break out of due to a lack of the kinds of education, training, connections, and other resources that governed access to the most productive urban jobs or businesses (K. Rao et al. 1991, 306). Nonetheless, urban employment for a few members of the family was still seen as a wise economic move, because rural agricultural land, primarily used for subsistence, could be retained and cultivated by a few family members (even the very old or young), while wages from the city brought in additional resources (Hershman 1981, 70).

The strategies adopted by various parts of Pramila's family illustrate the ways in which productive rural property and urban cash-earning opportunities could be optimized. In her natal family, her father and brothers originally had about eight to ten bighas land in Uttar Pradesh. They had worked to increase this *joint* rural property from the surplus urban wages of her three brothers and her father, who worked as mechanics and car and scooter drivers in cities. Meanwhile, the fourth brother stayed home and was in charge of maintaining the land, which he achieved mostly alone and with occasional family and hired help during planting and harvesting season.[8] Significantly, women's labor was invisible in this distribution of duties: several of her brothers' wives stayed in the village when their husbands came to work in the city, and helped with the rural household's upkeep and with agricultural tasks, yet they were not explicitly counted as productive workers in this family bargain.

While Pramila's father and brothers had put most of their savings into increasing their rural property, Pramila and her husband had actually sold urban property in order to invest in rural land. They had moved to SN just a few years ago and opted to stay in the "illegal" huts, having sold their low-income group (LIG) apartment in Delhi's Trilokpuri neighborhood when they needed a large amount of cash to avail of a very good deal on rural land. Because of the rush, the apartment allegedly fetched only Rs. 35,000, considerably lower than the value they could have obtained had they bided their time. They supplemented this money with a large loan obtained through her husband's employer, and bought two bighas of orchard land in her husband's name in their native village in Uttar Pradesh at Rs. 60,000 a bigha, from a childless widow who felt she could not manage all her land. Since then, they had been saving to buy another bigha and a half from the same person, who had promised not to raise the rates. This time, her husband had said, they would get it in Pramila's name so that "if he was gone, the children would feed and bathe her."

Most significant here are the diverse metonymic visions of property. Pramila's family had taken a loss on urban property that assured them better access to her husband's government job and superior educational facilities and career opportunities for her six children, and moreover gone into debt, in order to sink their savings almost entirely into rural orchard land that presently brought them only minimal returns, in an area where they would not live for about a couple decades. Yet this land represented not just an insurance scheme against the prevalent neglect of the elderly, but an idealized affirmation of where "home" really was, where they felt they would finally "return," and the kind of resources that they counted as significant investments in the future.

## Women As Property Owners

Women's situations as property owners (Table 2.3) reveals the ideological codes through which property distribution is culturally represented, and the ways in which women's ownership of resources is mediated and contained. Juxtaposed against the patterns of family property ownership, women's property ownership also vividly demonstrates the complex articulation between gender and class, and the difficulties with delineating women's "class" status.

Women's own economic contributions to the marital property fund appeared to be extremely important in determining whether

**Table 2.3**  Property Ownership by Women (in Percentages)

| WOMEN'S PROPERTY[1] | KE N=14 | KC N=16 | SN N=30 | TOTAL N=60 |
|---|---|---|---|---|
| **Urban** | | | | |
| LIG flat | 0 | 31.3 | 3.3 | 10 |
| MIG flat | 28.6 | 0 | 0 | 6.7 |
| 1 jhuggi | 0 | 0 | 33.3 | 16.7 |
| several jhuggis | 0 | 0 | 10 | 5 |
| <1 bigha land | 0 | 0 | 3.3 | 1.7 |
| >10 bighas | 0 | 0 | 3.3 | 1.7 |
| Business/Shop | 7.1 | 12.5 | 0 | 5 |
| Makeshift Shop | 0 | 6.3 | 6.7 | 5 |
| **Rural** | | | | |
| >1–5 bighas | 0 | 0 | 3.3 | 1.7 |
| **Future Ownership** | | | | |
| planned | 14.3 | 12.5 | 3.3 | 8.3 |

[1]Amounts of property were calculated per respondent, viz. 28.6 percent KE respondents said that they owned one MIG flat each; some women had multiple responses. 7.1 percent KE respondents and 10 percent SN respondents also reported cash assets as property.

they would be owners. 30 percent of the middle-class women were the formal owners of their LIG or MIG flats, and most had made a direct economic contribution toward acquiring those flats. Lata had bought her MIG flat entirely out of the earnings from her job; her husband had never held down a job or contributed to family income, so she considered their flat to be her own property.[9] 44.4 percent of the other nine women who had flats in their name said they had contributed their jewelry toward making the payments. In fact, *all* the women who mentioned contributing jewelry toward paying for the flat were also formal owners; this suggests that either women's property ownership became more likely where they put up some of the capital, or that only those women who had the property in their names pointed out their contributions of jewelry while others did not.

What I find most ironic here is that the potential empowerment represented by women's property ownership and their economic contribution to the capital fund was ideologically recuperated by reference to women's socioeconomic vulnerabilities, by invoking images of women's need and helplessness. In justifying their ownership of property, middle-class women frequently used tropes of male "responsibility" and female "need for protection" even though they themselves had contributed to the fund for acquiring the primary family resource. Bina, who owned a flat and a shop while her husband owned one other shop only, repeated her husband's remark in this context, *"tumhara hai, tumhare nam me rakkho"* ("it's *yours*, keep it in your name").[10] This assignment of ownership hints at the emasculation of accepting women's resources to build up common property (i.e., implying the man's relative lack of ability), and hence the need for overcompensation in the gesture of "giving" the property to the woman. While the reality of women's secondary status in the labor market is acknowledged in this decision, it is recorded in terms of the masculine role of providing women with a source of support, and men's independent ability to acquire other resources through work (or inheritance). However, women's fundamental alienation from marital and affinal property is also registered in the same gesture, because the obverse of the notion that property to which women have contributed any funds counts as "theirs" is the idea that property to which women have not directly contributed anything (a far more common situation) is never really "theirs."

Various *practical* causes were cited for the flats being in the women's names, a frequent one being that couples originally applied under both husbands' and wives' names when there was a lottery for the allotment of flats (to increase their chances of their number coming up), and the later registration was simply done in the name of the person whose name came up in the lottery. But other justifications clearly pointed to the negotiation of gender roles underlying the potential empowerment of "giving" women property. Several women from KC said their *husbands* wanted some property to be in the wives' names so that the women would not be left resourceless if their husbands died and people would not say their husbands left them helpless. Renu (who owned their LIG flat while her husband owned some additional land), even claimed that it had become common in their community for husbands to buy some piece of property in their wives' names for this kind of security.[11] Seema was the owner of their LIG flat, the couple's sole property, but even then, her husband reportedly said *"admi to apne kam-kaj se kar lete hain, aurat kanha jayegi"* ("men can make something for themselves through their own work, but where will the woman end up?"), validating his potential of acquiring resources although he had in fact bought nothing else for himself.[12] The woman's property was thus represented as a "gift" from her husband, symbolizing the man's responsibility, generosity and farsightedness, while her contribution to the family assets (acquired through marriage or paid work) was ideologically masked, even though her ownership may have acknowledged that contribution indirectly. However, this gesture may also have been a way for a husband to ensure that the property (including the woman's original assets) could be returned to her directly rather than being split among various heirs after his death.

Other women from KE and KC who were property owners had also expended their own economic assets or made acquisition of the property possible in some way. Rekha, now fifty-five, had used her "inheritance" upon being widowed, viz. her late husband's insurance and provident fund money, to buy the flat in the 1960s,[13] and two other widows from KC had also acquired flats in their names. In Indira's case, her wealthy father had given a flat to her and her husband jointly as a wedding gift, so her natal family had made the ownership of this asset possible.[14] Indira had no brothers, and was thus likely to get family property by custom, but the partial premortem inheritance in this case was unusual. Sushma, who lived with her family in SN while they were having a house and an LIG flat built elsewhere, was about to become owner of the flat while her husband would own the house. Significantly, she also had a natal "connection" to this flat; it was originally allotted to her maternal uncle and he transferred the privilege of owning a reasonably priced urban flat to her, even though her husband paid for it.[15] Thus, in all these cases, women's succession to property was connected to their own contributions, and relatively independent of the affinal family's resources.

"Ownership" of huts on squatter land had, as always, a very different significance from formal ownership of land or housing; it ensured a certain sense of security for women, but was ultimately a far more vulnerable and far less valuable form of owning property. Nevertheless, a large number of SN women were the formal owners of their huts: 43.3 percent of thirty women reported "owning" one or more jhuggis, that is they had the jhuggi cards made out in their names. This included 6.7 percent women who were widowed heads of households, who each owned several jhuggis, and 3.3 percent also had some other land. Many of the women whose names appeared on jhuggi cards reported doing this mostly for bureaucratic convenience and with their husbands' full agreement, in response to the requests/demands of the card-granting officials that the formal cardholder be someone who was home during the day when they made their visits. Given the negligible legal rights to formal property guaranteed by the cards, and the far greater attention devoted by these families to acquiring cultivable land or better urban housing, the larger number of women "property owners" from this area may not be very meaningful in the context of the total and preferred property of these families.

However, in a couple of cases, married women from SN had deliberately sought individual ownership because of their husbands' proven unreliability and their own responsibility for taking care of family needs. Shobha had insisted on being the owner of their jhuggi, having found out the hard way that without ownership she was unable to protect her family in the most basic ways. When her husband sold their previous LIG flat in a drunken fit, she had been unable to stop the sale by complaining about his diminished capacity and the rights of her and her children to stay in their home. The police had told her then that they could do nothing to save her home if she was not the owner. Similarly, Jaya had acquired the ownership to safeguard her choice to live in the city and her plans for her children's futures. She made sure that she paid for her jhuggi fully out of her own wages so that her husband's threats of selling their house and moving the family forcibly back to the village could not constantly be used to frighten her.[16] For these women who had experienced the vulnerability of economic dependence in graphic ways, and who were unlikely to inherit family property directly, even the relatively insecure ownership signified by the jhuggi cards constituted an empowering step in safeguarding their families' living conditions, being the best solution they could afford.

Poorer women as wives and daughters were sidelined from formal ownership of land resources, while their husbands often got rural land through inheritance, and hence were much wealthier in terms of disposable assets. Other than informal ownership of jhuggis, hardly any women in SN owned any other property. One woman (3.3 percent) owned a small amount of land (in an as-yet unbuilt area) jointly with her husband, bought from his savings, and one was going to get a flat in her name while her husband also bought a house. There was also the highly unusual example of Meena, whose father bought land in her name in their natal village before she was married; later she and her husband became joint owners after he added to it from his savings. These cases and one widow's land inheritance are the only examples of women from this group owning any property other than informal ownership of jhuggis.[17]

A majority of women from SN thus had nothing but the doubtful security of temporary huts in squatter areas, and perhaps token control over small parcels of rural land as widows; in contrast, several women from KE and KC owned the family residences (the prime immoveable property of that family) and some also inherited property in sonless families or as eldercare "payments." A majority of women in all classes did not formally own property, and rarely inherited from their natal or affinal families, putting them at a relative disadvantage with respect to their husbands or brothers. However, even middle-class women who did not formally own property or expect to inherit any reaped the advantages of living in neighborhoods which granted them access to prime education and employment opportunities,[18] thereby acquiring the tools to prosper in the contemporary political economy in ways that men in SN who owned substantial rural property but had low urban incomes could not.[19]

SN women, of course, were disadvantaged on both counts, lacking rural property as well as the resources necessary to make an independent living in the urban sphere; their situation vividly showed the compounded effects of gender and class subordination, as well as the hierarchy of urban skills and privileges related to notions of "development" in the contemporary postcolonial milieu in India. Their situation confirms studies of Indian women's economic conditions showing the greater exploitation of women in the "asset-poor laboring classes" (Bardhan 1994, 149–50). Rural households are becoming increasingly "proletarianized" as land gets concentrated in the hands of the emerging elite (Clark 1994, 128), and modernization "pushes" poor women into wage labor while "pulling middle-class women into salaried and professional jobs" (Bardhan 1994, 162). Processes of agricultural intensification related to modernization marginalize women further because of male control of land, incomes and credit (Ramamurthy 1994).

Perhaps the most contentious issue with regard to women and property has been the class-based nature of property itself, and the consideration of whether insisting on property for women is really a way of furthering class stratification. Rudmin's quantitative study of the cross-cultural correlates of private property ownership shows that private property is likely to exist in cultures with "social and material stratification," and that some women's lives may also be bettered in such cultures (1992, 78–79). Studies of dowry and inheritance, especially in Euro-American contexts, have typically focused on how royalty and the elite used women to channel property among the "upper" classes, strengthening class divisions while cementing the power of the patriarch.[20] However, elite women were not just conduits of property; they themselves also gained some material advantages and status through those resources. Moreover, historians have now also begun to show, through more methodologically challenging processes, that women with middling and even sparse resources owned, bought, and sold property.[21] Thus, any amount of property appears to be generally beneficial in easing women's economic situations and broadening their options irrespective of class.

Nevertheless, the very notion of property (and its association with social stratification) remains problematic in Marxist feminist analyses because the concept of private property appears to embrace ideas of continuing class disparities and impoverishment of the poor at the cost of the elite's consolidation of wealth. Sanghera and Malhana articulate a popular view among Indian women's groups, that asking for property rights is a form of "reformism" and "by postulating this demand a women's group is pitting the propertied class of women against working and landless rural women. How then can there be an autonomous women's movement cutting across class lines when class interests prevail and conflict?" (1984, 3). They argue that the primary referent is class, and that permanent change can only come from addressing the problem of landless families as a whole.

The situations described above point to some of the problems with such a rigid hierarchization of gender and class. As Moors points out, having to choose between gender and class priorities assumes that women/the poor are unitary subjects with fixed needs, rather than being fragmented beings with multiple needs varying by context (1995, 6).With systems of customary support from extended families having broken down, even more so in the urban context, and with national policies having turned increasingly from a socialist emphasis in postindependence times to a focus on "globalization" (Deshpande 1993), looking toward a class revolution to transform women's situations appears not only illusory but also ineffective, because a class revolution in itself will not remedy the violence and deprivation based on gender that poor women encounter. Even if an ideal revolution is the ultimate goal, current strategic considerations are important, and it is unrealistic to deny the empowerment of private property, however little, in a world of economic modernization, or the decreased vulnerability of poor (and middle-class) women through shared ownership of family resources.

## Property Distribution and Marital Status

Unlike men whose rights to property are most often affected by class, age, or birth order, women's ownership and access to property can be strongly mediated by their own status as properties, by whether or not they are married and thus which family affiliations determine their property entitlements. In some cases, being a married woman has been an impediment to property ownership: research on the United States and United Kingdom before Married Women's Property Acts were passed has shown, for example, that women often retained rights to property as widows or single women, but lost all independent control when married (Shanley 1986; Basch 1986). In other instances, the definitive factor has been postmarriage residence norms rather than marriage per se: uxorilocal or ambilocal residence is associated with women having greater rights over property, while shifts to virilocal or neolocal norms are associated with women's alienation from property.[22] Based on their study of Neolithic societies, Coontz and Henderson argue that virilocality may be seen as one of the *fundamental* principles underlying the accumulation of private ("kin corporate") property and the consolidation of social patriarchal power, because it allowed a group to get access to women's labor and that of their children, although women's labor became less crucial for the wealthy as class systems developed (1986, 129–48).

In this sample, marriage affects women's property in ambivalent ways, strengthening socially acceptable paths to gain access to property but also limiting property ownership. Through marriage, women are able to enjoy and even inherit affinal family resources, which is the preferred path for women to "get" property. However, because of this ideological preference they also forfeit claims to natal family property when they marry. Furthermore, in practice women are usually only indirect beneficiaries of affinal property, and grudgingly given token shares of natal property if they are single or divorced. Thus, marriage functions as one of the few viable (if indirect) ways to get both immoveable property and social approbation, while being outside marriage is both materially and ideologically an extremely vulnerable position.

The broad trends of property distribution in this sample indicate that the distribution of property was governed neither by legal guidelines nor customary notions of usufructuary rights for the extended family, but through mechanisms which *used* ideas of tradition, law, and entitlement to reproduce structures of gender and class subordination. A common practice, for instance, was for property to be held in the senior male's name until his death. While the specific shares he designated were divided up in some cases, often the property continued undivided after his death, especially if the senior woman was alive, in which case she was sometimes regarded as the de facto owner who had a say in the final division of the property, her honorable social rank in this matter held to supersede her legal lack of authority.[23] This system nodded toward hierarchies of age and ensured that property was formally consolidated in the male line, even while married women's entitlement to be maintained out of affinal property was acknowledged and contained.

Women's accounts of family property divisions underlined the predominance of inheritance in the male line. Senior males were likely to own and/or control family property in their lifetimes: in 26.7 percent of the sixty cases, the fathers-in-law were still alive and had control over the joint property, while in 33.3 percent of cases the women's fathers were in the same position. Even after their deaths, there was a tendency to leave common property undivided for a while: in 8.3 percent of the cases, the property remained officially undivided among heirs despite the father-in-law's death, and 10 percent women reported undivided property despite the father's death, plus there were 3.3 percent cases where the women's mothers and brothers had also left the property undivided in practice despite separate legal shares having been made. In other cases, property was divided up and almost inevitably went to male heirs: inheritances of immoveable property had already been equally divided between the women's brothers in 23.3 percent cases, and between male heirs, viz. husbands and brothers-in-law (including sole sons) in 10 percent cases pertaining to in-laws' property. In 15 percent cases relating to in-laws' property, the male heirs had received property in unequal shares, that is some sons had received a greater share than others.

These apparently different ways of distributing property all had in common the safeguarding of property for male heirs. The advantage of undivided property, whether the amount was considerable, as with Rani's father's estate of houses and businesses in Delhi, or more modest, like Kiran's family's joint urban home shared with her uncles and their families,[24] was that senior males and their household members could effectively enjoy the property without entering into potentially troublesome areas like formal division, where the rights of all legal heirs including women would have to be reckoned with. Sushila, for example, recounted how her father-in-law had benefitted from leaving the family property undivided: he, along with two of his brothers, had decided to keep their portion of the family land "joint," while the fourth brother had separated his share. The end result had been that her father-in-law had gained effective control of three-fourths of the total family land, about three bighas, by getting the portions of the two predeceased brothers, while having only to pay living costs for one widowed sister-in-law. The fourth brother who had separated his portion ultimately got to use only his quarter share.[25] Thus, unfragmented property was as much a signifier of consolidation of male control as direct shares to sons.

Women's best chances of having control over property were to have legal or de facto power over joint property as widows. In 15 percent cases, the mother had been designated as the official or de facto owner after the father's death, and in 13.3 percent cases the widowed mother-in-law was in the same position. In addition, 21.7 percent women reported that their mothers-in-law had got or would get official or de facto control over the joint property (only 10 percent definitively said they had or would not) and *over one-third* or 36.7 percent women indicated that their mothers had got or would get property (although 25 percent women also said they had or would not).

Women from KE and KC reported high numbers of property-controlling (whether of joint property or not) widows in their families (40 percent women reported this about mothers, 16.7 percent about mothers-in-law), as did women from SN (26.7 percent and 33.3 percent respectively). However, the meanings of controlling property was somewhat different between the neighborhoods, in terms of the entitlement and privileges gained by women because of the different nature of the properties. In the KE and KC cases, given the residential nature of the properties, this de facto ownership simply meant that the family continued to live in the common urban residence, with little other immediate financial benefit. But the ownership was more meaningful where rural land was concerned, as women in this position were sent money by their sons from the city, for maintenance but also as a "payment" for cultivating the common land. In addition, the actual distribution of specific pieces of land (and hence the dispensation of favors) lay largely with the mothers as well, and it was in the sons' best interest to stay on good terms with their mothers and support them financially.

While such de facto ownership was not the predominant means of property devolution, women's rights to property as widows *did* represent their best opportunities to get such resources. The significance of this mode of property access for women is that it represents a culturally sanctioned space of power for women that far exceeds their legal entitlements; if portions were broken up in strict accordance with law, widows would in most cases get smaller portions, similar to their sons' shares, and would not have effective control over entire estates. In Madhuri's joint family, for example, her father, the eldest son, had bought the flat that their extensive joint family all now lived in, using some funds obtained from selling a flat that was in his father's name, but mainly contributing his own savings. He had made his mother the formal owner of this "family home" because she was the most senior member of the family and thus honored as token head of household, even though the money was almost entirely his own.[26] This value accorded to maternal authority in the father's absence (though not in his lifetime) underlines the necessity of marriage as a route of obtaining property, but it nonetheless grants women symbolic access to power and property as mothers, which sometimes translates into effective control of family property.

This legitimation of maternal authority is particularly striking when contrasted with women's ownership of property as daughters. Only 3.3 percent of the women mentioned sisters-in-law getting shares of natal property, while 45 percent definitively said that sisters-in-law had not or would not receive property from their parents. Only 11.7 percent of the women said that they themselves and their sisters would get property, while 55 percent said they would not. The high proportion from SN in this respect (66.7 percent women claiming that sisters-in-law would get no property, and 46.7 percent claiming that they or their sisters would not, as opposed to 23.3 percent and 13.3 percent respectively from the middle-class areas) is a particularly strong indication of the minimal inheritance of natal family land in rural areas by women. In some other cases (6.7% of the women describing situations of sisters-in-law and 18.3% describing themselves and their sisters), daughters were said to have retained their property rights on the grounds that they had got or would get cash or jewelry (though not land or housing) after their parents' deaths, would be offered property whether they took it or not, or had indicated that they would take cash shares if the property was sold (but not if it was retained in its present form). However, these exceptions represent individual negotiations and optimistic projections, while the preceding sets of figures show the strong barriers against daughters succeeding to family property. In opposition to actual or symbolic *maternal* authority, which provided some avenues of property ownership, parity of *sons and daughters* with respect to family assets was highly unusual and customarily blocked.

Apart from the route of getting property as widows, most property inheritance for women generally occurred in unusual circumstances—for example, as rewards for eldercare or in sonless families—rather than as a matter of course. Other routes included making arrangements for unmarried or divorced women, and gifts from disproportionately wealthy natal families. But hardly anyone mentioned actual cases of women becoming equal inheritors of natal property in families where there were both male and female children. The only exceptions were Kalpana, who talked about some affinal relatives who had divided property equally between two daughters and a son "and were still friendly" (dismissing but evoking the specter of family discord that is supposed to emerge when property shares are extended to women), and Champa, who related that a female cousin in her village asked for her share of natal property and managed to acquire it in the face of initial resistance.[27] Even in these cases, the examples cited were distant and almost legendary for those families; there were apparently no instances of women amicably sharing natal property with brothers among the respondents or their immediate families.

Even the apparent ease of ownership for women as widows needs to be treated cautiously. In some cases, this appeared to give women actual powers of dispensation, including the addition and subtraction of heirs, while in others it seemed to be a superficial formality that was challenged if women attempted to transform the status quo in any way. Lalita's husband and three brothers-in-law had agreed that their mother would ultimately get to decide whether a widowed sister-in-law (a brother-in-law's widow) who had been living with her parents in a different village since her husband died would get a share of their ten bighas of rural land. Similarly, Poonam's mother-in-law had decided to leave most of the family assets (three apartments) to the youngest son, and had accordingly made her other sons pay her fully for the value of her husband's two other apartments for the right to live in them, with little reported protest.[28]

In contrast to these cases where the widow's decisions were abided by and accorded utmost respect, others reported that such lip service to seniority could also be merely superficial. As Prem

Chowdhry demonstrates, widows' access to resources is highly threatening to the patriarchal order; land disputes and reformulations of kinship in Haryana in the late nineteenth century were panicked responses to the potential crisis of "alienating" land through widows' ownership (1994, 102–34). Wadley's contention that "widows as potential inheritors are the biggest threat to landed families" (1995, 114) is borne out in numerous instances at thwarting widows' attempts to exercise control over property, such as the following situation in Kavita's family, showing that self-interest could override the symbolic power of the mother.

Kavita came from a prosperous middle-class family in Madhya Pradesh. Her father and uncles had been in military posts and involved in numerous businesses; they had each accumulated urban property from their own earnings, and moreover had inherited some rural land which was maintained as a joint property. When two of Kavita's paternal aunts were widowed, their mother, Kavita's grandmother, was concerned about the comfort of her daughters in their affinal households, and wanted to help them out by making use of their joint family land. But when she tried to reapportion the property in order to give some land to these daughters, she was vehemently opposed by her sons. The sons claimed that legally their mother could only have control over the equivalent of her individual portion, and magnanimously conceded that they would not object if she gave them something from that. Despite her reputation as a dominant and fearful force in the family, she had granted the validity of the claim by not pursuing it any further; instead, she began concentrating on trying to persuade Kavita's mother (her daughter-in-law) that she should give the land she had inherited as an eldercare reward from a neighbor to her sisters-in-law.[29]

This situation vividly depicts the resilience of male entitlements to various forms of property, women's alienation from property, and the slippery use of notions of family and tradition to safeguard these entitlements. While the sons in this case were willing to consider their mother as de facto "head" of the joint family when they got advantages from maintaining rural property as a joint unit, they would not accept the assertion of her authority in any way that altered the traditional division of resources and caused them to incur a loss of resources. The force of their moral outrage lay in their *male* entitlement to family property, and they could vehemently object to helping out their sisters whose need was clearly greater than theirs, because women's entitlement to natal property is fundamentally absent. Even though the brothers themselves no longer operated as a unitary family, and had completely separated financially into nuclear units, they still protested land going to their sisters in terms of it being "lost to the family." On the one hand, they could evoke such customary ideologies to emphasize their superior entitlement, while disdaining the other side of the customary contract that gave them this greater entitlement, viz. the continuing responsibilities to support members of the extended family (who were not direct heirs) that balanced the privileges of inheritance. On the other hand, they called upon convenient legal standards to support their claim, and their superior legal rights to property were of course iron-clad.

The situation of the women in this family highlighted the contradictions of property for women being mediated through marriage. Upon marriage, the daughters' entitlements to natal property were perceived to be severed, and yet as young widows they had little accumulated marital property, no husbands to mediate their enjoyment of affinal property, and were not senior enough to control an independent portion of affinal resources. In fact, their delicate entitlement was further vitiated by any show of support from the natal family, as discussed below, and they were thus caught between two sets of disclaimed responsibilities. Even Kavita's grandmother, who had benefitted from enjoying control of property as a senior widow, was able to exercise authority only if she did not challenge the pregiven distribution: she acquiesced to her sons' contentions and instead used her power to pressurize her daughter-in-law, whose inheritance (earned through her own caregiving) could be viewed as gratuitous and undeserved because as a married woman her "real" inheritance was the enjoyment of affinal property. Kavita's mother, too, was only able to hold on to her own property because the gift was made jointly to her and her son (none of her daughters were included); her son's right to keep any and all pieces of his inheritance, whatever the situations his sisters, aunts, mother, or grandmother might be in, was the only justification that could be used to retain the property his mother had earned.

Not only could widows' de facto inheritance signify a formal honor with little substantive powers to handle the property as full owner, but widows' rights to property could also be threatened by their simultaneous rights as daughters; that is, any financial support from the natal family could result in forfeiture of shares in affinal wealth (Jeffery and Jeffery 1996, 171), signifying that property could be received from only one of the two families. After one of Shobha's brothers-in-law bought or was given a little rural land near his in-laws' place, his widow continued to live there; Shobha claimed that her mother-in-law was unlikely to give the legal quarter share out of their joint five bighas to this widow because she had moved near her parents, despite her affines not knowing whether this woman had actually inherited anything from her parents. Similarly, Sushila's husband and two brothers-in-law intended to foil a widowed sister-in-law's request for a property share by pointing out to the *panchayat* (village council) that this woman had bought property near her natal family (it was not known if the natal family helped her buy this), hoping the panchayat would rule in their favor if they pleaded that the brothers' three bighas should not be diminished further when the woman already had some property. The fact that Sushila's husband and one brother-in-law also had urban wages and a jhuggi in the city did not, however, seem to diminish their own claims, which were based on male entitlement to rural land.[30] Thus, widows' rights to affinal property got eroded by proximity to and help from their natal families, and this apparently secure avenue of gaining control over property seemed to be attainable only at the cost of forfeiting property as daughters.

In any case, most women were even unlikely to succeed to property as widows. Numerous studies have shown that motherhood and seniority does bring women a certain authority and respect, but despite this symbolic power, widows' attempts to get land are often fraught with difficulties.[31] While the number of women who had got or expected to get legal or de facto rights to property after their husbands were gone was high, especially when compared to their nonexistent expectations as daughters, the highest estimation of 36.7 percent still left out the majority of women. This majority, usually bereft of natal property, at best enjoyed the benefits of affinal property mediated by their husbands' ownership.

### Relative Wealth

Even if women were to routinely inherit property through their affinal families or enjoy access to affinal family wealth, the question of whether affinal family property alone compensates for or balances disinheritance of natal property; that is, the extent to which the loss of natal property is significant, can only be answered by comparing the amounts of natal and affinal property and estimating how important natal family property was to the heirs' overall wealth. In this sample, inheritance was a moot issue in many cases: 18.3 percent of the women reported that their in-laws had no common property left and 13.3 percent that their parents had none. This proportion of propertyless families was lower than the 26 percent Indian average cited by Agarwal (1994, 31); a majority of families from all classes did, in fact, have property to bequeath. However, the lower proportion reflects the particular characteristics of the sample: 50 percent of the sample consists of middle-class families owning urban apartments, and the urban poor included here were not all rurally landless, sometimes even owning substantial rural property (only 23.3 percent of SN women reported that their parents were landless, and 13.3 percent that their in-laws were landless).

For many families, inheritance was relatively less important because self-acquired wealth played a more significant role, in cases where sons increased the family property or made individual wealth through their own earnings (25 percent of cases regarding in-laws' property, and 18.3 percent regarding parents'). Only 21.4 percent of the respondents from KE reported this about their in-laws, and none mentioned this about parents, while the proportions from KC were 25 percent and 31.3 percent and those from SN 26.7 percent and 20 percent respectively. Individual acquisition of property appeared to be all the more important for less wealthy families and large families, because even the disinheritance of daughters could not prevent the fragmentation of property into unproductive portions; inheritance per se only brought rights of common residence and common produce from farmland. For example, Champa's affinal family had twenty bighas of rural land, but her father-in-law had four brothers and each of them had between three and six sons, all of whom, along with their families, lived off the land.[32] In the urban context, Sharmila and her sisters had a standing joke that if ever there were to be an equal partition of their old family home, they could carry away a few bricks each as their shares! Her natal family had a large house in a prestigious neighborhood in Calcutta, but between her father and seven uncles/step-uncles, their adult sons and the families thereof, each "unit" (of married sons and families) had been able to lay claim to a couple of rooms at best. The only solution appeared to be for the heirs to sell the property and add the money to their own capital to make individual residences.[33] In such cases, virilocality determined direct enjoyment of property (and easy access to productive resources like crops or jobs) for sons, but led to no substantial material advantages if the daughters also had the benefits of living on affinal property.

However, the economic gains of inheriting property increase proportionately with the amount of land or resources at issue. Among the respondents whose families owned primarily rural land, in-laws and parents appeared in balance to own similar amounts of land,[34] although in individual cases one side of the family was often wealthier, especially when a family owned property at the extreme ends of the scale. But among the families owning urban land, the difference in amounts of property between the women's natal and marital families was more pronounced; among the in-laws there were more MIG and LIG flats (13.3 percent and 23.3 percent respectively as compared to none and 6.7 percent among the parents), but parents owned far more urban houses (66.7 percent of women reported this as compared to 16.7 percent about in-laws; houses are typically worth *much* more). Moreover, among those twenty sets of parents owning houses, a single house was the only asset in only 40 percent of cases; other resources included more houses, unspecified amounts of urban and rural property, substantial cash assets, businesses, a shop or shops. In 10 percent of those twenty cases, parental property consisted of several businesses plus unspecified rural property. These parents were thus reportedly far wealthier than the in-laws, in whose case such multiple assets were rarely mentioned.

In such circumstances, the disinheritance of daughters and the consolidation of wealth in sons' hands had substantial economic consequences, the most obvious being a marked disparity in living standards between brothers' and sisters' *families* in addition to the gap in assets among individuals. Not getting natal family property here appeared quite disadvantageous for the woman as an individual because of her resultant dependence on the husband (or father/brothers if the marriage failed), a dependence exacerbated by the statistical likelihood of her earning less than the men in the paid workforce. The disadvantage extended to the married woman's husband and children too, whose standard of living would be markedly better if they had proportional assets from both sides of the family.

## Non-Hindu Women and Property

While differences of social class, marital status, and age affected the amount and kinds of property owned by women in this sample, there was too little diversity by religion to make any predictions about how different personal laws and religion-based customs affect property transmission to women. In fact, the only three Muslim women interviewed were in family situations entirely different from each other with respect to property, and the variations in their situations also related to factors such as their regional/ethnic backgrounds or family wealth.

Among the Muslim women, Rehana's natal family situation was the closest to the legal norms.[35] Both her paternal aunts and her mother did legally inherit land from their natal families in West Bengal, although each sister's share was half that of a brother's as per Indian law for Muslims. The departure from law came in the informal arrangements these women made; the land was nominally theirs but was cultivated along with the rest of the family land by their brothers. The women "took their share" of this by consuming and taking back some crops on occasional visits, plus they expected help with their children's weddings. As seen in the discussion on wedding costs and natal family help, this situation meant that women got little economic benefit from property ownership since brothers rarely gave substantial help (chapter 3). However, in the larger Indian context the phenomenon of legal ownership itself was quite significant.

Shabnam's family situation, on the other hand, typified daughters' disinheritance from family property.[36] Both her father and father-in-law had bought the rural property they owned (fifteen and ten bighas respectively), and intended to divide it between their sons. Shabnam's comments on why daughters should not receive property reflected hegemonic ideologies: her brothers would break off social relations with her; she would no longer be able to make lengthy visits to her natal home; and she had already been given property in the form of wedding gifts.

Parveen's situation was the most atypical because she was involved in one of the very few reported instances of uxorilocal residence.[37] She and her husband had originally lived with her parents-in-law in the village, helping farm eight bighas but not making enough for themselves. They moved to Delhi to live with her husband's two elder brothers and their families, and finally moved in with her mother and two young sisters at SN at the request of her brothers who lived elsewhere, so that her mother would not be "alone." They had recently had their own adjacent jhuggi built, but though Parveen's husband wanted them to be separate and independent households, they still functioned as a joint household in terms of food and domestic work, with her mother being economically the head of household. The couple had in a sense become part of the wife's natal family, although they had only informal rights to a jhuggi, whereas her brothers had acquired "permanent" houses in their own names when exchanges had been offered for demolished jhuggis. Parveen's husband also expected to get a share of family rural land along with his brothers.

In effect, women had limited or no access to natal property in each of these Muslim families.[38] Customs of virilocality kept women even from enjoying the property they supposedly inherited—for example, in Rehana's family, which showed a formal adherence to legal precepts. Ultimately all these women were recipients only of occasional and uneven gifts from the natal family, and distanced from the full benefits of their natal family wealth. Their situation varied little from that of Hindu women.

## Blocking Women's Inheritance

In most modern nation-states, property rights are vested in the individual; in other words, one of the most powerful effects of Western legal systems has been to construct an individual jural subject with well-defined "rights" in place of collective, communal kinship-based rights where survival and fairness within the group were of primary importance. Yet many sociolegal systems still show a large degree of legal pluralism; that is, the articulated operation of both systems.[39] The persistently thorny question with regard to women's property rights under situations of legal pluralism has thus been whether their lot is in fact improved as jural subjects under the alleged protection of the modern nation-state.

The inscription of women within law has a troubled history: for example, the push to inscribe women as legal individuals in colonial milieus was often connected to the need to establish politico-cultural hegemony or to extract economic surplus (T. Sarkar 1996; Robertson 1997), and the development of property laws for English and American women has been connected to the need for adjudicating debtor relief and legal clarification of equity questions (Shanley 1986, 72–74; Basch 1986, 103–104). The benefits of women appealing to a formal legal system in the modern state continue to be ambiguous. On the one hand, there is compelling evidence that customary notions of resource distribution and usufructuary rights are not useful for seeking equity; in fact, these notions become the basis for women's increasing impoverishment as insertion into the capitalist world-system gives men superior access to the monetized economy.[40] Under the modern state and often the colonizing influence of Christianity, notions of "households" with male heads have gained strength, and traditional forms of women's property and marriage prestations have been devalued, leaving women much more dependent than before.[41] However, other scholars have pointed out that the death of customary law need not be mourned; many sexist biases underlie customary law, and the equity-based and individualistic principles of modern legal systems are much more likely to be empowering for women (Starr 1984, 107–13).[42]

The account of property transmissions in this chapter indicates that it may be misguided to frame the advantages of formal versus customary law for women in terms of an either/or debate; rather, both may operate simultaneously to secure hegemonic privileges. As described earlier in this chapter, allegedly customary practices of inheritance and "traditional" ideas of women's expectations were most often invoked, and formal law ignored, when women were deprived of natal family property. However, when necessary, formal legal avenues were also used to reinforce customary law. That is, promises such as continuing goodwill between brothers and sisters if women took no property formed the discourse that kept this uneven distribution of resources flowing smoothly, but legal recourse was promptly resorted to as an appropriate tool to combat women's recalcitrance, because women were believed to be less knowledgeable about legal maneuvers.

Thus, women were at a distinct disadvantage under legal pluralism, having few rights under customary law and few of the
socioeconomic resources necessary to pursue their rights enshrined
in formal law. However, in the presence of formal law the disadvantage could be mitigated if women were in a position to resist, because those who pursued legal avenues could get some protection
and support (see chapters 5 and 6). The strategies used by families
to block women's inheritance of property, as discussed in this section, provide fascinating insights into how law is used to intimidate
women. These maneuvers show how women's natures and desires
are represented, what makes legal documents fluid or firm, and the
incredible mathematics of tallying across genders.

One of the most common devices for disinheriting daughters is
to bypass testamentary succession altogether and leave the property
directly to sons as premortem gifts.[43] The beauty of this method is
that legal challenges from female heirs can be avoided altogether,
eliminating any possibility of discord. Yet in the following episode
narrated by Vimla,[44] it is important to note how this legal device
manipulated between men to solidify male inheritance was justified
through the specter of female greed, disloyalty, and unpredictability.

Vimla's father-in-law had bought his two elder sons property in
their own names, and as for his youngest son, Vimla's husband, it
was assumed that he would inherit the common residence where
his parents had lived with him, as an eldercare reward. Nothing
had been said about the father-in-law buying anything for his
daughters. Yet, according to Vimla's account, in a conversation with
her husband, her elder brother-in-law told him:

> Get the flat in your own name now (*apne nam karva lo*), your
> father is here now but he might be dead soon. Look, between
> us brothers there is a lot of love, but these "ladies" who are
> there, they can say this is the house that belonged to the
> father and so they too have a share in this, but if father had
> willed it already then no one could have any complaints. . . . I
> can give you a surety about myself, that I will say I want this
> to go to my younger brother, but I cannot say anything about
> my wife, she could make a claim later on.

Both wives and sisters were cast in grasping, mercenary roles here,
in opposition to "pure" and selfless sons. In contrast to the ideal of

mystical love between brothers and sisters that should not be soiled by mercenary matters (evoked by many women in explaining refusals of property, chapter 4, Table 4.1), which frequently comes up as a reason for women declining property shares, here there was a startling inversion; it was the brothers plotting against unsuspecting sisters who portrayed brotherhood as solidarity and the brother-sister relation as being riddled with potential treachery. Sisters and sisters-in-law are also usually depicted as having conflicting material interests with regard to property (chapter 4, pp. 131–32), and so it is notable that here women from both sides were seen to have a common overreaching greed. Here it was those without property who never protested the unequal division, and the relatively propertied and powerful who constructed a negative representation to consolidate their own position.

While legal strategies were used by male heirs to settle the situation once and for all in the case above, in other cases the law was treated as flexible and irrelevant when women did voice a legal claim to property. Ganga told me about an ongoing family conflict that in a way recreated the horror projected by Vimla's brother-in-law.[45] Ganga's husband and one of his brothers had looked after an old bachelor paternal uncle, and upon his death it was apparently assumed that her husband and his *four* brothers (i.e., not just the ones directly responsible for eldercare, but all the male heirs, there being no other male cousins) would share the uncle's cash savings. When the brothers went to the bank and courts for this purpose, however, they were told that because of the uncle dying intestate the money belonged to all nieces as well as nephews, and the men needed signed releases from all the female heirs. As the brothers anticipated, the female cousins signed a document saying they did not need the money and that it could go to the males. But their only sister decided that she was entitled to an equal share. From the total pot of Rs. 200,000, each brother offered her a couple of thousand from each of their shares, but being a political worker and hence relatively savvy about financial matters, she saw through their ploy and brought a legal case against them. According to Ganga, their extended family and community felt she should be able to get a share if she wanted it (some of these people also felt that the brothers killed off the uncle for the money), and that the courts would see that her claim was legitimate if she persisted, but the brothers were so outraged that they would not even let her into their houses, and were determined to use their political clout to influence the outcome of the case.

In this instance, the property being contested was not a direct ancestral inheritance of indivisible rural land to which men might claim privileged access (though it was disputed whether some of this money might have been Ganga's father-in-law's originally), nor was it a precise "payment" for eldercare because all the recipients were not the caregivers. The sister had been deserted by her husband and now had a small business besides doing political work, so it was not as if she were enjoying property from her affinal family. The rage against her was simply because in her assertion and persistence she had rudely violated the gendered boundaries of property entitlements. As in the previous case, brotherly solidarity was viewed by the men as benevolent, whereas the sister was seen as treacherous because she had revealed the embarrassing conspiracy to keep the money among the men.

In yet another family conflict revealed by Vimla,[46] even brotherly solidarity broke down completely when the crisis of women getting an inheritance share tested family ties. This occurred in Vimla's sister-in-law's (husband's brother's wife's) natal family, where the father had said his daughters would be given some property. Thus, there was a clear testamentary intention to include daughters in this case, although they were hardly treated as the equals of male heirs; according to Vimla, the father was a landlord who had a "huge" amount of property, and the token inheritance for his three daughters was *one* piece of land between them. But the sons were horrified at the thought of "their" property being diminished even by that small amount, and reportedly went around hinting at the father's probable senility.

After numerous reminders from the sisters, one strategy was to bypass the designated land, sell a portion of less profitable property elsewhere, and give the sisters the money from that sale, which came to about Rs. 10,000 for each woman. While this resolved the matter in the brothers' minds, all the sisters did not consider it settled, and ironically the issue progressed with a falling-out among brothers over their respective shares. As the brothers began fighting among themselves, they approached the sisters separately and offered them greater shares of the total property if they would side with a particular brother. Vimla reported that all this had resulted in a complicated legal standoff and a complete breakdown of social interactions among siblings. While the amount of property at stake here may have been primarily responsible for the conflict, it is fascinating to mark the flow of brotherly solidarity, holding firm against women's encroachment but crumbling as soon as individual self-interest was threatened. It is clear that property was perceived by the brothers with a profound possessiveness, and sisters were viewed as being fundamentally disentitled to those assets. Yet in what became a parody of pure brotherly relations, sisters were enticed with prospects of property mainly as a way of foiling another brother's rapaciousness and reducing his share.

The perceived ridiculousness of women's property shares is perhaps best exemplified by the bargains offered to women in lieu of property. In the last two cases, the cash amounts offered in exchange for the money or land at issue were paltry, and lacked the basic criterion necessary for a rational trade, viz. that the item offered be attractive enough to justify forfeiting what one might have got instead. The women in these cases seemed to have realized the unfairness of the deal, but other women were cheated through similar calculations. For instance, in Shipra sister's case described in the following section, she got Rs. 2000 in exchange for a share equivalent to at least a hundred thousand rupees, but was villified for asking even for that amount.[47]

I read this mathematical naivete on the part of male heirs not as an attempt at fair compromise at all, but as a product of assumed entitlement. Those who considered themselves to be the legitimate heirs wanted the minuscule amount to stand as a "gift" of magnanimity that would make the pesky problem go away, ignoring the validity of the claims of female heirs. A rejection of this gesture was then seen as sufficient cause for moral outrage. Simultaneously, there was also the threat of dragging the matter through the courts if the trade was not accepted, and women's alleged inferior knowledge of legal maneuvers and their difficulty with going to court regularly for years could be used to drive home this bargain.

### "Hishabey to Ami Pai" ("Well, I Get It According to the Calculations"): Shipra's Family Property

The trades that Shipra and her sister had made with regard to her natal property illustrate the complex binds from which women often made property decisions, showing the paucity of ways for women to be accepted as property owners. Shipra had come to SN about seven years ago, immediately after marriage, and had two daughters at the time I met her. Her husband owned a very small store. She was the youngest of three sisters and a brother, and had lost her mother as an infant and her father at ten. A paternal uncle and his wife had primarily raised her, and later she had also lived in her brother's household with him and his wife. While her father had been alive when her two sisters got married and had reputedly bought all the appropriate gifts for those weddings, her brother was responsible for her wedding costs.

Shipra came from West Bengal, where succession for Hindus follows the *Dayabhaga* system, under which daughters can get far larger portions of property than under the more prevalent *Mitakshara* system (Diwan 1991, 347–49). As Shipra's family divisions show, however, this legal advantage has no significance if women are persuaded to give up their shares. Here, there were about eighteen bighas of land and two large houses owned by her father and uncle at stake, as well as a portion of her mother's inheritance which her maternal uncles had been controlling, and the male heirs managed to acquire it all. The deals offered to the women indicate that the male heirs were all too keenly aware of legal guidelines that needed to be delicately bypassed, while they simultaneously emphasized their naturalized right per custom in taking the women's shares.

According to Shipra, her brother said to her, "Why don't you register the property in my name, and [in return] I'll give you all the right gifts and jewelry when you get married." Shipra told me, "Well, I did have it according to the calculations, but let it be, I decided why not do as they say." There were no role models of propertied women in the area, and Shipra saw little realistic chance of directly enjoying her property. Additional pressure was brought to bear on her because she lived in her brother's household and was reportedly often ill-treated and beaten by him and his wife. Thus, her decision to give him the land was made both in the hope of better treatment at home and the option of escaping the home in the only socially acceptable fashion, through her brother spending enough money so that he could arrange a marriage into a family that was financially comfortable. Similarly, her maternal uncles made her sign with the promise that they would give her gold earrings for her wedding.

It turned out that by giving up the land Shipra perhaps traded in her only bargaining counter. Not five months after she signed the deed, her brother found a husband for her and had her married off almost overnight. The groom had been visiting briefly from Delhi, and had actually been hoping to marry a different woman, but had decided not to at the last minute because her family demanded a large sum of money from him. Because the groom would go back to Delhi very shortly and had no family with him, Shipra's brother believed himself to be exempt from buying the slate of gifts which mark relations of alliance in marriage (chapter 3), and gave her only a few saris; in fact, her husband insisted that her brother had *taken* some money from him to defray whatever wedding costs had been incurred. The maternal and paternal uncles also contributed the smallest of gifts. The husband was estranged from his own family, and thus there were no affinal gifts either. After nine years of marriage, Shipra was completely dependent on her husband's meager income from vending, and did not even have their jhuggi in her name. Perhaps most ironically, her fear that taking the property would have alienated her from her natal family proved moot: they had not maintained connections anyway, she did not know the way or have the resources to travel that far, and her husband had refused to take her because he claimed he would get only a lukewarm welcome as a son-in-law in a home without her parents.

Shipra's sister, on the other hand, appeared to have challenged the passive surrender of land. She was already married, and she and her husband were trying to extend the land they owned near her affinal home. The brother and uncles were seeking her signature at right about the same time as one of her affines was selling off land, and so in exchange for giving up her natal land, she asked them to pay her some cash. Among their families, this gesture had been cast as a fundamental violation of cultural norms, greedy and overreaching. However, it turned out that she took only a minimal amount of Rs. 2000 for a share worth at least a hundred thousand rupees, and was allegedly applying it toward buying land that would cost at least Rs. 30,000.

In these transactions, it is not difficult to see that the ideal of family harmony and lifelong support to daughters functions as a powerful persuasive tool to deny women natal property, but one that is easy to disdain in practice. Like many other women in this study (chapter 5), Shipra believed that owning property could be beneficial for women and could bring them economic security, but could see no realistic way to do so given the other prescribed roles and actions that governed her life. The promised returns to the relinquished property in the form of dowry seemed more a way to make property alienation amenable rather than a realistic bargain. As her sister's case shows, retaining any amount of property or getting any amount of cash instead would likely be no better, and would have brought on her the cultural ostracism that she feared as a single woman dependent on her brother for support. Both owning property and declining property were thus ultimately fraught with difficulties.

## Conclusion: Stable Systems of Disentitlement

In this glimpse of property relations, women's rates of property ownership were better than the abysmal 1 percent world average cited in the UN statistics,[48] but the overall picture did not get much better than that. While property ownership appeared to be a source of security for women of all classes, they had few opportunities to profit from it. As widows, whether in urban or rural areas, or middle-class women married in the 1960s, they had the best opportunities of being formal owners of property, although even that was far from ubiquitous and came with varying degrees of control over the property owned. The relationship between urban and rural wealth and differential access to prime resources in the capitalist economy also played a significant role, and women among the urban poor were particularly cut off from rural family wealth enjoyed by males. Most property divisions were supposedly in the spirit of customary law and ignored newfangled changes, but those who benefitted from such property were entirely ready to use legal remedies to their advantage, and thus the continuance of seemingly old traditions were in fact a consolidation of postcolonial regimes of privilege. Within this old/new scenario, women's role (in different ways depending on class) was always to have access to property mediated through marriage, and to experience property through the gendered codes of protection and vulnerability, rather than in terms of acquisition of power and wealth.

# 3

## Gifts for Alliance

### Marriage and the Flow of Goods

The shadow of marriage and the related transfer of goods looms large in theoretical discussions of women's property. In explaining why women are disinherited from natal family property, myths about the transfer of resources at marriage are frequently called upon: the idea that women's entitlements to family property are transferred from natal to affinal households on the occasion of marriage, that dowry or marriage prestations constitute women's share of inheritance, and indeed the basic notion that marriage itself constitutes the primary form of property for women in patrilineal contexts, whereas men's route to property is grounded in family resources and the labor market or the realm of business. Marriage is thus intricately entangled in the discourse about property; while hegemonically represented as a structural twin of patrilineal property distribution, it is less an avenue of women's property and more a conduit for class formation and the consolidation of wealth, and the strengthening of alliance systems.

This chapter explores how these myths about marriage function to regulate the contemporary distribution of property, by examining the meanings of marriage alliances and wedding prestations, and the significance of dowry as putative property. This is done by focusing on the breakdown of wedding expenses by kind of goods, payer and receiver, and kin-related debit and credit patterns. Families *do* incur a substantial expenditure on the occasion of weddings, often disproportionately more for the bride's family in the North Indian communities studied here. The issue of significance is: Can these expenses be designated primarily as "dowry," and could dowry in

79

that case function as women's property? Wedding costs for daughters and sons are compared in order to evaluate whether the equivalence between dowry and inheritance is merely symbolic. A corollary is that inheritance is forfeited in expectation of long-term dowry, the hope that brothers will continue to send gifts over the years if women's property is not "extracted," and will help with her children's weddings: this idea is checked by examining who pays for weddings and the financial assistance to women from their natal families for children's weddings. These analyses help to reveal the ways in which cultural constructions of family responsibilities, distribution of resources, kinship and gender roles seen in marriage sustain the present system of property transmission.

Wedding prestations are analyzed in this chapter in terms of the two central ways they are characterized in anthropological debates: as tokens for establishing kinship ties between uniting clans and families, or as mechanisms for granting premortem inheritances to daughters. In the first approach, social relations are viewed as being fundamentally marked by gift exchange between groups,[1] and the exchange and circulation of goods and even women through marriage not only determines the accumulation of resources but is the basic building block for reproducing culture and defining the social system.[2] The other popular notion, related to research showing that women's property rights often came about as a way of consolidating class interests,[3] is that women's inheritance comes through their dowry—that is, that the transfer of resources at weddings marks transfers of wealth to women.[4] In the following sections, the analysis of the content of and meanings assigned to wedding prestations is used to evaluate which of these two concepts most effectively explicates the data.

## Setting Up Matches: Gifts for "Alliances" Only

My mother would not have had any objections if I had gone in for a "love marriage," but it's just that I never fell in love (laughs) and I could not have one, so it had to be an arranged marriage, and if it had to be an arranged marriage it had to be within the same caste, because my mother said "With a love marriage I would not have objected but if you want me to find a match then I will have to look in my extended friends' circle etc. so it will have to be from the same caste." (Uma)[5]

The Indian norm is for families to "arrange" marriages and be involved in approving the affinal connections to be formed through marriage; a prevalent attitude among people of marriageable age (Sharma and Shriram 1979; Sprecher and Chandak 1992) is that marriages establish alliances between families and hence must be carefully arranged in the best interests of everyone. "Love" marriages or self-arranged marriages (the "romantic" or companionate marriage model predominant in contemporary Western culture) are regarded with much greater suspicion because they are believed to result in minimal bonding between marrying families, although they are associated with the attractive rhetoric of contemporaneity and "progressive" attitudes. The dividing lines between the two forms of marriage may be broached further by allowing limited or extensive social interaction between the couple. Ultimately, however, family-arranged marriages are not only a frequent default option for those who might have no objections to self-arranged marriages, but are most important because of their significance in establishing kinship systems.

Self-arranged marriages were very rare among the families included in this study: among the sixty women interviewed, only one (1.7 percent, from KE) had a self-arranged marriage, and the women mentioned only five other instances of such marriages among their relatives. Significantly, Ritu, the one woman who had found her own partner, had been completely cut off from her family. The ostensible cause of disapproval was the groom's different religious background (he was Sikh and her family was Hindu), but Ritu was convinced that her brothers' ire was fundamentally a question of her family losing control over "their" woman, particularly because of her high earnings as a lawyer.[6] This statement echoes the opinions of several other women that it was less socially acceptable to the women's families that they make self-arranged marriages.

Even the three single women and one married woman (6.7 percent of all respondents, all from the middle-income neighborhoods, and all below thirty, i.e., among the youngest) who claimed that their individual choices of marriage partner would be acceptable to their families, focused on the choice to find spouses more as a way to highlight their families' alleged progressiveness rather than as a realistic option for themselves. Limited venues for social interaction between "suitable" men and women in an urban setting (especially women who do not go out to work or study), subcaste endogamy and lack of ethnic and social mobility tend to make self-arranged marriages difficult to achieve. Moreover, they visualized the ideal marriage as being akin to family-arranged marriages, in the crucially important dimension of closeness between the families (rather than the individual characteristics of the couple) being the primary deciding factor.

Uma's comment at the beginning of this section illustrates this gap between hypothetical possibility and common outcome. As she indicated, there were few social opportunities of finding a partner, and given the inevitability of marriage within her cultural nexus, her family took over the task. In her case, her mother began to look for a groom while she was finishing her Master's degree, but ultimately one of her professors came up with the proposal that his brother might be a suitable groom, and the suggestion was followed through by her family. Implicit in her comments is the notion that "suitability" of the groom was measured in terms of narrowly defined class, ethnic, and professional parameters, whether the spouse was selected by the individual or the family.[7]

The majority of weddings had been arranged by finding brides and grooms from broad kin and affinal networks. Of the forty-two marriages where data about the mode of arranging weddings was available, 57.1 percent had been fixed by looking among distant relatives and affines, and to a lesser extent in the subcommunity/jati.[8] For instance, Medha married her sister's husband's brother, and Shashi's eldest daughter found grooms for her younger sisters among her affines.[9] Even among the 28.6 percent cases where friends, neighbors, colleagues, or business associates had facilitated matches, the extended family was usually involved in some way. Poonam's paternal aunt suggested a match between her niece and her neighbor's brother's son, and Sharmila's maternal grandmother was a friend of her eventual husband's paternal aunt.[10] Other paths, viz. marriage brokers or newspaper advertisements, constituted only 7.1 percent of cases, and in one case even a match initially set up through a response to an advertisement turned out to be among extended kin.[11] While social class, education, and employment were said to play a major role in determining choices on both sides, one of the major criteria was still endogamy, within the subcommunity or at least the larger ethnic group (Paul 1986, 8, 187–88). This similarity also facilitated a certain unity of expectation with regard to wedding and postwedding exchanges of goods and distribution of resources.

The most significant correlation between marriage transactions and the mode of arranging weddings was that *only* family-arranged marriages were associated with the network of gifts between families. Self-arranged marriages were placed completely out of the loop of prestations and the corresponding establishment of affinal ties.[12] In the self-arranged marriages, whether the wedding took place at a marriage registry office or was a simple ceremony at a temple or *gurdwara*,[13] there were no customary ceremonies or gifts exchanged, although the marriages were accepted within the families (except for Ritu who had all connections with her natal family severed). In these cases, marriage gifts or dowry were clearly not seen as premortem inheritance; rather, it was assumed that such marriages provided relief from customary gift obligations. The one exception property-wise was Bina's daughter, who had been given a flat by her paternal grandfather ostensibly because her family had given no wedding gifts; however, the primary purpose behind the gift was to help out the couple, who were economically in a worse situation than their families.[14]

The other cases of completely giftless weddings were from SN: the one instance of second marriage, and the three cases regarded in the community as "bridal sales," where the groom paid for the wedding (paying the bride's brother for "wedding costs" in two cases, and in one case paying a man who demanded payment for a distant relative whom he had brought from the village).[15] These marriages were also accepted by the community, but the weddings were accompanied by no more celebration than a small blessing ceremony by the women of the community in two cases, and a gift of a few utensils and a meal for relatives and friends in one case. In these weddings, where the brides were previously married women or fatherless daughters with brothers who claimed to have no money to pay any wedding costs—that is, women who were disadvantaged in an already difficult marriage market—contracting the wedding in itself appeared to free the family from customary obligations. Again, this did not translate into women getting shares of their natal family property instead; rather, it was a way of placing them within marriage (the sanctioned path to property) and discharging a natal family's alleged obligation. In the cases of these "difficult" brides, the objective of extending kinship relations through marriage was forfeited in favor of a goal that could be more problematic for the families: the possibility of nonmarried women claiming natal property or expecting long-term help from natal kin.

Methods of spouse selection thus determined the cultural networks set up between families, and marriage prestations served as tokens of family alliances. In a system validating Maussian analysis, family-arranged endogamous marriages were seen as being within the circle of gift exchange and kin network consolidation, whereas self-arranged marriages, remarriages or bridal sales did not have the benefits of facilitating relations within the subcommunities and hence were not cemented through gift giving. From this perspective, any personal dowry given to the woman was a small part of wedding prestations, secondary to the aim of extending kin networks. Women's forfeiture of all gifts in atypical marriages, as well as the strong cultural preference for strengthening kin networks through marriages, thus indicates the relative insignificance of property concerns in wedding prestations and underlines the centrality of gifts for founding kin relations instead.

### Wedding Ceremonies: The Framework for Gifts

In Hindu communities, while the "Vedic Marriage" is held up as the ideal, most weddings contain diverse ethnic and local customs and limited scriptural commonalty.[16] Customarily, several ceremonies precede and succeed the actual wedding, often including occasions for exchanging gifts between the families entering into the alliance. Though names varied according to the community and region of origin, some of the most common ones in this sample were: *roka* (celebrating that the match had been finalized, "booking" the groom); *chunni charhana* (event held at the bride's house when groom's family brings her gifts of clothes and jewelry); *sagan* or *tilak* (when gifts are taken to the groom's home, this may occur several times but usually takes place a few days before the wedding); a ring ceremony or an engagement (hosted by the bride's family, when the couple exchanges rings); *lagan* (when gifts are sent to the bride's family but are reciprocated in equal or greater amount); and *gowna* (a postwedding celebration, held one to three years after the wedding. The bride returns to the natal family after the wedding and goes to her affinal family a few years later).

Although different names are assigned to similar ceremonies within and between ethnic groups, and there are variations even within families at different weddings, there were some common patterns. In every case, even where the wedding was fixed in a matter of days or hours, there was a prewedding ritual where the bride and/or groom were blessed by members of the other family and given a gift. In some families, there were several engagementlike ceremonies (*rokna, chunni charhana, sagan, tika, tilak, thaka, engagement, ring ceremony, paka dekha*, etc.), always involving food and gift giving.[17] During the actual day or days of the wedding (*shadi*), the responsibility for feeding, housing, and entertaining the wedding party or *barat* was on the bride's family, including the main wedding meal to which several hundred guests from both sides were often invited. More rarely, the groom's family had a reception or celebration only for their own guests before or after the wedding.[18] Some families also had extensive postwedding ceremonies such as the gowna.[19]

Despite the seemingly long list of ceremonies, however, each family participated in only a couple of pre- or postwedding ceremonies. Only 7.3 percent of weddings were reported as having more than three ceremonies (including the *shadi*/wedding itself). 41.7 percent weddings reportedly had two ceremonies including the shadi, and 38.6 percent had three.[20] Several respondents claimed that financial concerns, time constraints, and the diminished significance of old rituals had led to an abbreviation of ceremonies. While a breakdown of weddings by decade could not definitively demonstrate this trend, several women narrated the ways in which urban modifications had altered the customary elaborate forms of ceremonies perceptibly. For instance, Madhu's sister and Uma, who had both got married about five years ago, had the wedding party at hotels in Delhi, and the nature of this site determined a time limit for beginning and ending the party.[21] In contrast, Uma dimly recalled attending cousins' weddings in their village home as a child, when the bride's family had to invite neighbors and the wedding party for various different kinds of meals (for example, fruit and sweets one day and "cooked" food, e.g., fried rice and vegetable dishes, another day) in the week before the wedding. Jaya, who was married fifteen years ago in her village and frequently went back there to attend weddings, testified to the influence of urban abbreviation having carried over to villages, resulting in grooms' families making much shorter visits than earlier. This view is contested by rare accounts like Medha's (also married about five years ago), who described a full fortnight of festivities with myriad rituals including kin and women from the whole village.[22] Many families had thus begun to shorten the process (and hence the repeated expenses), but a few still observed the full range of ceremonies, especially, as in Medha's natal family's case, as a marker of status.

Compared to Hindu weddings, Sikh and Muslim weddings are ceremonially far simpler, even though they involved a similar volume of expenditures overall. Sikh weddings involve the couple circling around the Sikh Holy book, the *Granth Sahib*, and exchanging garlands, followed by readings from the book and religious songs. However, in terms of prewedding ceremonies, the pattern described was identical to Hindu weddings, including *rokna, sagan, tika,* ring ceremony, *chunni charhana.*[23] In Muslim weddings, the *maulavi* (cleric) officiates between the two families, and the main ceremonies involve getting the formal assent of the bride and groom and settling the amount of *mehr.*[24] But here too, the women narrated a series of prewedding ceremonies: a ceremonial occasion when the match was first settled, involving a meal and presents for the groom's family and a small gift for the bride, and a later occasion when gifts were exchanged between families, even the observance of a turmeric-and-oil ceremony prototypical of Hindu weddings. In these cases, it was not necessarily the dominant presence of Hinduism that influenced the ceremonies, but the fact that norms for prestation ceremonies were to a certain extent determined by community practices.

The diversity and extensiveness of wedding ceremonies among the various communities attest to elaborate ritual frameworks for marriages, where community and affinal relations were cemented on a variety of occasions. Although these ceremonies were often telescoped in the interests of time or money, their traces still functioned to strengthen relations with wider kin through gift exchange. If gifts needed to be given on fewer occasions at present, they were also likely to cost more and to include ever-trendier commodities among all social classes. Thus, the current pattern of ceremonies appeared to preserve the practice of establishing ties with affines through extended gifts, while optimizing the time and expenses required to do so.

### *Jo dena hota hai* (What Has to Be Given): The Nature and Parity of Wedding Gifts

The ways in which wedding gifts (dowry or bridewealth)[25] demarcate roles and hierarchies have long been used by anthropologists to study kinship and cultural systems. At the heart of these debates are the meanings of such marriage payments: What are they meant to be "payments" for? How does their significance change as customary practices are articulated with transformations in the political economy? How are class and gender status marked through wedding payments?

In the Indian context, the form of wedding gifts clearly reflects transformations in the political economy connected to the worldwide migration of white-collar and blue-collar workers from India, a huge rise in conspicuous consumption standards particularly among the middle class, and the dominance of market-driven agendas and development ideologies in shaping the lives of people, even those living in the remotest of areas. With greater educational opportunities and salaried jobs becoming available, as well as an apparent oversupply of marriageable women, amounts of "dowry" and "groomprice" have increased in several communities, and have even displaced bridewealth.[26] In contrast to studies that continue to relate marriage prestations to socioeconomic hierarchies (e.g., Schlegel and Eloul 1988, 295), dowry appears ubiquitous in all classes. Agarwal shows that many "tribal" groups who until recently lived by communal land ownership, and who have diverse forms of marriage prestations linked to customary notions of property distribution and responsibilities, are also changing their practices of gifts and land access in response to the effects of the hegemonic mode of production (1994, 154–67). Thus, while the form of wedding prestations is diverse, based on customary gifts in the ethnic groups or community or subcaste in question, their elaboration and modification reflects dominant ideologies about class and consumption.

At most weddings, there is a complicated traffic in gifts between affines and gifts to the marrying couple. The simple duality of whether these gifts are markers of alliances between families *or* women's inheritance is thus difficult to resolve because gifts are rarely unidirectional, and are typically given to a number of people for a variety of purposes. In a Hindu wedding with Vedic rites, for example, one of the central ceremonies of *kanyadan*[27] is characterized by a token payment or *varadakshina* to the groom during the ceremony—that is, these payments from the bride's family are interpreted as being part of scriptural prescriptions (Teja 1993, 53; Paul 1986, 6).[28] *Stridhanam/stridhan*, or women's wealth, is supposed to be part of the wedding payments as well, typically visualized as jewelry or vessels given to the bride herself as a personal fund (Paul 1986, 4), though not necessarily portrayed as an equal inheritance share.[29] The situation is further complicated by the fact that in most Hindu weddings both families do exchange gifts despite the disproportionate expenses by the bride's family.[30] Indian Muslim weddings, which incorporate the customary payment of *mehr* from the groom's relatives to the bride, though often only in token form, also commonly incorporate (as do Indian Christian weddings) the pattern of gifts to the bride, groom, and groom's family associated with Hindu weddings (Shukla 1987; Ahmed and Naher 1987, 38–42).

In this sample, except for self-arranged marriages, second marriages and bridal "sales," there were no giftless weddings. Though the specific amounts and presents given at any one event varied in every family, there appeared to be well-established norms of appropriate prestations. Mapping the patterns of expenses and gifts from either side provides a revealing portrait of the different roles that the couple's families are supposed to play, and the related cultural constructions of family, responsibility, and wealth.

Data for total costs of weddings in the respondents' families was difficult to obtain. When asked to estimate the cost of their own or recent family weddings, only a few women (23.3 percent in all, but only one or 7.1 percent from KE) responded with precise figures about expenses incurred by the bride's family. Most women could not provide specific amounts because they claimed it was too difficult to calculate the total amount, especially when considering that some major items like jewelry might have been bought years earlier, that relatives might have contributed some clothing, jewelry, or furniture as gifts, and that no tallies of expenses for various occasions were retained. Many were uninformed about the actual cash required even when they knew about the expenses, especially if they had no income or credit sources of their own and relied on income earners (often males) in the family for money. They were particularly in the dark about expenses for their own weddings, either because they had been too young at the time of marriage to comprehend the transactions, or because the seniors in the family (often parents) had handled the disbursements directly even if they had been married when in their twenties and in paid employment. The disjunction from financial awareness was partly related to age and parental responsibility for handling weddings (even for grooms), but gendered notions of women's dissociation from direct fiscal resources undoubtedly also played a part in their ignorance of expenses. As Ursula Sharma found, women tended to be fully involved in the negotiating process but did not usually take on the actual financial procurement (1980, 144).

It was expected that total wedding costs would be relatively lower in SN, given families' lower incomes and also the fact that most weddings took place in rural areas where costs of food, space, and entertainment were likely to be lower. This was confirmed by two women (6.7 percent of SN sample) who mentioned expenses between Rs. 10,000 to 30,000, and three (10 percent of SN sample) who mentioned expenses between Rs.30,000 to 50,000. The comparative cheapness of rural weddings was also attested to in Bina's decision to have her daughter married near her in-laws' village (though they had no regular contact with the area otherwise); she spent only Rs. 10,000 to 20,000 excluding jewelry, whereas some extravagant urban weddings among her relatives had allegedly cost up to Rs. 1,000,000.[31] In contrast, only two women from SN reported a high cost for the bride's family at a rural wedding, although Medha's wedding costs of over Rs. 100,000 were partially explained by an unusually high cash dowry of Rs. 30,000, supposedly demanded because of her father's wealth.[32] Women from KE and KC reported much higher costs for current urban weddings, between Rs.70,000 and 200,000.[33]

Income, social class, and rural versus urban norms of spending did seem to affect the total expenditure. It is also important to remember that these figures represented average costs, and that in fact the scale of expenditure could vary widely at either extreme. While Medha's and Bina's relative's weddings were far more costly than other weddings in their families and communities, others also described weddings that were pared down from community norms. Uma made it clear to her fiance that the marriage would not take place unless his family rescinded their demand for cash to cover their expenses, and because of her strong antidowry feelings the only expenses her family incurred were for feeding the wedding guests at a hotel and buying a few saris for her.[34] When Bindu married a man from Haryana who worked in transportation (she was from Uttar Pradesh), her husband was sensitive to her widowed mother's lack of money; he forbade prewedding gifts for himself, claimed to be happy to be given just a suit as a gift, and brought her some clothes and jewelry himself.[35] Thus, individual families could negotiate gifts and expenditures on either end of the scale, though the baseline was no doubt set by class, regional, and ethnic norms.[36]

Although even fewer women had estimates for the total costs of weddings for groom's families, the range of expenses varied widely, and no conclusions could be drawn about comparative costs of brides' and grooms' weddings. From SN, one woman (3.3 percent of SN sample) reported that it was between Rs. 5,000 and 10,000, and two women (6.7 percent of SN sample) said it was between Rs. 10,000 and 30,000, the amounts being expectedly lower than quotes from the other neighborhoods. But three women from KC (10 percent of middle-class sample) cited amounts that spanned a huge range: from between Rs. 50,000 and 100,000, to between Rs. 100,000 and 200,000, and the third over Rs. 200,000. While the details of gifts described in the following pages indicates that bride's families usually incurred far more expenses, it is difficult to draw this conclusion merely by comparing the few estimates of total expenses, without knowing how much of these expenses were recycled into family assets as jewelry or spent on entertaining business associates.

However, the reported expenses for grooms' families were important in emphasizing the gap between ideological notions (of compensating daughters but not sons through dowry and wedding expenses) and actual expenses of sons' and daughters' weddings: the differences were not large enough to account for women's wedding gifts being an inheritance share. Table 3.1 and 3.2[37] show a far longer list of expenses for brides' families, but only a third of the fifteen women who discussed comparative costs said daughters' weddings actually cost more, and only Parvati said that in her community in central Nepal grooms' families usually spent much more.[38] Significantly, 60 percent of responses in this category reported the costs of sons' and daughters' weddings as being comparable. Only one response from SN (6.7 percent) conveyed this, indicating that grooms' families among poorer people may have had lower expenses for sons' weddings than for daughters, while the parity of expenses was far more prevalent in middle-class families. Given that weddings mark an overdetermined "display" of social class through food, entertainment, and gifts, the stakes are indeed higher for wealthier grooms' families, with the entertainment and jewelry having to be of a standard that showcases their perceived status appropriately. Importantly, in such cases, wedding costs or dowry for daughters (though also potentially larger as markers of status) become even less of a substitute for inheritance, because equivalent family assets are spent on sons' weddings.

Expenses of daughters' and sons' weddings being *similar* should not, however, be taken as evidence of total *parity*; the breakdown of expenses and the kinds of gifts (Table 3.1 and 3.2) are crucial indicators of different purposes for the expenses, which lead to an accumulation of assets in line with prevailing hierarchies. Table 3.1 enumerates the gifts given from bride's families; for most families, the bulk of the items were clothes and/or jewelry for the bride, groom, and the groom's extended family (this sometimes included cousins, and indeed anyone who came with the wedding or engagement party). Other gifts reflected the class backgrounds of the families: while wealthier families gave the trendiest electronic appliances and furniture (e.g., color TVS, VCRs), more middle-class families went with less expensive versions of the same, and relatively poor families gave utensils, luggage, or bedding.[39] As Table 3.2 shows, grooms' families' gifts were principally for the bride, and reciprocal gifts were rarely given to the bride's *family* (Hershman 1981, 213). Thus, the bride's family added to the resources of the groom's family and endowed their daughter with personal gifts, while the groom's family usually gave gifts for the bride only.

Table 3.1 and 3.2 also indicate that a higher volume of gifts were reported from KC as compared to KE, where incomes were substantially higher and hence displays of status may have been expected to be more elaborate. But in many weddings described by the KE respondents, there had been a conscious effort at keeping prestations simple, whereas in weddings reported by KC women, the latest fashions in dowry goods were often followed. However, families from KE (including grooms' families) spent a lot of money on entertaining guests, indicating that this mode of displaying status (entertaining business associates, friends, and neighbors) was more

**Table 3.1** Gifts Given by Brides' Families per Wedding (in Percentages of Total Number of Weddings)

| GIFTS BY BRIDES' FAMILIES[1] | KE N=24 | KC N=25 | SN N=47 | TOTAL N=96 |
|---|---|---|---|---|
| Clothing and/or Jewelry: | | | | |
| For Bride | 83.3 | 96 | 87.2 | 88.6 |
| For Groom[2] | 66.7 | 72 | 63.8 | 66.7 |
| For Groom's Family[3] | 54.2 | 72 | 38.3 | 51 |
| Utensils | 4.2 | 12 | 57.4 | 32.3 |
| Furniture | 20.8 | 60 | 17 | 29.2 |
| TV/VCR/Refrigerator/ Kitchen Appliances | 16.7 | 32 | 6.4 | 15.6 |
| Bed/Bedding | 0 | 0 | 12.8 | 6.3 |
| Suitcases/Trunks | 0 | 0 | 8.5 | 4.2 |
| Land/Property/Livestock | 4.2 | 0 | 4.3 | 3.1 |

[1]Brides' families' expenses also include hosting the wedding party.

[2]Gifts to groom usually include clothing plus *varadakshina* gifts, which may be jewelry, a watch, and even a radio or a bicycle as part of the varadakshina package.

[3]Recipients of gifts in groom's family include groom's parents, siblings, and their families. Other relatives who are part of the wedding party are also usually given small presents.

**Table 3.2** Expenses Incurred by Grooms' Families per Wedding (in Percentages of Total Number of Weddings)

| EXPENSES BY GROOMS' FAMILIES | KE N=24 | KC N=25 | SN N=47 | TOTAL N=96 |
|---|---|---|---|---|
| Clothing/Jewelry for Bride | 25 | 40 | 53.2 | 42.7 |
| Clothing/Jewelry for Groom's Extended Family | 4.2 | 0 | 0 | 1 |
| Entertainment/Reception | 29.2 | 20 | 8.5 | 16.7 |
| Cash Gift to Bride | 0 | 0 | 8.5 | 4.2 |
| Utensils | 0 | 0 | 2.1 | 1 |
| None | 12.5 | 4 | 4.3 | 6.3 |
| Unknown | 45.8 | 56 | 36.2 | 43.8 |

important in this wealthier area than personal items included in the dowry.

Contrary to the common perception of dowry as large amounts of cash, it was far more common in this sample to give small amounts of cash to the groom and his family, on various prewedding and wedding ceremonies.[40] Only 3.1 percent weddings had reported cash expenditures between Rs. 10,000 and 50,000, and 8.3 percent included cash gifts between Rs. 5000 and 10,000. In fact, in 20.8 percent of weddings the total cash gifts were reported to be less than Rs. 2000, and in 14.6 percent no cash gifts from the bride's side were reported at all. Thus, cash appeared to play a relatively small part in total wedding expenses by the brides' families.

Though relatively less, the expenditure of cash was still disproportionate, as revealed by a tabulation of cash given by the *groom's* families: there were no cash gifts described by the KE respondents, only two cases (8 percent of KC weddings) of gifts over Rs. 1000 to the bride reported from KC, and eleven (23.4 percent of SN weddings) instances of cash gifts to the bride named by SN respondents. Cash gifts to the bride were popular in SN because grooms' families who could not afford much jewelry gave a token sum of cash instead. Yet these amounts were much lower than the amounts given to grooms' families, more so in SN where 45.4 percent of the cash awards to the brides were less than Rs. 500, and 81.8 percent were less than Rs. 1000. The gap in reciprocity between brides' and grooms' families in this area reflects the broader lack of parity between the responsibilities of the two sides.

A concrete example of the lack of parity in gifts between families is provided by Rani's son's wedding.[41] Paying "homage" to the doctor groom and the senior scientist father-in-law (the bride herself was also a doctor), the bride's family gave, in addition to clothes and jewelry for the bride, a set of gold jewelry for the groom's mother, gold rings for the groom and his father, a bedroom set and a refrigerator, a cash gift of several thousand rupees for the groom and smaller amounts of cash to the whole wedding party, and clothes for twenty-five to thirty relatives. In fact, they asked Rani and her husband to choose the clothes for the groom's extended family (which the bride's family would pay for), so that the gifts would be of a sufficiently high standard. Rani thought that as the groom's family they showed exemplary decency by declining such gifts as a TV and VCR (although the rationale she used was that they already had them and that the duplicates would simply rot in boxes, a denial marked by an emphasis of the groom's family's resources).

Furthermore, apart from buying jewelry and expensive clothing for the bride, Rani and her husband were atypically generous in buying clothes for the bride's parents, feeling that this would reassure the bride's family about the prosperity of their affines. The major expenditures on the groom's side were the postwedding reception for six hundred people—colleagues, neighbors, and relatives—and a prewedding reading of the Holy Book which lasted three days and to which all these people were invited. However, only the bride's parents and siblings were invited to these events, whereas the groom's side took three hundred people to the wedding to be fed and entertained by the bride's family. Rani's son's wedding expenses are significant because total costs for both sides appeared similar; however, a breakdown of expenses reveals that the reciprocity from the groom's family in giving gifts to the bride's family or entertaining them was minimal.

Ritu, whose family wealth lay in a chain of medicine shops, surmised similarly, based on her experiences of her brothers' weddings (her own had been performed by a magistrate), that total expenses by the families involved often seemed equal but expenses made by the groom's family mostly went toward their own assets:[42]

> They have basically the same expenses, for the girl one is going to give a sort of dowry, like household goods or clothes which are not that expensive, but I have seen in my family that they buy more gold for the son than for the daughter so the total amount is the same. Also any 'ancestral' jewelry is given to sons' wives but they buy from the market to give to daughters, and the sons' wives jewelry is also heavier.

Ritu and Rani's examples point to a significant fissure in the myth of reciprocal gift giving: the bulk of the groom's family's expenses— the bride's clothes and jewelry, entertainment of their own guests— helped to enhance *their own* wealth and prestige (if the bride's "personal" things are regarded as being part of the groom's family's total assets).

The disproportionate expenditure points to the potential hierarchical relationship between the two families and the bride's inscription as an asset of the marital family. For example, in delineating the greater expenses for the bride's family, a principle she followed for her daughter's wedding two years ago despite the dire economic hardship of being a widow and the only meager income earner in a family of seven, Hema said,[43]

> For every Rs. 100 of things they give, we [the bride's family] have to return Rs.151 in some form. . . . See, if one does not have the ability to be able to take those things, then one can just keep Rs.51 or Rs.21 from that plus the sweets and return the rest. And those who want to and are able to can give back more than what is given by the groom's family, they can keep the clothes and give double back to them. See, that's why in these expensive times people generally return the things, and those who do keep the clothes keep them for their own fancy because they are the clothes from the *daughter's family* [emphasis mine], her in-laws have sent them.

Here, the symbolic principle of reciprocity of gifts between the families entering into alliance is underlined, and it is seen to be emotionally and socially important to the bride's family to receive gifts from the groom's side as a token of establishing kinship relations. However, as the tabulation of gifts shows, any reciprocity from grooms' families requires a minimal outlay of resources, and the weight is overwhelmingly on the bride's family in terms of having to give more, on more occasions, and more expensive things than the groom's family (though the content and amount might vary across class and rural-urban divides).[44]

As Ritu implied, grooms' families spend a lot of money in increasing assets that, though ostensibly the brides', are seen to belong within the bride's affinal family, whereas the bride-"givers" transfer substantial assets as they appear to hand over responsibility for the bride. While grooms' families may give gifts to signify kinship, the onus is upon brides' families to fulfil any wishes of their affines, making hypergyny-related notions of the disproportionate responsibility of the bride's family more important than reciprocal relations of kinship. The model of gift giving that emerges from this data thus confirms that there is minimal reciprocity between affines,[45] even though marriages are important for establishing community alliances. However, despite brides' families' greater outlay for goods going to their affines, daughters' wedding costs still did not equal sons' inheritance, because many families, often prosperous ones—that is, those likely to have more property and wanting to display status—incurred substantial expenditures for both daughters' and sons' weddings.

These principles seem in line with Tambiah's (1989) contention that in North Indian weddings, prestations from the brides' families add to the resources of the joint family that the bride is joining, from which the conjugal unit gets a share only if the joint family is split. In contrast to the European model where the dowry and trousseau build up the resource base of the couple, here the groom's entire household/family is the focus of gift giving. I would add that at the wedding, *both* families' expenses seem to be directed toward increasing the assets (through gifts) and status (through hospitality) of the groom's family, which is supposed to be the "joint" family into which the bride merges, and whose continued prosperity makes it less likely that the daughter will turn to the natal family for later help or property shares. Simultaneously, the bride's family also enhances its own position/status by displaying due propriety in ceremonies and prestations.[46]

### "Ladkiwale ko to dena hi parta hai" ("The Woman's Side Does Have to Give Things, of Course"): Issues of Dowry and Demand

> My daughter and son-in-law got everything from us—furniture, crockery, utensils, refrigerator and TV—in their rented flat when they got back from the honeymoon. There was only a mug and a bucket in the flat before we got stuff. Her father-in-law and mother-in-law brought those and then came to see our things. They had said, "Tell us what you are giving so that there are no duplicates with what we give" [SB: But you gave everything!] That was just a way for them to ask what we were giving, so we would tell them what we bought, there was never any question of duplicates. (Lata)[47]

As the Maussian analysis of gift giving emphasizes, ritual gifts carry profound meanings about cultural bonds; dowry is no exception, being an exceptionally fluid and powerful signifier imbued with a variety of meanings. While some of these meanings are invoked to protest outrage against dowry deaths, others are called upon when gifts to affines are made, and yet others are drawn upon in women's affectionate remembrances of their dowries. The many characterizations of dowry in this sample include: dowry as token of parents' love, dowry as voluntary gift exchange, dowry as inheritance, dowry as addition to affinal resources, dowry as coercion, dowry as extortion. The following analysis of dowry and demand reveals how these characterizations serve as metonymic representations of individual family dynamics and societal transmission of resources. The power of dowry lies in its multiple meanings, in its very ability to be simultaneously a voluntary act and a compulsory one.

The effect of dowry or "indirect dowry" on women's status is a complex issue.[48] In contrast to the popular anthropological contention that bridewealth is associated with a high valuation of women's labor, whereas dowry is related with a lower economic status for women, possibly because dowry coexists with class hierarchies and hence a greater availability of hired labor (Schlegel and Eloul 1988: 298–99), several scholars have argued that it is not dowry per se but access to the goods and the relations between marrying families that determines women's status. Thus, rise in dowry may be connected with a decline in women's status in some cases (Kapadia 1993; Paul 1986; Heyer 1992), but as Heyer found, the decline may be connected to increased capital outlay for weddings rather than a fall in the value of women's labor (1992, 434). Increased dowry may not be necessarily disempowering for women, depending on women's control of the gift and the hierarchy between the affines (Bradford 1985; Upadhya 1990).

In popular discourse, however, dowry is most often represented as an evil institution bringing about a decline in women's status, characterized as the satisfying of extortionist demands from the groom's family disguised as premortem inheritance. Feminist political critiques of dowry in this vein seek legal changes such as the criminalization of dowry, or social alternatives such as women's greater insertion into the labor force,[49] and most importantly, frequently emphasize enforcing women's inheritance rights as a way to render the practice of dowry irrelevant.[50] The fact that wedding gifts have not diminished in the slightest either with legal restrictions against dowry and women's legal rights to inheritance, or with women's greater educational and employment opportunities,[51] indicates that these solutions not only idealize the role of law and education in social change, but also have failed to address the representations that make dowry appealing. In characterizing dowry demands as use of force and an act of coercion, they have differentiated dowry from its more common disguise: a consensual agreement, an unspoken contract, an act of affection and welcome rather than a submission to violence.

As Kishwar points out (1994a, 10; similarly Teja 1993, 71–72), it is not marriage prestations per se but dowry demands that are viewed with social contempt;[52] in a majority of so-called dowry deaths encountered by her organization, causes other than dowry were given as the excuse for torture (1989b, 5). One of Kishwar's crucial contributions to the analysis of dowry has been to point out that brides themselves are far from averse to wedding prestations: in response to Kishwar's own call for strengthening inheritance rights, many women told her that with scant chance of receiving property shares, dowry was the only thing they could realistically expect from their natal families. These attitudes are echoed in other studies including different classes, educational levels, and age groups that show women's enthusiastic support for dowries, particularly with regard to items for themselves and the conjugal home, even though high *demands* for dowry are frequently seen as a social evil.[53] Perhaps even more importantly, the gifts appear to be deeply linked to women's pleasures, to feelings of being done right by and of being loved by the natal family, to being for once the sole vehicle of the family's expenditure and status.[54] Disturbing as these criteria seem to be as markers of self-esteem for women,[55] they represent women's scant hold over resources and emotional wealth, and are extremely difficult to erase through legal proscriptions.

The phrase prefacing this section, *"ladkiwale ko to dena hi parta hai"* ("the woman's family has to give things, of course"), juxtaposed by several women against the notion that it was indeed unseemly to ask for things, reveals the ambivalent meanings of "demand" and contested definitions of what constitutes acceptable forms of dowry. The very silences of leaving demands unarticulated speak of the need for the bride's family to give a certain expected amount. The idea of *jo dena hota hai* (what has to be given) or customary gifts are powerfully formless signifiers, with an apparently unspecified content but an immanently readable form that families seem to have no difficulty materializing. Such gifts, commonly perceived to be uncoerced, are variously interpreted as expressions of the brides' families' wealth or a reflection of the groom's "value."

The social illusion that alleged dowry is a voluntary gift of affection from the bride's family was widespread. In 39.6 percent of all weddings mentioned, the overwhelmingly predominant norm with regard to gifts was that "bride's families give what they want." In 14.6 percent weddings, the groom's family said they wanted nothing but the bride herself (except for hospitality), though they did accept gifts nonetheless; in one case from KE (1.04 percent of total weddings), they expressly forbade the bride's family to give gifts. This indicates a strong consensus across social classes that leaving it up to the bride's family to do the right thing was most preferable, since it appeared to ensure customary gifts without showing visible greed (only 5.2 percent of weddings were in fact completely giftless, or included only a few saris or utensils given by the bride's family).[56]

However, negotiations over the amount of prestations were common. In 19.8 percent of weddings, the groom's family made explicit demands (much higher in weddings likely to be held in the rural areas, 27.7 percent of weddings reported from SN as opposed to 12 percent and 12.5 percent of weddings reported from KC and KE respectively). In contrast, 3.1 percent of weddings (all instances from the middle-income areas), had "indirect demand," that is, demands were not expressed but hinted at (e.g., Lata's story at the beginning of this section), showing that even when objects desired were basically similar in content to those demanded explicitly, it was more common to use subtle pressures, apparently deemed more tasteful. There were also cases of demands negotiated by both families, either by the bride's family bartering down the amount, or by the bride's family making an up-front bottom-line offer, which the groom's family could accept or else refuse the match (5.2 percent of weddings).

Uma described a prototypical dowry demand situation that they had been encountering in trying to find a groom for her sister-in-law.[57]

Generally you ask them, "how would you like the marriage to be performed?" and then it starts, the groom's father is usually the one who brings up the list, and sometimes the whole list will be presented to you, where it will be written "cash: Rs 2,000,000; Oneida Color TV with Remote Control Model 21SSE." They even have the model number, you feel like they are trying to suck your blood.

Uma strongly associated this situation with Bihari ethnicity, that is, she felt the demands reflected the "market" for Bihari grooms with moderate education and/or a middle-class job, both in Delhi where she and her husband worked and in Bihar where her in-laws lived. That it was a broad market value was further evident in the fact that it was not a sum that recognized the resources of the bride's family: Uma's husband worked as an engineer in a firm, her father-in-law was retired from government service, she worked in a publishing company, and the only immoveable affinal property was the house in the village where her in-laws lived, so even the cash amount was far beyond their total savings. Importantly, Uma's description of dowry demands, though real enough in her case, were also the ultimate specter of the evils of dowry, a widespread representation that most families consciously distanced themselves from, and that made it easier to depict more nuanced demands as consensual gifts.

The raising of "demands" in such crass ways was socially unacceptable to many families, and it was repeatedly conveyed that families making high demands were unsuitable affines. For instance, Kavita's sister had got engaged and the groom's family seemed agreeable to the fact that her family would be unable to give much. But when the groom's family took further stock of her family's transportation business in the city of Bhopal, and learned that they had recently bought a TV and also a second car for the business, they (the groom's family) started demanding that a refrigerator be given for the engagement. Kavita's mother insisted that relations be broken off immediately "because people who start asking for things from the very first time will keep on asking for a whole lifetime."[58] Similarly, Sushila's brother-in-law canceled his daughter's wedding when his son went to the groom's village and overheard someone in the groom's family saying they wanted Rs.10,000 cash and a scooter because the groom was educated (at high school level) and the bride had many uncles with jobs in the city (Sushila's husband who worked as a floor polisher was one of them).[59] Voicing explicit demands could thus be a cultural gaffe, whereas token refusals and subtle hints could be far more profitable.

Yet, even through emphasizing their distaste for "demand," women revealed their underlying allegiance to ideologies of women's families buying gifts in disproportionate amounts, and the existence of tangible expectations. To return again to Rani's son's wedding (see pp. 93–94), Rani's retelling of her daughter-in-law's parents' attitude eloquently revealed the politics of nay-saying: "they asked if we wanted anything and we said 'nothing,' . . . but they still gave quite a lot; they had a very nice wedding."[60] The implication is that a social consensus about "nice" weddings including a specific level of gift giving clearly exists. Thus, Rani knew she had little to lose by appearing to want nothing from her affines; she gained social/moral currency by the token refusal, appearing both nongreedy and sufficiently wealthy to be able to spurn prestations, but was actually in no danger of forfeiting gifts. Rani's family had two high wage earners (before her daughter-in-law joined the household) and wanted to display their socioeconomic status through the wedding; significantly, *both* the stylized refusal and the numerous gifts were important tools in achieving that status. The prevarications of Lata's daughter's in-laws (described at the beginning of the section) provide a similarly vivid portrait of the subtext of ingenuous refusals of dowry; while not naming specifics to save face, the groom's parents made sure they described exactly what they really wanted by pointing to the empty apartment in KE and hinting at its fullness.

The actions of Poonam's in-laws showed the hypocrisy of such refusals in the most blatant way.[61] They repeatedly said that they wanted nothing, but clearly had a higher standard in mind than what they got. After the wedding there were many taunts about the content and quality of the things given, and numerous incidents of physical and mental cruelty. The sanctity of actual gifts was thus absolute even though dowry *demand* was discursively antisocial; as Poonam's case shows, polite refusals could even be more dangerous than outright demands, because the threat of violence and harassment went unnoticed.

These situations of overt and covert demand also indicate the complex meanings of dowry. As the giftless weddings indicate, amounts of wedding prestations were related to the sorts of alliances formed and were not necessarily proportional to the bride's family's wealth—that is, *not* directly related to a woman's premortem inheritance. However, depending on the socioeconomic dynamic between the affines, there was a wide variation with regard to what dowry was supposed to be a payment for: the groom's value, the bride's attributes, or the wealth of either family could all function as determining factors.

In the canceled weddings of Kavita's sister and Sushila's niece described above, a high dowry was sought on the basis of the bride's family's wealth and the groom's qualifications. Paro, whose husband had been an agricultural laborer when they were wed twelve years ago, also conveyed the norm that dowry is a payment for the groom's worth, by relating that for her wedding, her father gave the groom hardly any customary gifts because he did not have a stable job. When her husband did find steady work in agriculture later (and thus raised his "price"), her parents "made up the loss" by giving him a bicycle on the occasion of her sister's wedding; the sister's husbands got a full range of customary gifts because of their better earning capacities.[62] Similarly, when Maya said she had made no demands for her two sons' recent weddings (although her sons were just starting out as contract laborers, her husband had a good government job by SN standards and they could have expected a good dowry), she commented that "people should not ask for things because it is like selling one's sons,"[63] also implying that the dowry pays for a groom, perhaps one of the reasons why explicit demands from the groom's family were viewed negatively, as trading one's children.[64]

Yet in other cases, the bride's value appeared to set the standard for exchange. Rani said about her daughter-in-law's family: "they asked if we wanted anything and we said 'nothing,' because we got such a well-educated girl, a doctor. If a girl has finished only tenth or twelfth grade a dowry may be ok, but this is a 'line-wali' (i.e., in a professional "line"!) woman earning Rs.5000/month."[65] Here, the bride's own earning power was highlighted as the chief economic asset transferred through the wedding, and dowry inscribed as potential compensation for a woman's perceived shortcomings.

The resources of the respective families rather than the qualities of a couple were also significant factors determining dowry. Gita, who was from one of the most prosperous households at SN, with a flour shop in her name and a husband who was a construction contractor and who had been buying up valuable rural land with his savings, was quite open about wanting dowry for her sons' weddings because the bride "is going to get a nice place to live and we have enough to live on, so anyone wanting a good alliance is going to have to pay."[66] She explained that a family seeking an alliance with them would have to pay for the comfort the bride would be lucky enough to experience. Many others also said that large dowries were necessary only when the groom's family was very rich, and unnecessary among socioeconomic peers.

The obverse of this, the perceived economic prosperity of the bride's family (closest as a rationale to dowry as premortem inheritance, though much of the "dowry" does not go to the bride herself), appeared to be connected to some of the most overt dowry demands, viz. in Kavita's family (as described above) and several instances of postwedding demands found in all three neighborhoods (also Chanana 1993). Medha's father and grandfather had over one hundred bighas of rural land while her in-laws' joint land was about twenty-five bighas. Even though Medha married into her sister's affinal family, her elder brother-in-law took Rs. 30,000 from her father (ostensibly to buy a scooter, which would bring Medha and her husband income if her husband drove it commercially). Because of this expense, Medha herself received very little jewelry despite her family's wealth, nor did the couple get this dowry cash. But after five years of marriage, her husband now wanted his father-in-law or brothers-in-law to set him up with a garage on their land.[67] The repeated demands in this case seemed clearly linked to the difference in wealth between the families, and were framed as measures to bring the bride's standard of living more on par with her natal family's, literally the opposite of Gita's situation where the bride's family would be paying more because her standard of living would be higher. Yet in both these cases, the onus was on the brides' families to pay extra whether they were substantially richer or poorer, evoking again the notion that brides' families are responsible for adding to the prosperity of the grooms' families.

The question of *mehr* payments in Muslim weddings also dealt with notions of value paid for the bride, but in proportion to the groom's family's status. The idea of mehr is that the groom's family agrees to pay or put aside some money for the bride as her own resources, or her insurance in case of divorce. Under the Muslim Women's (Protection of Rights in Divorce) Act (1986), this is the only form of compensation available to Indian Muslim women upon divorce other than three months of maintenance. Yet as the Muslim women in my sample narrated, and as I also witnessed following a Muslim wedding at SN the gift was often symbolic. Mehr frequently entailed promising to put a piece of land or a sum of money or jewelry in the woman's name (the amount depending on the groom's family's resources), but on the nuptial night the groom usually pled inability to pay and asked to be forgiven this "debt," while the bride was usually told by her in-laws that the "nice" thing to do was agree.[68]

As Parveen said, the mehr debt was seen to be an extremely solemn religious matter and extended even beyond death unless formally forgiven. Her in-laws had only eight bighas and four sons, and her husband sold cheap clothing from a hand-cart, while her mother and brothers had land and houses, so the mehr was quite small. Yet she had not been paid either the Rs. 1000 promised about ten years ago, after the wedding, or the ring her husband promised her instead. She and a visiting friend of hers both agreed that it was better for a woman not to forgive the mehr because then the husband was no longer as attentive and could easily divorce her. Yet, they also repeated the community belief that people were said to be selling their daughters when a very high mehr was set.[69] Thus mehr (often characterized as either deferred bridewealth, or indirect dowry going from the groom's family to the bride's family and then to the bride, and in India coexisting with dowrylike prestations from the bride's family), rarely functioned in the form of a woman's fund of resources as intended.[70] Instead, it worked as a religiosocial bargaining counter for women rather than a security fund proportionate to the groom's family resources.

An important measure of dowry being even partially the woman's inheritance is the degree of access and control a bride has over the wedding prestations. Did women attain control over any portion of the dowry, or was "giving to the daughter" merely a facade for the woman's in-laws acquiring things for themselves? Tabulations showed two distinct niches for the ways in which cash and goods from the wedding were distributed: the bride's gifts and jewelry remained most often with the bride herself (75 percent women claimed this),[71] but the cash from the wedding as well as the household goods acquired were usually used within the in-laws' household (21.7 percent women claimed so).[72] Only three women each from KE and KC (21.4 percent and 18.8 percent respectively) said that in-laws kept brides' jewelry, and despite the high number of women from SN reportedly holding on to their personal jewelry, 36.7 percent of them simultaneously claimed that in-laws also retained and even used some of the brides' jewelry (Jeffery and Jeffery 1996, 107). In-laws keeping jewelry connoted both a harmless safekeeping as well as more contentious episodes of women's jewelry being sold or pawned or given at others' weddings. One woman from KE (7.1 percent) and one from KC (6.3 percent) also claimed a "shared" jewelry fund between mother-in-law and daughter-in-law, situations where the amount of free access remained unclear. Besides these somewhat ambivalent instances, there were a few cases of grooms' families directly claiming cash dowries: 18.3 percent respondents reported that the groom's father or brother directly took the cash, 6.7 percent that the groom took the cash, and 6.7 percent that the cash was given jointly to the couple.

Thus, cash and goods from the wedding seemed to benefit the affinal household directly. At best, clothing and jewelry (which might however have been one of the major expenses on either side) came to the woman for her use and control; women's access/control over these goods may have reflected her rights over stridhan or woman's wealth/assets, over which she customarily had absolute rights. In all, the pattern that emerged here too was the principle of enhancement of total assets of the bride's affinal joint household, along with gifts to the bride that substituted for (though it did not equate) inheritance.

The discourse surrounding demand and dowry articulated by women such as Rani, Lata, Sushila, and Parveen in this section treads between the language of "usual," unmentioned customary gifts (with specific form nonetheless) and that of commerce, of dowries (or mehr) being a price for a bride or groom or a compensatory value for evening a bargain. While overt high demands seemed generally socially repugnant, large differences of wealth between affines were sometimes cause for explicit pressure to give high dowries and continual gifts. In these cases, the concept of "balancing" and improving the daughter's standard of living became a somewhat acceptable veneer for demanding things from the woman's family. Significantly, this last idea invoked the notion of equitable distribution of family property, with the daughter getting a large proportion of family assets rather than merely wedding gifts; yet the woman was unlikely to benefit directly from many of the items demanded, which were more likely to enhance the whole affinal family's standard of living. In fact, most rationales about dowry, whether focused on the bride's and groom's "value" or the families' wealth, revolved around the issue of enhancing the groom's family's total assets.

## Paying for Weddings

In the orchestrated links formed through ceremonies and gifts, the identities of the people liable for expenditure are important because substantial contributions for wedding expenses indicate certain roles and responsibilities within the family structure, and also reveal networks of intimacy. The examples from weddings discussed here reveal that many ideal/customary pathways of giving and receiving are both reconfirmed and contradicted in reality, revealing again the use of ideological specters and the change in customary practices along with changes in political economy.

The conventional notion is that the joint family, that is, the bride's father's family, is liable for wedding expenses. In fact, unmarried daughters (not sons, who actually get the property) can legally ask for their marriage expenses to be paid out of joint family property. However, as the chapters on property illumine, concepts of joint and extended family are very fluid now, especially in urban areas, with some entitlements held firm as before but others having dissipated with urban residential scatter. Wedding costs seemed to be one of those areas that have ceased to be the responsibility of the joint family in practice, even though the *idea* of joint family contributions to weddings is still used to rationalize patrilneal property distribution.

According to the respondents' accounts, the parents or fathers were the ones mainly paying for the weddings (62.7 percent of daughters' weddings, and 44.8 percent of sons' weddings).[73] Mothers were the main contributors usually in cases where the father was no longer alive or the mother was the main earner (11.9 percent of daughters' weddings, and 6.9 percent of sons' weddings). Many parents supplemented their savings with office/provident fund loans or loans from other sources, and only in a few instances (6.3 percent of weddings) were mortgages or sales of property necessary, so that the immovable property fund remained intact despite the large expenses. Thus, while families' liquid assets were usually severely strained by weddings, the bulk of long-term assets like property were held over by parents for inheritance, customarily going to sons.

Wedding expenses were expected to be borne by what Paro called the "guardians" in the family,[74] fathers being succeeded by brothers in this respect. After parents, the other major contributors to wedding expenses were indeed brothers (38.8 percent of sisters' weddings, 21.4 percent of brothers' weddings). The proportion was particularly high in SN (51.5 percent of sisters' weddings), where it was common for brothers earning urban wages to pay for an extensive portion of rural weddings of sisters. As Sushila narrated, at her sister-in-law's wedding the groom's family expected the dowry to be commensurate with that of a woman who had three brothers with city jobs, and so they had shopped for good clothing and even radios and other appliances in the city before going back for the wedding a couple years earlier.[75] For Jaya's rural wedding fifteen years earlier, too, the expenditure was lavish even though her father was a recluse who earned hardly anything, because her four brothers had shops and waged jobs in the city.[76] During Parveen's sisters' urban weddings, her mother, who vended clothes, spent relatively little, while her brothers who had more money from their jobs were responsible for the bulk of expenses and even had the weddings at their home.[77] While Parveen's brothers were not gaining any economic resources by contributing this money, in Jaya's case and in others like Seema's (where her son put up considerable money for his own and his sister's wedding),[78] brothers' contributions defrayed expenses while helping preserve immovable property for male heirs. Without their help, the parents would have been forced to sell or trade in property to pay for the wedding.

Conventionally, sisters are not supposed to bear major expenses, either because of Hindu religious ideas of kanyadan mandating that women never give but only receive from their natal families (which some women did cite), or economic reasons of women having few independent resources. However, while these proscriptions acted as deterrents in most cases (and also resulted in women making fewer claims to property because they had not helped), the taboo was ignored sometimes, especially when the parents were no longer alive or the mother by herself was unable to afford much. Unmarried and married sisters (and also aunts) helped financially with 14.9 percent weddings of sisters and 14.3 percent weddings of brothers. In Sharmila's family, her eldest sister had stayed single and helped pay for the second sister to get married out of her wages even when their father, a teacher, was alive. Later, after getting married herself, she had continued to fund the weddings of three other sisters and their brother with some help from the other siblings.[79] Poonam's elder sister's husband had also helped out at weddings even when her father was alive, but after her father's death he bore the major cost of Poonam and her sister's weddings. For later weddings of brothers and sisters, Poonam and her husband and other married sisters and husbands shared the costs.[80] The contribution of brothers, while much more prevalent as shown above, was also naturalized, being viewed as a part of their responsibilities; sisters, however, took a participatory role despite ideological proscriptions, particularly in cases of dire need. Like their help with eldercaregiving or with giving other resources (Chapter 4), women's assistance was needed and accepted by the natal family despite discursive proscriptions. Significantly, sisters' help in marriages came with little expectation of inheritance in return.

Those getting married also contributed to the costs sometimes, depending on whether they had jobs and enough savings. Grooms reportedly contributed to 34.4 percent of weddings (of males' weddings tabulated); the percentage from KC and SN was even higher, 42.9 percent and 41.7 percent respectively, including several cases where the groom not only helped out but bore major costs of the wedding. Brides' contribution was reported in only 4.5 percent of total weddings of females; none of the brides in weddings described by SN respondents made any financial contributions. The low number from SN reflected the early age of marriage among women from these families, long before entry into the paid workforce. But the minimal figure in the total sample should also be interpreted in light of the high ratio of men to women in the paid labor force and the difference in wages and labor force participation between classes; men worked more often, earned more, and could have more savings.

Brides' contributions were not simply a question of women having savings to contribute; women's money seemed to be put in only if deemed necessary, recalling again the taboos against "taking" from women to discharge the obligations of their natal families. Bharti's husband paid for his sister's wedding in their parents' absence, and insisted she save her share of the cash she inherited from their parents; Lata did use her daughter's earnings, but felt for that reason that she should also give her something in later life for "taking" that money.[81] In these cases, daughters' earnings were not perceived as part of the natal family's resources in the same way as the sons', and were used only in tight situations rather than as an extension of the household's assets.

One of the most significant absences among wedding contributors was the case of uncles, both maternal and paternal. Paternal uncles' resources are of course traditionally regarded as part of the unified joint family property, but this seemed to have completely broken down in areas where siblings had separated and set up independent nuclear units. Paternal uncles helped substantially in only 2.9 percent of niece's weddings (both from SN, i.e., 6.1 percent of women's weddings tabulated from SN) and with no nephews' weddings. In the two cases where uncles did help, a rural joint family nucleus existed, making all members somewhat responsible for wedding expenses in the family; but significantly, many other families also had joint property where uncles did not help in that way.

The absence of maternal uncles' contributions is even more significant in light of property issues because one of the largest transfers of resources from the woman's natal family for her use is supposed to go into bearing a chunk of expenses of her children's, especially daughters', weddings. These expenses, including clothes and jewelry for the bride and clothes for the bride's natal and affinal family members as well as the cost of a major meal, are often cited along with dowry by many women (chapter 4, Table 4.1) as the equivalent to a share of property. Yet in fact, only one maternal uncle substantially helped pay for a nephew's wedding (3.6 percent of total weddings of males), and only 7.5 percent made major contributions to niece's weddings (12.1 percent of niece's weddings from SN).

Most women in all the areas reported that the contribution of maternal uncles were on a par with those of other uncles and aunts, that uncles gave a wedding gift rather than paying for a hefty share of the wedding. For example, Harjinder said she reciprocated her brother's gifts with equal gifts to his daughters, not wanting her son to be under an obligation in the future.[82] Seema had literally declined her share of natal property a decade earlier to help her brother while his daughter was getting married, but her wealthy brothers eventually gave far from adequate returns when her children were married; together, they paid Rs. 7000 at her daughter's wedding.[83] Thus, her brothers did not even reciprocate with an amount on a par with her contribution as an aunt, let alone shoulder a substantial portion of wedding expenses in lieu of her refusal of natal property, despite their enormous natal inheritance.

The structure of payment for weddings thus reflects the cultural nexus of wealth, responsibility, and property. Within the nuclear family, parents and brothers, those who usually had control over family assets, were accountable for wedding costs as part of the responsibility for getting property. Women's exemption from responsibility for payments is related to their lack of economic resources as well as constructions of kinship which render them "alien" in their native families. Although proscriptions against women's contributions served to distance them from natal property by refusing to let them share in the family's responsibilities (and thence, correspondingly, privileges), women did break these taboos when their families could not have done without help from daughters. The lack of help from uncles demonstrates not only nuclearization and the shrinkage of extended kin ties, but indicates for women that dowry is the one substantial transfer of resources to them and that natal property is unlikely to come their way at their children's weddings.

## Protima's Life: The Instability of Marriage

The myths that marriage itself compensates women for property, that affinal families are a haven for women, and that natal families heap gifts upon married women lifelong as tokens of love, are perhaps realizable in the best of circumstances. I use Protima's life to consider the very obverse of those notions: the systemic vulnerability and the inherent disempowerment for women created by the excessive dependence on marriage for women's well-being and the emphasis on dowry as women's property. As Protima's situation shows, the fragile correspondence between marriage and security, and hence the false equivalence between marriage and property, must be exposed if the myths of marriage are to be deconstructed.

In the middle of asking Protima demographic questions in a common courtyard in SN, I was interrupted in midsentence by one of her neighbors; "She's from your village," he said, meaning she was a Bengali. But Protima herself hardly remembered any Bengali any more, having lived about nine years in Delhi with hardly any contact with her natal family. I knew already that her affines were from Uttar Pradesh, and because ethnic group exogamy is so rare, suspected that the circumstances of her alliance with the affinal family might be atypical. Indeed, her life story[84] turned out to be a vivid example of the articulated effects of gender and class subalternity.

Protima's family had crossed the Bangladesh border and migrated to West Bengal in the mid-1970s, and had settled in rural Midnapore. They had sold their land in Bangladesh, after repeated police brutalities and feuds between different religious and caste groups in the village left them in constant fear of losing everything. Her father had died while they were still in Bangadesh, and while her mother and brothers shared the money from the land sale, they did not acquire any common property in Midnapore; each brother concentrated on accumulating resources for his own family. The eldest brother sold fish, the middle one manufactured raw alcohol, and the youngest brother, whom she and her mother had stayed with, occasionally worked as a weaver in a factory. Protima and her mother, as well as her brother, also tried to make a living tying *bidis* (leaf-wrapped cigarettes) and selling them to a broker, but had made only Rs. 8 or 9 daily between the three of them in the early eighties, which had not been enough to secure them even a basic minimum of food and clothing. They were so poor and vulnerable that her brother had been coerced by the head of a neighboring village into marrying a woman from a very poor family, who too could not afford to spend anything on the wedding.

Protima's brother had always told her that he wanted her to be married in a "nice" home where there would be no difficulties and no grief; she too had thought about leaving the village and being married in the city, believing her life could only get better. The need for Protima to be married seemed all the more urgent after her brother got married and there was another person to feed in the house, and so he asked a man (a brother-in-law of theirs among extended kin) who was visiting from the city if he would take Protima with him when he went back, and try to arrange a "good" marriage for her. This man had allegedly already accepted Rs. 1600 from a man in his neighborhood in Delhi to bring back a woman from Bengal; the putative buyer was allegedly old, impotent, and alcoholic and had been unable to find anyone to marry. Although Protima had few options, she did balk at this deal when she came to know about it, and was upset enough that her "host" made inquiries about other prospective grooms and located her present husband. He was above the customary marriageable age and had never been married, but seemed a more pleasant prospect in general. His family, too, was delighted, and his three brothers helped him come up with the Rs. 1600 to repay the original deal. They had a registered marriage in court, and a get-together for neighbors and family at SN where she got a few clothes and utensils as gifts.

Marriage, however, proved to be no haven. Within a few months, Protima found out about her husband's excessive drinking, which got steadily worse, and after about a year he started beating her regularly in drunken rages. At the time that I was in SN, he would beat her nearly every night for many hours, and her screams would ring through the neighborhood. Sometimes she escaped with her children to sleep at her sister-in-law's or at a neighbor's, but there were usually severe repercussions for this, with her husband and even brother-in-law beating her on the pretext that women who were not in their homes at night were morally rotten. Protima's husband had all but given up on his work as a vendor by this point; she got no money for household maintenance for him, and barely survived by selling coal garnered from the wagons or with handouts from relatives. Her affines occasionally helped her out and felt sorry for her, but also joined in condemning her character at other times. And she had lost all contact with her natal family: she did not have the money to go visit them in West Bengal, and doubted that she and her children would be welcome in her brother's penurious home anyway. Her mother had come to stay with her in Delhi after her first child was born, but had been so frightened at witnessing the daily beatings that Protima had insisted she go back and consider her (Protima) to be dead to the family.

In many ways, Protima's situation was obviously related to her family's economic circumstances; their migrant status and landlessness put them in a very difficult position for accumulating resources and cultivating relations based on alliance. However, the gendered effects of this poverty were notably different. Her brothers shared the small pot of money from the sale of their land in Bangladesh, and were attempting to determine their economic status through the labor market. They theoretically also acquired the responsibility of taking care of their mother and sisters, but it was only the youngest, unmarried brother who did this, and he too tried to dispose of these charges with haste soon after he was married.

Marriage was supposed to ensure women security and happiness in their homes. And yet, Protima's mother felt neglected and unwelcome at her sons' homes, and was frightened and forced to leave at her daughter's. Like Protima, her brother's wife too had been married off with alacrity and forced into a family unwilling to have her there; the brothers in both families had been unwilling to continue supporting sisters from their own resources, no matter what circumstances the sisters ended up in. The transaction for Protima freed the brother and made a profit for the broker, but had no economic advantages for Protima at all. Since such payments were typically made by men who had been unsuccessful in finding brides through regular channels, the odds of making a favorable match were not good. There was cultural capital to be gained by being married, but also the risk that the broker would make a sale to a brothel rather than a potential husband (although whether that would put her in a worse situation than the one she was in is debatable). The prime fate envisaged for women, that they could only be "saved" through marriage and should take their chances with marriage roulette, thus screened the other registers of their dependence: their relative disadvantage in the labor market and their alienation from inheriting whatever common resources the family possessed.

### Conclusion: Marriage and the Transfer of Wealth

In her study of dowry and inheritance in coastal Andhra Pradesh, Upadhya stresses the importance of the two separable faces/uses of dowry: dowry's role in transferring property to the woman; and its "marriage payment" dimension, "in which wealth and material goods are transferred between the bride and groom and/or their families or kin groups as a central part of the marriage contract" (1990, 37). While in her sample, dowry payments fulfilled both dimensions (women often got substantial land in their dowry), in the portrait emerging from my respondents' accounts, the inheritance profile was substantially in shadow, while the prestations-for-kinship face was emphatically in the light. Here, wedding gifts were primarily a form of establishing favorable kinship networks, marked by a mildly bilateral exchange of gifts but with the onus strongly upon the bride's family to give in greater quality and quantity. Unlike other groups where establishing favorable community ties were helpful for economic purposes (Heyer 1992; Bradford 1985), here there was little economic interdependence between marrying families. The prestations primarily showcased the status of the two families for their larger community, while also celebrating the establishment of new kin.

This pattern of gift giving was also crucially important for maintaining existent property relations. Given the patrilineal norms of property distribution and the ideology of virilocality, the largely one-sided pattern of gift giving was meant to ensure that daughters stayed happily within the affinal family and laid little further claim to natal family resources. The fulfillment of (often unvoiced) criteria for "dowry items" was also an insurance scheme with the same intended effect, having the aim of pleasing the daughter's in-laws and reminding her of her family's continuing expenses.[85] Moreover, the flow was overwhelmingly unidirectional to the extent that according to ritual nothing was accepted in return from the daughter, further distancing the woman from claims to property on the basis of shared contributions to the family. This inscribed women in a position closing off their adult agency in helping out their families *or* laying claim to property shares, both of which could break their gendered passivity and put them on a par with their brothers.

The idea of dowry gifts compensating for property was largely discursive. In one of the instances of social class cross-cutting gender, wedding costs and gifts were generally much higher for wealthier families, and sons' weddings often ended up costing as much as daughters' because of higher jewelry and entertainment costs. Thus, disproportionate expenses for daughters' weddings were often a myth. But even where the expenses for daughters' weddings were higher and gifts were given to daughters on a variety of occasions afterward, these combined costs (about Rs. 200,000 for the wedding being the highest reported among the respondents) were still much less than the woman's proportionate share of family property (although the money may have represented a substantial portion of the family's total liquid assets at the time of the wedding). Also, for the most part a woman's natal family's compensatory obligations were extended to her for a few years at best and rarely lasted until her own children's weddings, despite the financial help on those occasions being part of the implied dowry-property contract. The alleged "extra" cost of gifts for married daughters did not fairly balance out against a direct share of family resources. However, *because* property was relatively independent of dowry and women did not get inheritance shares even when they had weddings without prestations, women's own acquiescence to dowry/ prestations is more easily understood, prestations being the only conduit of transferring some natal resources for women's benefit.

While "dowry" in these circumstances was distinctly different from the Eurocentric notion of the term, there was indeed a substantial transmission of resources at weddings. In terms of material goods, the dowry mostly built up a small fund of clothes and jewelry for the bride, with the rest of the goods being for her in-laws' consumption, adding to the total prosperity of the bride's affinal family (Table 3.2). At the ideological level, both families and even the marrying couple, including the bride, not only accepted a certain version of dowry but even found it pleasurable, as a celebration of the status of the two families, and one of the few social signs of affection/duty for a daughter expressed through concrete expenditure. This also explains why few families changed their social practices in response to the legal criminalization of dowry. Marriage prestations, largely token in terms of actual calculations when compared with property shares, were immensely significant in their metonymic and mythic representations of cohesive, fair and loving kin networks.

# 4

## "Wo Ayee Hak Lene" ("There She Comes, to Take Her Rights")

### The Dreadful Specter
### of the Property-Owning Woman

*Oi jaye, Oi jaye, Bangalir meye*
*Kheye jaye, Niye jaye, aro jaye Cheye*

There she goes, the Bengali's daughter;
She eats from us, takes more with her,
And wants even more.

The Bengali saying above plays on the alleged fears associated with women's claims to natal family property, which make the *woman* responsible for taking an infinite parade of prestations from her family.[1] This specter of daughters' insatiable greed and one-sided lifelong drainage of resources from the natal family is used to construct a good/bad daughter model that valorizes women's refusals of inheritance shares and demonizes those who would pursue claims to property or resources. Yet this placement of the onus upon women is an inversion of the facts surrounding the majority of property transmissions: transactions between groups of men where women function as tokens of exchange; sons inheriting the bulk of natal family resources despite numerous gift-giving rituals where small amounts of assets are transferred to daughters and their affines; and strong cultural sanctions for the estrangement of women from their natal families. The simplest of rhythms and words in this couplet appear to naturalize a "timeless" truth, but these supposedly ancient cultural beliefs serve to counteract postcolonial reform of inheritance law.

The title of this chapter, *"Wo Ayee Hak Lene"* ("There She Comes, to Take Her Rights") invokes a similar ideological barrier that deters women from seeking family property. It is a phrase used by one of my interview respondents to describe a hypothetical specter akin to the previous one: what she imagined her brother, sister-in-law, and other relatives saying if she ever tried to claim her legal share of natal family land. The phrase brilliantly captures the double entendre of the words *hak* as well as the translated term *right*.[2] Even while *hak lena* or "taking rights" has a strong pejorative connotation in this context, implying greed, a selfish focus on individual rights, and a monetization of family relations, ironically the notion that availing of one's "rights" is the right or correct thing to do by standards of legal equality cannot be erased.[3] This tension between the fairness represented in enforceable legal equity and the invaluable family ties which allegedly rise above legality may explain the hostility directed toward the *haklenewali*, the woman who would claim her rights.

In this study, which places women's subjectivity centerstage, however, it is also important to mark the limitations in the power of such sentiments. Women, while partly constituted within and limited by such ideologies, are not simply manipulated by them; they also contest such beliefs in overtly rebellious or subtly resistant ways. With regard to property transmission, some women show a desire to assume equal social and financial responsibility toward parents and to maintain empowering connections with the natal family, while others separate themselves from the natal family except for receiving occasional gifts, and are possessive about other women's claims to "their" affinal property. Between the extremes of a perfect echo of patriarchal ideologies about women having no right to property (representing the hegemonically "conquered"), and of ideas about a scrupulously equal economic division of property (often portrayed as the "correct" feminist position), lie a range of other positions reflecting women's negotiations of various factors.

This chapter attempts to identify the network of nerves and sinews beneath the visible body of property divisions by examining such negotiations surrounding property division. As Brettell argues in her analysis of nineteenth-century property bequests in Portugal, property transactions "both shape and are shaped by relations between men and women, parents and children, brothers and sisters," constituting "moments when the rights and obligations between people are negotiated" (1991, 447). Thus, notions about kinship and gender fundamentally undergird the intergenerational transfer of wealth and "an understanding of cultural constructions of gender difference are [sic] of utmost importance" for interpreting property transmissions (1991, 462). Similarly, Moors shows that awareness of property rights may be widespread, particularly in urban contexts, but that women pursue taking family property only in vulnerable socioeconomic positions or in culturally prescribed ways (1995, 49–50).[4]

Ideological notions that mediate women's attitudes toward accepting inheritance shares from their natal families in India are examined closely in the following sections as a way to explore myths and realities about kinship. These notions include the construction of eldercare and family responsibility, women's role as surrogate males in sonless families, dowry and other prestations or lifelong help as substitutes for inheritance, and the relation between accepting property and women's total severance from the natal family. Within each parameter, there is evidence both of fundamentally intransigent male entitlements to property and women's negotiation of alternate spaces.

Beyond the particular issue of grounding Indian women's low rates of property ownership in larger sociocultural frameworks, the broader question investigated in this chapter is the relationship between individual agency and ideological apparatuses, a problem that goes to the heart of cultural theory. Is some women's acceptance of their own lesser entitlement merely a reflection of their position within dominant power systems? The Marxist notion that such beliefs were merely "false consciousness" has long been out of favor for cultural theorists, who have marked that people's beliefs are fundamentally constituted within certain ideologies, rather than alien notions being forcibly imposed upon them. Moreover, the idea that certain notions can be transparently called "false" is problematic, because "ideological" beliefs are not experienced separately from lived social relations and cultural sensemaking. As Eagleton puts it in his extensive summary-discussion on the meaning of "ideology,"

> Part of the opposition to the 'false consciousness' case stems from the accurate claim that, in order to be truly effective,

ideologies must make at least some minimal sense of people's experience, must conform to some degree with what they know of social reality from their practical interaction with it.... They must be 'real' enough to provide the basis on which individuals can fashion a coherent identity, must furnish some solid motivations for effective action, and must make at least some feeble attempt to explain away their own more flagrant contradictions and incoherencies. (1991, 14–15)

Although Eagleton's view of ideology still appears to imply that there is an external imposition of harmful views by interested parties, his notion that ideology contributes a seemingly real and rational basis for identity formation is very important to the argument of this chapter that attitudes to property division occur in a universe of perceived cultural tradeoffs, and are not simply a result of ideological manipulation. While dominant ideology often strongly influenced women's decisions, many complex constructions of self were also at work, and, even where it could be shown that certain expectations were "false" in the sense of being contradicted by "real-life" events, this did not necessarily mean that women were oblivious to the fiction or unaware of the affective benefits they gained by refusing material resources.

## Multilayered Attitudes toward Natal Property and Women's Property

Most women cited a variety of reasons for not taking natal family property (Table 4.1), indicating a complex internal reaction to the issue. However, the responses could be grouped into certain broad categories reflecting prevailing ideologies about women and property. At one extreme were the responses that reflected the allegedly progressive and "feminist," paradigm, that women should take family property and people should not distinguish between sons and daughters (#6). The opposite extreme was represented by views that did not challenge or question dominant ideology at all, where it was claimed that "custom" was the barrier against women getting natal property (#7). "Custom" was a broad opaque concept in such responses, amorphously combining inheritance norms, family dynamics, and diverse ethnic, regional, and religious practices.[5]

**Table 4.1** Respondents' Attitudes toward Taking Property (in Percentages)

| | ATTITUDE TOWARD TAKING NATAL PROPERTY[1] | KE N=14 | KC N=16 | SN N=30 | TOTAL N=60 |
|---|---|---|---|---|---|
| 1 | Don't want, it causes rifts with brothers/sisters-in-law; want smaller share to prevent rift | 50 | 37.5 | 40 | 41.7 |
| 2 | Get dowry/lifelong gifts instead | 28.6 | 25 | 50 | 38.3 |
| 3 | Share husbands' wealth and affines' property instead | 50 | 25 | 40 | 38.3 |
| 4 | Could get property in sonless family | 14.3 | 6.2 | 36.7 | 23.3 |
| 5 | Want natal family's prosperity instead | 7.1 | 37.5 | 16.7 | 20 |
| 6 | Women should take natal property | 0 | 18.8 | 26.7 | 18.3 |
| 7 | Can't get property as per "custom" | 0 | 12.5 | 26.7 | 16.7 |
| 8 | Not enough property for multiple shares | 7.1 | 12.5 | 23.3 | 16.7 |
| 9 | Property goes to eldercaregivers | 14.3 | 25 | 0 | 10 |
| 10 | Should take if woman poor or in trouble | 7.1 | 18.8 | 0 | 6.7 |
| 11 | Have own wages instead | 21.4 | 0 | 0 | 5 |
| 12 | Other | 35.7 | 18.8 | 10 | 18.3 |
| 13 | Do not know/Unknown | 7.1 | 6.2 | 0 | 3.3 |

[1]Percentages show frequency of responses in partricular categories; since some answers could be multiple, the percentages do not add up to 100.

**Table 4.2** Respondents' Attitudes toward How Property Should be Distributed Ideally (in Percentages)

| IDEAL DISTRIBUTIONS OF PROPERTY[1] | KE N=14 | KC N=16 | SN N=30 | TOTAL N=60 |
|---|---|---|---|---|
| **1  All children should be equally entitled** | **64.3** | **75** | **63.3** | **66.7** |
| 1a  Equally between all children; to all children in very wealthy families | 50 | 43.8 | 60 | 53.3 |
| 1b  According to children's needs/abilities | 14.3 | 37.5 | 10 | 20 |
| 1c  Parents should give to all children; refusing share is daughter's choice | 0 | 25 | 3.3 | 8.3 |
| **2  Should go to sons** | **28.6** | **43.8** | **43.3** | **40** |
| 2a  To sons, while daughters get from affines | 21.4 | 37.5 | 10 | 20 |
| 2b  To sons, while daughters get dowry | 0 | 18.8 | 20 | 21.7 |
| 2c  To sons, per "custom"; to sons, to prevent family rifts | 7.1 | 6.3 | 20 | 13.3 |
| 2d  Daughters should not demand share; can take property if offered by brothers | 0 | 12.5 | 6.7 | 6.7 |
| **3  Should go to daughters and sons, but unequally** | **28.6** | **25** | **33.3** | **30** |
| 3a  Small token to daughters only; immovable property only to sons, other shared | 28.6 | 18.8 | 20 | 21.7 |
| 3b  To daughters, if family sonless | 0 | 6.3 | 16.7 | 10 |
| **4  To eldercaregiver** | **7.1** | **25** | **10** | **13.3** |

[1]Percentages show frequency of responses in partricular categories; since some answers could be multiple, the percentages do not add up to 100.

As the descending order in Table 4.1 shows, women's responses evoked different paradigms for achieving a fair social distribution of resources. Most numerous was the fear that taking natal property would lead to rifts with brothers and sisters-in-law (#1, brought up by 41.7 percent of the women in all), that leaving women's share as part of their natal family's assets allowed family relations to be harmonious and supportive. Next in importance were responses that brought up the idea that marriage placed women in a different mode of entitlement: that women got dowry and other gifts instead of property (#2, evoked in 38.3 percent of the responses); and that daughters "got" marital and affinal, rather than natal, resources (#3, mentioned by 38.3 percent of the women). While 23.3 percent of the women believed that women could get property in Hindu families if they were brotherless, per certain scriptural prescriptions (#4), others saw themselves as being generous (rather than afraid) in being able to keep their natal family more prosperous by not withdrawing their share (#5, 20 percent). In addition to these rationales based on the idea of women's separation from the natal family at marriage, other paradigms invoked property being a reward for eldercare (#9, 10 percent of responses), or property as a compensation for a daughter's economic hardship (#10, 6.7 percent of responses).

There was no strong statistical correlation between age and attitudes toward taking natal property. The idea that property should be equally distributed among children had a very small negative correlation with age (-0.2, P-value 0.13); that is, younger women appeared more likely to hold this belief. Notions of the natal family prospering if women did not take property shares was also negatively correlated with age, but even more weakly (-0.1, P-value 0.46), as were notions that women get affinal rather than natal property (-0.025, P-value 0.85). Positive correlations between age and particular attitudes—that is, the likelihood of that attitude being more prevalent among elder women—were also quite weak: 0.05 (P-value 0.68) for caregiving being the basis of property distribution; 0.12 (P-value 0.36) for refusing property for fear of rifts; and 0.13 (P-value 0.32) for believing dowry compensated for property. Hence age per se was not a significant variable delineating differences in attitude.

Certain variations in responses between neighborhoods did seem significantly connected to socioeconomic circumstances (although the lack of responses in a particular category did not necessarily signify the absence of those beliefs). For example, given the difference in women's education and the kinds of jobs held by women between KE and the other neighborhoods (chapter 1, Tables 1.14 and 1.16), the KE women's assertions that they could do quite well on their earnings and did not need property had some justifiable basis, while others were hardly in a position to make that claim. Similarly, some women from KE and KC said that they would have taken natal family property in the hypothetical case that they were really poor or in some trouble, while women from SN who were far more likely to be in such situations never brought this up. Perhaps this latter group had a clearer sense that they were unlikely to get substantive property no matter how poor they were, and instead were better off leaning heavily on their natal families in lean times if they had not severed their ties by asking for property.

On the other hand, no one from SN mentioned a relationship between eldercare and inheritance, even though there were actual situations in SN in which this was the dominant principle, even to the extent that a daughter was the sole heir because she was the caregiver. This indicates that, although the belief was not articulated, it was a part of that cultural universe. While responses were stratified on the basis of class, Tables 1.7–1.15 show that there were also substantial differences by neighborhood in criteria like ethnicity, rural versus urban upbringing, education, and age, for example, SN had a substantially younger profile than the other areas. Thus, the prevalence of a particular response in an area could not always be analyzed as an effect of class, and could be related to other demographic characteristics.

The fluidity of the categories is further demonstrated in the discrepancies between Tables 4.1 and 4.2, in the difference between women's reactions to their own natal property versus their views on how they would distribute property *ideally*. Many of the same rationales appear in both, but in different proportions. In all, 66.7 percent of the women supported ideas of not discriminating between children by gender in distributing property (#1), whether by including them all as heirs or choosing heirs based on need or ability rather than gender. In sharp contrast to Table 4.1, where only 18.3 percent of women in all contemplated taking natal property in equal shares, 53.3 percent in Table 4.2 thought that ideally both daughters and sons should get property in equal shares (#1a). However, alongside widespread support for giving property to children regardless of gender (Table 4.2, #1), a substantial proportion of women preferred sons as heirs (#2, 40 percent in all) or as preferred heirs (#3, 30 percent in all). Among the diverse rationales for leaving property to males, the idea of giving property to sons to prevent family rifts was brought up by 13.3 percent women (though it was considerably less consuming than the 41.7 percent seen in Table 4.1), along with ideas of women getting dowry and affinal property (other popular attitudes in Table 4.1). Eldercare was evoked as an ideal standard by a similar number of women overall (Table 4.2, #4, 13.3 percent versus Table 4.1, #9, 10 percent).

Like the notion that women contributed to family prosperity by not subtracting their shares (#5, Table 4.1), ideas that women need not be entirely sidelined from family property were articulated by several respondents in contemplating ideal divisions of property, even as they confirmed male preference; they suggested giving daughters some moveable assets in the parents' lifetime, or allowing them the option of refusing (Table 4.2, #1c, #2d, #3a). Along with the much larger number of respondents in Table 4.2 who wanted daughters to be equal heirs, this indicates that women were acquiescent in supporting women's disentitlement to property in the present social circumstances, but envisaged bequeathal of property to women in an ideal situation.

### Equal Love: Conceptions of Equitable Distribution

> *If parents gave both daughters and sons something then both might think that their parents loved them.* (Reena, SN)[6]

Notions that daughters should be equally included in property distributions were the commonest way in which women conceptualized ideal inheritance (Table 4.2, 53.3 percent, and also evoked by 18.3 percent of the women in delineating their own attitudes to natal family property, Table 4.1). This idea was often visualized in association with images of property as a vehicle of love, as typified by Reena's comment above. The youngest woman in my sample, 18-year-old Reena, was still in seventh grade and with no marriage imminently in sight, and her response was unencumbered by many of the "social" obligations or considerations that married women in particular took upon themselves. Yet though atypical in those ways, Reena's response matched the theme running through women's ideas about giving and getting equal property: showing and earning love.

Women's rights to property are often viewed as being a "modern" and feminist demand, appearing proportionate to education and high social class (connoting more "enlightened" views) and irrelevant to the majority of women. The voices of Reena and many women in her neighborhood refute the eliteness of the above claim. Despite the overwhelming impression that Indian women tend to refuse natal property, it is important to remember that a large number of the women in this study supported the idea of equal property, especially when it came to visualizing how they might distribute property ideally without restraints (53.3 percent), as opposed to what they could actually see themselves demanding (18.3 percent). Moreover, in either case, women from SN were the ones who supported equal distributions of property in far greater proportions (as high as 60 percent followed by KE with 50 percent, Table 4.2). In this sample, high education and class were definitely not correlated with ideals of women being equal inheritors of property, and it was not women's own "backwardness" or disinclination that was keeping them from sharing natal assets.

Furthermore, the images used by SN women revealed a significantly different paradigm for claiming property, evoking neither the alleged brashness of rights-based claims nor the pathos of victims' needs associated with demands for legalization of women's rights to property. Instead, inheritance issues were coded in emotional and affectional terms. For example, several of the women who unqualifiedly supported equal property for sons and daughters used their experiences of motherhood and images of the womb as a symbol of equal entitlement for all children. As Meena, twenty-two and mother of two daughters, put it:

> If parents make equal shares of everything for all their children, then no one can say they have been given less or more, they can say that the parents having given birth to them all gave them all equal shares. After all, daughters and sons come from the same cells in the body, not different places, and one feels the same empathy/tenderness (*darad*) for both.[7]

A comment from Paro, a thirty-three-year-old mother of two sons and a daughter, is another example of women connecting the dispensation of property to their mothering/parenting duties: "It would be nice if everyone could get a share since they are all equal (*barabar*) to the parents; we don't clothe one and keep the others naked or feed one sweets and starve the other."[8] In these images, the economic dimensions of property were muted; women's profound connections to their natal families were emphasized. While it is impossible to tell if this was a conscious strategy on the women's part, this line of argument provided a much more comfortable entry to the discourse on property because it did not evoke the specter of the woman rudely claiming her "rights." In defiance of dominant ideologies which proclaim women's complete severance from the natal family upon marriage, it also emphasized the importance of ties of birth for women and hinted at the need to feel recognized by natal kin through gifts of property.

In contrast, women from KE and KC often used calculations of relative amounts in justifying their choices, focusing on a more precise financial division. Ritu, a thirty-five-year-old lawyer with one son, said, "Parents should divide property equally, or proportionately depending on marriage expenses. But nowadays they spend a lot on sons' weddings too, so it should be equal."[9] Uma, a twenty-seven-year-old mother of one son, proud of her dowryless wedding and aware of her lesser claims on her mother's house compared to her brother, contended that if she had daughters she would prefer to give them no dowry but equal shares of property instead.[10] Forty-two-year-old Indira asserted, given her experience of her own lavish wedding but also her expectation of natal property, that things bought for weddings were gifts and should not be taken into account in the dispensation of property.[11] While the absence of womb imagery from these responses cannot be tied to a class-based conclusion, here equity of assets was far more of a direct concern. Although talking about women's "rights" was just as socially taboo in these milieus, tangible economic fairness apparently could be voiced as a standard.

However, despite the 53.3 percent of respondents who visualized and voiced culturally acceptable metaphors for women to get property, only 5 percent in all actually felt they would be able to pursue their justifiable claims. Only one woman from KE (7.1 percent of KE responses) and two from SN (6.7 percent of SN) were absolute about pursuing shares, and four women overall (6.7 percent) expected to get property because of the serendipity of brotherlessness. Others who thought they were entitled to shares felt inhibited either because there was not enough property to divide, or because they felt the simultaneous pull of contrary ideologies such as having received dowry already. While it is important to note that women themselves were often supportive of daughters' equal rights to natal property, ultimately few could realize these professed ideals in the face of other cultural pressures. Thus, for a transformation of property relations, a broader nexus of cultural fears and tradeoffs, rather than women's will to property, needs to be the focus of change.

### "Naihar Tut Hi Jaye" ("The Natal Home Is Broken for Me"): Fears of Natal Abandonment

*Babul ki duya-e leti ja*
*Ja tujhko sukhi sansar mile*
*Maike ki kabhi na yad aye*
*Sasural me itna pyar mile*[12]

Take your father's blessing/prayer as you go;
Go, and [may you] get a happy household;
May you never remember your mother's home;
[Because of] all the love you receive
at your in-laws' place.

A significant number of women (41.7 percent in all, Table 4.1) also evoked the theme of a daughter's love and love for a daughter in delineating their rights to property by calling upon apprehension rather than affection, saying they would not claim full or any shares of natal property because they were afraid this would sour relations with their brothers or cause their brothers' wives to hate them, and that as a result they would no longer be welcome in their natal homes. This attitude represents one of the dominant metaphors mediating women's refusal of property (Teja 1993, 70; Hershman 1982, 75), that of the greedy shrew or the *haklenewali*. There was also a close connection between these feelings and the apparently obverse ones, the desires for continuing to be part of the natal family by actively contributing to its prosperity or being available for its crises (Table 4.1, 20 percent). Significantly, these attitudes articulate women's desire for closeness with the natal family with an agency that is invisible in, and indeed contrary to, the dominant discourse on women's needs and feelings.

The opening phrase heading this section (quoted from a well-known folk song) and the song that follows (sung in the persona of the bride's father) are examples of the dominant discourse whereby the wedding is represented as the event that marks the watershed of the woman's pleasures, affections, loyalties, and memories.[13] Ties to the natal family are supposed to be severed, and she is to become an inseparable part of the affinal family. The *bidaii* ceremony, when the bride leaves her parents' home after the wedding, is an occasion of bittersweet sadness over the cutting of deep emotional ties.

Without dismissing the parents' sorrow at this rite of passage, made worse by rituals of eternal severance, it is difficult to miss that the mourning veils the consolidation of patriarchal property relations. As Kolenda (1984) vividly demonstrates in her study of two Hindu communities, groups (often North Indian) that ritually sever the woman's natal connections upon marriage tend to pack her off with dowry and little subsequent inheritance, while those who have no concept of "losing" the woman upon marriage and who believe couples "belong" to both families often give land to daughters to persuade them to live nearby and help the family. Among the communities studied here, the woman's complete change of identity underlined by Hindu wedding rituals that permanently alter her name and caste (and even religious and funerary affiliations), along with the concept of kanyadan, the gift of the daughter, symbolize her severance. Thus, property comes to be the brother's, because he remains "in" the family.

Yet, contrary to these hegemonic expectations, many women do not internalize this severance from the natal family in the ways represented by the songs; if they cry "the natal home is broken for me," they do so with regret, longing to keep that tie unbroken, to retain their connections with the family associated with love, as opposed to the affinal family, which represents the realm of dutiful work (Jeffery and Jeffery 1996, 155). Numerous studies that examine North Indian Hindu women's relationship to their natal families emphasize repeatedly that women challenge the notion of "losing" their natal families and affirm profound emotional connections with them.[14] Raheja contends that women's assertions of their natal connections are not just about sharing wealth and resources of their families, but "a poetic discourse on power and the possibility of

women's resistance to patrilineal authority and patrilineal pronouncements on female identities . . . contesting the power relations that
make them so vulnerable when they marry and go away" (1995, 26).

One of the commonest traces of such love for the natal family
is seen in fear, that claiming property will break the last residual
ties with the natal family and that women will no longer be welcome in their brothers' homes. The haklenewali, the woman who
"takes her rights," is evoked here as the specter to be avoided if all
natal links are not to be broken. In claims such as "where the sister
takes her share all those things [gifts, respect] are not there any
more, they say 'now you've got your share so go away, why are you
back here again?,' "[15] the connection to the natal family can be seen
as a concrete fund, and taking property exhausts that link, such
that women are cut adrift from customary gifts, emergency shelter,
and even affection.

The tension-fraught instances of women claiming property in
chapter 2 show that these were not idle threats. To prevent such
rifts, some women tried to leave a residual share in the natal
family fund by not separating their portion, as among Rehana's
aunts who told their brothers to keep the land and farm it, and
that they would visit and take crops once in a while.[16] But several
others (20 percent of the middle-class women, plus 3.3 percent of
poor women) legally signed over their portions to the brothers to
emphasize the affectional connection over the material one. This
was usually done at the brother's request to show good faith, but
was in fact a legal safeguard, an official insurance against the
woman's claims surfacing later.[17] It is important to note that, given
the paucity of *actual* gifts or sustained help from the natal family
(as described in a later section), no economic consideration was
usually expected in return; women usually made such "gifts" because of the fear of loss of the *emotional* space represented by the
natal family, the fragile realm already threatened by marriage and
residential separation.

Bringing up property and hence monetizing the brother-sister
relationship was seen as undesirable;[18] that is, brothers resented
any financial claims made by sisters, and could apparently be
munificent based only on "pure" love. Brothers' relationships, on
the other hand, were not perceived to be adversely affected by
having to divide property. At most, according to Rani,[19] "between
brothers the quarrel is about a bigger or smaller share, but when

sisters are involved it will turn into such a quarrel that they won't even want to see each other's faces anymore."

However, such notions of brotherly love being untainted by economic transactions was not borne out by the many stories about brothers' resentment over having to share resources (Jeffery and Jeffery 1996, 45). These incidents also gave the lie to the ideal of the joint family having unified interests in building up a common stock of property. For example, Meena's husband was waiting for his father to pass away before he bought rural land in his own name (they had three bighas in her name), hoping to get his share of the ten bighas controlled by his father without being the only one sending home money for land, and having to share what he purchased with the others.[20] Similarly, Sushila said that her father-in-law wanted them to buy rural land, but she urged her husband not to buy it while the father-in-law was alive, because all the brothers would take shares of it.[21] Medha's husband kept sending money for buying joint family land in the village to his brother, who continually spent the money on himself; Bindu's brother-in-law mortgaged her husband's land in his absence.[22] In KC, too, several cases of family discontent among brothers were reported: Seema and Renu's elder brothers-in-law sold their fathers' property in rural Punjab and ex-West Pakistan and kept nearly all the money; and Sharmila's father and uncles had long-standing disputes with their stepbrothers over which rooms each brother would get in the family house.[23] In all these cases, the breakdown of alleged joint family values and the entrenchment of the separate interests of "nuclear" or individual units were clear.

Yet even in cases of disputes involving brothers' shares, the source of discord was often perceived to be other women's greed; that is, the spectral figure of the property-hungry woman was made the repository of blame even where males contested over property.[24] As Medha narrated, she worked hard to get their new jhuggi registered in her name (her husband already had one in his name), but her brother-in-law got the formal ownership while she was briefly away. When she chided her husband over allowing this to happen, he told her that the jhuggi was still "in the family" and that wives try to destroy love among brothers by such requests.[25] *Her* wish to have property was overrun by the brotherly solidarity ideal.

Fear of incurring the wrath of brothers' wives figured prominently in women's reasons for staying away from natal family property. It was alleged that mothers could no longer give gifts once sisters-in-law were there because they claimed rights over all possessions; and that women would no longer be welcome in the natal home managed by sisters-in-law if they had asked about property.[26] The putative jealousy of daughters-in-law has a justifiable basis: if women are supposed to get property only through their in-laws, as daughters-in-law they might well feel possessive toward their only sanctioned (albeit indirect) access to resources (Jeffery and Jeffery 1996, 142). Some women did indeed express resentment at the idea that their husbands' sisters might diminish the property of their in-laws, such as Pushpa who said about her sisters-in-law: "Why should they take anything? *I'm* not going to give them anything from my share."[27] But the jealous sister-in-law can also be regarded as the metonymic transformation of the wrathful brothers themselves (the wrath supposedly brought on by sisters demanding property). With sisters-in-law being the only "strangers" to women in the natal home, it seemed emotionally more comfortable for women to scapegoat them as the disapproving ones, thus preserving parents and brothers as sources of unvarying love and generosity, and denying the collusion of their own relatives in erasing their natal connections.

Women's fear of estrangement motivating their refusals of natal property is a widely articulated belief, but there is also a positive face of that desire: women's active urge to contribute to the well-being and prosperity of that family. Ritual connections with brothers observed by North Indian women, such as the wearing of two toe rings for the husband and brother to symbolize natal and affinal connections (Wadley 1995, 97) or the similar mourning rituals for husbands' and brothers' deaths (Raheja 1995, 34), signify the most profound of emotional ties. Thus, in what Moors terms the "problems of dependence and the pleasures of identification," women may not take shares of inheritance as a way to retain rights in the natal family, "to share in its status and feel a special closeness to their natal household," which "enhances their status and by implication her own and accentuates their obligations towards her" (1995, 53–54).

As Table 4.1 shows (#5), 20 percent of the women claimed that they wanted their brothers to have all the property not because they were afraid of soured relations, but because they did not want to diminish the resources of the natal home further and wanted it to flourish as much as possible. Whether these women had independent financial resources to help their families or not, they could contribute passively by "not taking." As Pramila put it, women want that *"mera naihar bana rahe"* ("my natal home remain prosperous/well-endowed");[28] they take pride in this first home being joyful and smoothly run, and indeed draw esteem from preserving that part of themselves.

The related notion that the natal home should continue to exist as a site of love and indulgence in a world of duty and work also powerfully propels the distribution of property. A woman without natal family members to visit described herself to Jeffery and Jeffery (1996, 201) as "toasted on one side." As Seema put it, "the son should be given more property so that he can give his sister enough love to make up for her parents' absence at every festival, every important day, every occasion."[29] Lata also stressed the seemingly contradictory idea that her daughter would lose if she and her brother divided up and sold the parents' apartment in KE, because she would no longer be able to come back to the emotional space represented by a natal home.[30] In these instances, the poignancy of feeling toward the natal family completely undercuts the ritual, patriarchal prescription of severance, and reveals women's ambitions for and dependence on ties of blood.[31]

### Property over Time: Dowry and Long-Term Help in Relation to Property

Another popular notion about the ultimate fairness of the social distribution of resources is that marriage is the path for daughters to "get" affinal property, and that daughters also get parental property through gift-giving rituals associated with weddings, childbirth, and other festive occasions. 38.3 percent of the respondents claimed that they would refuse natal property because they had been given dowry and continued to be given presents, and 38.3 percent also mentioned that once married, they were supposed to "get" property through husbands' families (Table 4.1). The idea of equity according to this scheme is that daughters ultimately get as much as sons through a lifetime of gifts, and even more because of access to affinal wealth.

This myth of equivalence between dowry and premortem inheritance can be disproved by contrasting dowry payments with total wealth. In many middle- and upper middle-class families, sons' weddings often cost as much as daughters' (chapter 3, pp. 90–91). Furthermore, except for cases of landlessness (in which case dowry was still given), even the smallest unit of property (except for informally acquired jhuggis) was worth more than the higher-priced dowries mentioned. For instance, while Medha's wedding did cost Rs. 100,000 and included a Rs. 30,000 cash dowry, she reported that her father had at least one hundred bighas of rural property, including cash-crop and commercial land, so her three brothers would get far more than her wedding expenses if there was a customary division.[32] Even when several male shares needed to be made of more modest estates, the *value* of property was always much greater (except in extreme cases, for example, Uma's sister-in-law's wedding negotiations where many families sought Rs. 2,000,000 cash[33]).

Another vivid proof of the mutual exclusivity of dowry and inheritance is in the expensive weddings of women in sonless families, where women who fully expected to inherit natal property also got as many (or more) wedding prestations as other women in the community. Both Indira and Vimla described unusually elaborate gifts and entertainment at their weddings, given to them because of their fathers' wishes to display status as prominent businessmen, and not at the request of their in-laws.[34] Shobha also claimed that people in her village who had given property to brotherless daughters usually gave at least as much if not more dowry/gifts than others.[35] In these cases, inheritance was a supplementary distribution of assets and was not affected by the amount given at marriage, while dowry related to establishment of kin ties and demarcation of status.

When inheritance consisted of "joint family" living quarters or land for subsistence agriculture, there was no immediate monetary profit for males from the inheritance, whereas dowry always resulted in out-of-pocket expenses; but property was a heftier chunk of resources nonetheless. The contentions of 38.3 percent of the respondents that they would not take property because they had already been given dowry (or expected to get presents), or attitudes such as Gita's (who had no daughters but unmarried adult sons herself)—"If there is such a law [for daughters to always get shares], then why did we need to get our daughters married at such great expense?"[36]—revealed a common ideological connection drawn between dowry and property. However, this could not be supported in economic terms, and was rather a rationale to justify disinheritance.[37] Dowry cannot be regarded as equitable premortem inheritance unless it is assumed that women are inherently entitled to smaller shares of family resources, or that they should get less because they "take" liquid assets rather than immovable property.

The idea of women receiving natal property in addition to dowry plus affinal resources invoked a fear that women would thereby get "a double share" and impoverish the brothers. This assumed that not all nuclear units would get property from both sides, that women's inheritance of natal property would not become ubiquitous. But these fears were also tied to legitimate concerns that enforcing women's property rights might lead to in-laws pressuring women to claim exact inheritance from the natal fund—that is, an extension of dowry harassment. The position of daughters-in-law at the bottom of the chain of control makes manipulation and coercion in such cases likely.

This angst was used to manipulate women in various ways. As a mother-in-law in a household with very meager resources and despite having a son who was keen to get his in-laws' help in raising their living standard, Harjinder used this fear to enforce her authority over her daughter-in-law in forbidding her to take natal property. She claimed that they would lose social dignity if *the in-laws* (i.e., she) were perceived to be taking things continually from the daughter-in-law's parents.[38] On the other hand, Renu narrated an incident of clear dowry harassment where her niece-in-law's in-laws were pressuring her wealthy brother-in-law and his wife to give them money for adding on to their house.[39] Significantly, the (niece's) in-laws were using the rhetoric of women's right to receive natal property to validate their claim on their daughter-in-law's parents, while the parents were using the facts of the in-laws' harassment to raise the accusation of dowry demands and denying the daughter property. In such family situations where young married women had little control over any financial resources, it was hard to postulate a realistic empowering way for daughters to claim and retain control over natal property. Given the current structure of domestic control and hierarchies between bride-givers and bride-takers, the prospect of increased harassment of women and their families if there were fewer taboos against women's property is hardly unrealistic.

Many women pointed out that parents had to spend a lot of money not just for daughters' weddings but also for the years afterward, sending gifts when grandchildren (particularly grandsons) were born, and at other festive times, with an especially large role during the marriages of grandchildren. Parents' responsibility in this matter was supposed to be transferred to a woman's brother. However, as seen in the calculations of wedding payments (chapter 3, pp. 109–110), women's natal families or brothers rarely helped with the major expenses of their children's weddings. Kalpana voiced a common contention,[40] that wedding contributions from the woman's relatives were more like gifts, and that sisters usually reciprocated with equal amounts at brothers' children's weddings, unwilling to impose on brothers to that extent or to be that indebted.

Besides gifts, other kinds of economic assistance from natal families were also rare in the middle-class areas, despite ideological assertions about the family's long-term responsibility for their daughter's well-being. From KE, only 21.4 percent of fourteen women (14.3 percent were widowed early) were given occasional financial assistance by their brothers, and one woman (3.3 percent, from a sonless family) was helped substantially by her father. From KC, there was only one case (6.3 percent) of a mother helping out with childcare, one of a brother giving gifts when the sister visited, and one of general financial help.

The extent of help was much greater in SN. Ten percent of thirty women reported widows being extensively helped by their natal families, 36.7 percent mentioned getting gifts from brothers on a regular basis, 10 percent relied on the parents for financial assistance for living expenses, and one (3.3 percent, with husband and children) lived in her mother's household.[41] Perhaps most importantly, 20 percent of respondents described living in their natal homes for several months in the year, especially during lean times, using the natal families' resources to ensure their survival and that of their husbands and children. This latter circumstance is one of the few genuine examples of foregoing a concrete property share in exchange for economic benefit over years. Such family help was largely absent in middle-class families except in unusual circumstances like widowhood, but a more realistic possibility in poorer families who (as shown in pp. 151–52) had fewer taboos of financial help between parents and daughters.[42]

Yet, help given to married daughters was likely to be a source of conflict, because brothers resented sisters getting a substantial share of what they believed to be their assets, despite the sister's financial need or the disparity in wealth between the families (see Kavita's family situation, chapter 2, pp. 63–64). Even though help given was rarely equivalent to an inheritance share, any alienation of resources became grounds for family rifts. For example, Preeti's maternal grandfather, who was quite wealthy and had a high-paying job in addition to substantial semiurban land in Uttar Pradesh, had given Preeti's parents a house and land in addition to regular monetary help, largely because her father had never been able to hold down a good job. After the grandfather's death, the maternal uncles, who were also independently wealthy from their jobs, said that there was no legal validity to the gift and took the property back; Preeti's father and brother lacked the financial resources to challenge this usurpation.[43] In contrast to the ideal that daughters are looked after by their natal families lifelong, in times of trouble or joy, brothers could be quite resentful of *any* transfers of property to sisters, and women had good cause not to seek help from natal families for fear of causing rifts and severing connections.

As Table 4.3 shows, married women did not primarily prefer to seek help from natal families, making the gesture of refusing property in order to leave a residual claim to natal wealth largely symbolic. A majority of married women from the middle-class households (50 percent from KC and 81.3 percent from KE) said they would mainly turn to their husbands for help, and many did not even consider the husband as being a separate economic pool. Thus, the resources of the nuclear unit formed the primary basis of reliance. In SN, where many men spent most of their income on drinking and gambling and women sought informal sector work to feed their families, this number was noticeably lower and the family funds were rarely joint; neighbors, rather, were cited by 43.3 percent of SN women as the most important resort for help.

Sons were an important source for the middle-income families (cited by 26.7 percent of middle-class respondents), but in the low-income neighborhood, little expectation was placed on children. Few women from SN had adult sons, and the sons of those who did contributed little to household income on a regular basis.[44] Next in

**Table 4.3**   Sources of Financial Help Preferred by Respondents (in Percentages)

| PREFERRED SOURCES OF FINANCIAL HELP[1] | KE N=14 | KC N=16 | SN N=30 | TOTAL N=60 |
|---|---|---|---|---|
| Husband | 50 | 81.3 | 26.7 | 46.7 |
| Neighbors | 0 | 0 | 43.3 | 21.7 |
| Parents | 35.7 | 12.5 | 20 | 21.7 |
| Parents-in-law | 7.1 | 25 | 26.7 | 21.7 |
| Bank Loans | 21.4 | 25 | 3.3 | 13.3 |
| Sons | 21.4 | 31.3 | 0 | 13.3 |
| Friends/Colleagues | 28.6 | 12.5 | 3.3 | 11.7 |
| Loans from Moneylenders | 0 | 6.3 | 20 | 11.7 |
| Brothers | 7.1 | 12.5 | 13.3 | 11.7 |
| Brothers/Nephews-in-law | 7.1 | 18.8 | 6.7 | 10 |
| Distant Relatives | 7.1 | 0 | 13.3 | 8.3 |
| Workplace Loans | 0 | 12.5 | 3.3 | 5 |
| Sisters | 7.1 | 12.5 | 0 | 5 |
| Pawning/Selling Something | 0 | 0 | 6.7 | 3.3 |
| Maternal Uncles | 14.3 | 0 | 0 | 3.3 |
| Daughters | 0 | 6.3 | 0 | 1.7 |
| No one | 7.1 | 18.8 | 10 | 11.7 |

[1]Percentages show frequency of responses in particular categories; since some answers could be multiple, the percentages do not add up to 100.

importance as sources of help were parents and in-laws at 21.7 percent each. In addition, many more named parents as a possible last resort when other avenues were exhausted. In-laws were referred to by the poorer families more frequently, but middle-income families, especially from KC, also mentioned them as potential sources of help. However, reliance on parents and in-laws was more prevalent among younger women; only 30.8 percent of thirteen women naming parents-in-law as resorts of help were over twenty-nine, and only 15.4 percent of thirteen women citing parents as sources were over twenty-nine. Given that women generally had lesser access to financial resources, they were rarely named as possible sources of help whether as daughters or sisters. These figures indicate that the extended *family* was not a frequent source of support; while spouses of middle-income women were named as important resources, poorer women relied less on spouses and more on neighbors. Only about a fifth of all the respondents felt they could rely on parents or parents-in-law, and reliance on brothers, brothers-in-law, and sisters was even lower. Thus, refusing property in expectation of financial help from family was largely a social illusion, especially in the urban context where wage incomes were the means of subsistence, and there was no possibility of living off the land with the family.

Nonfamilial sources of financial help were significant, showing the strength of employment- and residence-related urban ties. Revealing the eddies of family politics in answer to the hypothetical question about sources of help, many women insisted that they specifically preferred not to turn to relatives when they were in trouble, because the embarrassment of asking family members for money could haunt their prestige in a way that asking relative strangers could not. Middle-class women said they would prefer to ask friends or colleagues (20 percent), or to get money through easy, low-payment bank or work-related loans (6.7 percent), that is, through paths which bypassed kin. Women from KE were particularly apt to name friends and colleagues (28.6 percent), because they were often employed and hence had networks of acquaintances who were not in contact with their families. The issue was far from hypothetical for the poorer families, who could promptly name possible avenues of help. Even if they could face the embarrassment of approaching family, their family members often had little extra income, so the most common sources were neighbors at 43.3 percent (especially if money was quickly required, nonrelative neighbors often being preferred) and professional moneylenders at 20 percent (whose rates were far higher than bank or work loans).[45]

Furthermore, families from SN were less likely to have their loans forgiven because they frequently borrowed from nonfamilial sources or distant relatives who were unlikely to write off debts. Even close kin that they borrowed from had little money to spare and could rarely forgive loans. Seventy percent of the SN respondents said they needed to repay any loans they took and 20 percent said they needed to repay loans with interest, while only 21.4 percent of women from KE and 50 percent of women from KC reported the necessity of repaying loans. Some women from KE and KC (26.7 percent, as compared to 6.7 percent from SN) who relied on parents, in-laws or children for financial assistance looked upon these sources as extensions of the family who would usually expect no repayment unless a specific deal about payback had been struck.

While married women both ideologically and practically relied on the resources of their nuclear unit, and rarely on parents except for cases of extreme economic hardship, women who were outside of marriage, for example, single or divorced women, clearly had a much greater need for the resources of the natal family, having no access to marital or affinal resources. In these cases, some families made provisions for daughters, but in others property was still believed to be fundamentally a male entitlement and was only grudgingly or temporarily put in women's control.

In contrast to very rare instances of married women sharing inherited property with their brothers, single or divorced women were more likely to receive some property from their families. With no male heirs in Kanta's maternal family, her mother had foregone a share of the total property (two apartments and some cash) in favor of an unmarried sister, who was seen to deserve special protection.[46] The parents of a divorced friend of Kavita's had built a set of separate rooms for her in their house, ostensibly so that she need have no dependence or conflict with her brother or sister-in-law.[47] Within Sharmila's affinal family, her husband had been saying that when the family property, a house, was divided or sold, a share should be given to one unmarried sister, though the other (married) sisters were apparently not to be given anything.[48] In these cases, families clearly recognized the special vulnerabilities of women who had no access to the means which were believed to be women's paths to wealth.

However, families were far from unanimous about the support extended to women in such situations. In the case of Sharmila's affines, it was not known how the other brothers felt about the one sister getting a share, but in a similar instance, when Kavita's paternal grandmother tried to give shares to two widowed daughters, her sons vehemently resisted attempts to have their shares curtailed even by a small amount, even if it meant helping their sisters.[49] Jaya's mother-in-law, widowed early in life, was given property and looked after by a relatively well-off sister, but the father and brothers had been unwilling to do more than give crops or, occasionally, cash.[50] These situations reflected an ambivalence about the daughter who could get no property through a husband yet who nonetheless could not be given a full entitlement; while some family members contended that custom should be set aside in these exceptional circumstances, others were unwilling to curtail habitual male privileges.

Even women who had not encountered any such situations hypothesized that women without access to marital or affinal wealth would not get rights to natal property easily, although their families might try to make some alternate economic arrangements for them. Rani speculated that "even if a woman is not married her parents or brother are not going to be happy giving her a share, they will say 'let her get married,' and if she does not, they can say 'stay with us and we will look after you,' but nobody will want to give property."[51] Bina felt that parents-in-law might look after widowed women, and parents and brothers were supposed to be responsible for widowed or deserted women, but "nowadays in case the share gets less, they [brothers] try to further educate those sisters," that is, hoping to make sisters employable so that they no longer needed to be given property.[52] These comments reveal that women realized property was viewed as a profound male entitlement whatever the woman's situation, giving the lie to the idea that women do not usually get natal property *because* they "get" shares from in-laws.

Given that women had little hope of receiving assets from the natal family whether married, unmarried, or married but poor, and with the only potential sources of regular support being affinal or marital resources or personal income, it is not surprising that women opted to stay within marriage even when there were severe marital troubles. Relatively few women (18.3 percent) said that women should never leave their marriages under any circumstances[53]; in other words, marriage was not viewed as an immutable bond that should never be broken, and women who opted to stay in problem marriages were perhaps deterred for sound economic reasons rather than cultural prescriptions.

Divorced women's ties to the affinal family were perceived to be severed, and alimony or maintenance was rare, with no cases from the poorer areas. As Table 4.4 shows, 41.7 percent of women supported the *idea* of women getting maintenance for their own upkeep after divorce, and another 15 percent felt that they ought to get maintenance for child support. Yet a large number expected that divorced women would go into other forms of economic dependence like another marriage, or reliance on parents or brothers, or

**Table 4.4**  Respondents' Attitudes toward Divorced Women Receiving
Maintenance Money from Husbands/In-laws

| ATTITUDES TOWARD DIVORCED WOMEN RECEIVING MAINTENANCE MONEY FROM HUSBANDS/IN-LAWS[1] | KE N=14 | KC N=16 | SN N=30 | TOTAL N=60 |
|---|---|---|---|---|
| **Should get maintenance** | | | | |
| Should get, for taking care of herself | 57.1 | 43.8 | 33.3 | 41.7 |
| Should get, for help in raising children | 14.3 | 12.5 | 16.7 | 15 |
| **Should not get maintenance** | | | | |
| Should not get, her parents should be responsible for her care | 21.4 | 18.8 | 33.3 | 26.7 |
| Should get only if husband was at "fault" | 21.4 | 6.3 | 33.3 | 23.3 |
| Should not get, can remarry instead | 0 | 6.3 | 23.3 | 13.3 |

[1]Percentages show frequency of responses in particular categories; since
some answers could be multiple, the percentages do not add up to 100.

else seek employment, all scenarios averting women's direct need
for natal property.[54] Given these alternatives, women's best economic options were to stay within marriage where they were likely
to have a higher standard of living and greater social acceptability.

It thus comes as no surprise that of the total of thirty-five cases
of marital disputes cited among family and close friends of the
respondents (12 from KE, 11 from KC, 12 from SN, including cases
of problems with the in-laws, problems between the couple, or situations of male bigamy), there were 28.6 percent cases of reconciliation, 20 percent of remarriage following the divorce (in 31.4 percent
cases, the dispute was ongoing or an informal separation had taken
place). Only 22.9 percent cases had resulted in the woman formally
severing the marriage without entering into another conjugal relationship, indicating that women were not wont to depend solely
upon their own earnings or rely on dubious help from the natal
family. In the absence of good economic opportunities or inherit-

ance for women, being married was indeed one of the few ways to enjoy property with any security.[55]

In sum, the ideology of dowry and ongoing gifts to women being equivalent to inheritance does not bear up in practice. Not only are marriage expenses (whether for sons or daughters) and other ritual gifts relatively less in value compared to property, but there is little expectation of other help from the natal family for children's marriages, annual gifts, or more serious economic crises. With nonfamilial sources of financial help counted as most important, and marriedness being crucial to financial well-being, it is not surprising that dowry gifts come to be regarded as the major socially sanctioned path of receiving some resources from the natal family. If not for dowry, women would have no assets other than personal savings and resources of the nuclear household.

### Surrogate Sons: Brotherless Women Inherit Property

Among Indian communities with patriarchal inheritance norms, transmission of property through daughters in sonless families has been a historically popular device for keeping assets in the family line.[56] Among certain ethnic groups, daughters' full inheritance in sonless families is explicit in customary law.[57] In many other communities, the frequency of this practice, though not formally articulated in law, can be inferred from family histories of uxorilocal residence.[58] A geographical transfer of "home base" to live among women's natal kin is the hushed secret of many family chronicles. In terms of the gender codes enshrined in property relations, it is fascinating to note that in such cases the husband of the property-owning daughter is culturally depicted as an emasculated, slothful, and ridiculous figure, presumably because his lack of paternal property is a profound signifier of powerlessness (Hershman 1981, 75–79; Jeffery and Jeffery 1996, 123). It is seen as impolite and cruel to remind him of his "unusual" and "unmanly" residential situation. The very term *gharjamai*, literally meaning the domestic or at-home son-in-law in several North Indian languages, is significantly asymmetrical, with no parallel term for women living at their in-laws', whose enjoyment of affinal property is naturalized.

In the present study, brotherlessness was indeed one of the rare situations in which women received natal family property. All

of the five brotherless respondents (8.3 percent of total respondents) whose parents had property had already inherited or expected to inherit (this included two women from SN; one other SN
woman who was brotherless had no parental property). In the last
few generations, daughters (rather than sons-in-law or nephews)
seemed to have become preferred heirs. Uma's grandmother, for
instance, had inherited her parents' rural house in Bihar as the
only daughter and it had always remained in her name.[59] The nine
bighas in Punjab farmed by Ganga's father lifelong had all been
given by her sonless maternal grandfather to his daughter.[60] In a
recent case, a couple from SN had just bought some rural land
fairly cheap from a woman who had inherited her natal family land
and cash in the absence of brothers, but who was selling it because
her postmarital residence was far away from the land.[61]

The preference for daughters as heirs in sonless families can
also be connected to other cultural changes such as the erosion of
notions of joint family unity and a greater attention to individual
"nuclear" branches. Shobha's comment on this subject, "those who
don't have sons give property to their daughters; they think that if
their own daughter stays there then no-one else can seize it,"[62]
hints at this contemporary emphasis on one's immediate family
that has superseded ideologies of preserving joint family property
in male hands as the ultimate goal.

Whether or not women were brotherless, many of them believed
that this was one of the few ways in which property could come to
women; 23.3 percent women, mostly from SN (Table 4.1), brought
this up as a criterion, and 10 percent mentioned it even in contemplating shares for women in *ideal* divisions of property (Table 4.2).
In fact, many women from SN were insistent that brotherlessness
was the only *legal* way for women to get property. Sushila, who had
got a share of her father's savings along with her step-siblings,
declared that "the legal right [to property] is for those who are the
only daughters and have no brothers or if they have only one brother
who has no children. Once the brother has children then the woman
has no right any more."[63] Even Medha, who believed she should be
able to share some of her father's substantial property with her
brothers, proclaimed that daughters' rights did not even "develop"
(*hak banta nahi*, alternatively translatable as "rights were not even
'created'") when there were sons in the family.[64] They based these
assertions on situations in their villages or among their kin. This

mode of inheritance for women was interpreted as the "new" and modern reform that had come about under the postcolonial state, viz. the preference for daughters as heirs over distant male relatives or sons-in-law that was more common in the last century was regarded as being *the* new law of "property for women."

In this inscription of the property rights of brotherless daughters as both an exception to the rule and one of the only rules, the spectral quality of women's property entitlements is highlighted. Propertied women can be ideologically contained within this rationale, with no spillover into "normal" families with sons. The absent presence of male heirs mediating this standard is best revealed in the niches of these proposed transmissions, where women's ownership of property is repeatedly marked by surrogate male presences. For example, Vimla's parents wanted her to have their house, and often said to her, "you are our son." She took this to connote not just that she would take their property but that she would also be responsible for their eldercare "like a son," feeling that she could not have taken property if there had been a brother, except in the unlikely situation that he was very wealthy and she very poor.[65]

Furthermore, Vimla was the surrogate heir not just in her brother's but also in her son's place. Even though she had a sister, she was treated as the only designated heir; her sister had indicated that she did not want any natal property because her in-laws had a lot of land, and also that she thought of the natal property as being for Vimla's son, the only male grandchild (Vimla also had a daughter). Similarly, although in Indira's natal family women had been offered property even when they had brothers (predictably, the divorced aunt had accepted part of her share and the other aunts had written away their shares "because they did not need it"), Indira considered herself to be the main heir to her father's considerable wealth. This was not only because of the prosperity of her sister's in-laws, but mainly because her elder son had been raised by her parents and her father loved and depended on her husband "like a son."[66] In these cases, the women inherited not only "as" sons but also "for" sons, underlining rather than erasing the fundamental male entitlement to property. Significantly, this also made the so-called modern form of the practice a mirror image of the scriptural notion of the *putrikaputra*.[67]

Women's inheritance of property in sonless families is a vivid example of an apparently empowering avenue for women with little radical potential. Here, women's access to property depended on genetic accidents, and even actual ownership was haunted by ghosts of unborn and future male heirs. Meanwhile, this route of property transmission appeared in discourse as a sanctioned "modern" way of giving women property, while the rarity and subversiveness of the practice were muted.

### Property as Payoff: Eldercare and Other Family Responsibilities

> Both daughters and sons should be given something. But further-more the son, or daughter, who looks after the parent the most should be given the property, because usually all the others have separated themselves, are living and eating by themselves and do not even ask about the parents. Just when it is time for the parents to give things [before dying], they all show up and start calling them "mother" and "father"; then all they have to do is to put them on the funeral pyre, feed some people at the funeral to hide their shame, and get ready to take the property and live it up." (Parvati)[68]

An alternative paradigm to viewing inheritance as the transmission of family wealth over generations is the commonly recurring standard of eldercare, that elderly parents give children property as a reward for tending to their physical, financial, and emotional needs. While only 10 percent of respondents overall (none from SN, Table 4.1) pointed to it as a rationale for property division, one SN woman had actually received all of her mother's property in exchange for caregiving, and many other instances of eldercare awards across generations were cited by the respondents. Though not the commonest basis of property division, this was nonetheless an important path of noncustomary property devolution.

Parvati, a widow of fifty, who was often perturbed by her four sons' alleged lack of attention to her needs, framed the concept of eldercare-based property division in the gender-neutral way cited above. But the rationale of eldercare was more commonly used to justify male inheritance, by invoking the customary gendered division of labor among siblings whereby sons are supposed to be responsible for elderly parents' financial needs, medical crises, and even funeral costs. Ironically, the consistent application of the gender-neutral eldercare principle has the potential to be especially significant for women, who more often take on caregiving, marking one of the negotiable spaces for women to get property in defiance of norms of male inheritance. And yet, the standard of eldercare can also be one of the most intransigent bases to deny women property, if customs against accepting help from married daughters set the standard. To understand whether property indeed devolves precisely in proportion to eldercare, or whether this rationale is simply a screen to justify giving property to sons, explicit eldercare rewards and the barriers to women assuming these responsibilities need to be examined closely.

Using property as a reward for services rendered or for potential responsibilities (as 1.7 percent of the respondents did) is of course symbolically the raw opposite of the view that property is a gift of love toward all children (and also distant from the perception that ancestral resources are carried on through inheritance). Parvati's comment makes explicit the vulnerability and fear of abandonment that runs through the idea of using property to pay caregivers, fears especially tangible for people with meager resources. For instance, Durga related that her mother was afraid to cash in the remainder of her natal family's land in Bangladesh, fearing that if she went with her sons and they took the money, they might then abandon her and she would no longer have the inheritance to hold over them.[69]

While women were likely to be more neglected in this respect because they typically owned less property, men also felt the vulnerability of age and tried to use their property to obtain financial or social security. Lakshmi's grandfather wanted to divide up his land among his sons in exchange for Rs. 250 a month as *khoraki* (maintenance, literally money for food) from each son, but they were unwilling to give this money for what they perceived to be a family entitlement, while the son who he was staying with thought he should get more land if he was going to bear the entire financial "burden."[70] In a world governed by capitalist relations, the elderly without liquid cash were increasingly vulnerable; disposition of family property was one of the few avenues of power.

The above dynamics illustrate that eldercare is far from being the natural, loving duty it is ideologically proclaimed to be; rather, "payment" for eldercare more often shows traces of disintegration of usufructuary rights in family land and a greater reliance on concepts of individual property and conditional inheritance. In addition to financial vulnerability, physical frailty also appears as a frequent cause for concern: expectations of caregiving frequently evoke images of bodily fluids, a recurrent theme being that the person who does the actual work of taking care of an elderly relative without bladder or bowel control is the true heir.

Numerous examples of women receiving property in return for taking on eldercare, in preference to customary male heirs, bear evidence of male heirs' abandonment of the elderly despite lip service to sons' responsibility in this area. A dramatic instance where property was left to nonkin or neighbors who had been caregivers was that of Kavita's mother looking after a widow in their neighborhood, who left her land to Kavita's mother and brother.[71] Another atypical example was that of Jaya's mother-in-law who, although widowed early and largely supported by her natal kin near their place, had brought her (the mother-in-law's) father-in-law over to her home and looked after him in his last years. She was rewarded with his entire property, while his son, Jaya's uncle, was disinherited for staying away from his father and living near his own in-laws.[72] In other cases it was daughters who had looked after mothers and been given family assets; for example, Uma's paternal aunt who had lived in the rural home in Bihar with Uma's grandmother was treated as de facto owner of that house and property, while Uma's father had opted to live in the city and travel abroad.[73] In these instances, women's caregiving conferred direct economic benefits, to the extent that customary heirs had been disinherited.

In one of the clearest cases of commodification of eldercare, Bindu's mother had come to live with her and her family, and had given Bindu her savings of Rs. 15,000 because she had agreed to look after her.[74] None of the other sons or daughters received anything. Bindu's mother had lived earlier with one of her sons, but when he died the other married sons had not been willing to assume responsibility for her. Thus, Bindu received the privileges of being a default/surrogate son along with the work, and she felt she had lived up to taking the money by paying entirely for her mother's funeral (typically a son's job), and taking care of all her mother's food, clothing, and also bodily care while she was alive.

Given the gender division of labor whereby women are responsible for domestic work, including the management of intimate body fluids as part of childcare and eldercare, it is not surprising that women had the advantage in getting unexpected eldercare awards, by extending their caregiving to people not included in the customary scheme. (Within the customary scheme, women are expected to be eldercaregivers to parents-in-law, and their husbands are given property in "return.") In terms of the standard as contemplated by Sushila, (twenty-five years old and with a four-year-old male child)—"whoever is going to clean up my urine and feces and is going to put up with taking care of me, that's who I want to give everything to"[75]—women stood to get the upper hand.

Several women related the provision of eldercare to inheritance and wanted daughters to be included as equal heirs, making similar connections about the superior quality of daughters' caregiving. For instance, Maya, with two married sons and a married daughter, proclaimed that "she [the daughter] plays an equal role in taking care of her parents, helps in their troubles, she comes by when her mother feels sick, so she should have a share."[76] Madhuri, having experienced only daughterhood and not marriage or parenting, was even more extreme, saying "when do sons help nowadays, it is the daughters who take much more care of parents; they might get some share of property but they help more than sons do."[77] If property division were indeed proportionate to eldercare, women could thus have a favorable claim based on their physical care (if not financial assistance).

However, as the portrait of property divisions showed, women rarely inherited any property, and the examples of property awards cited above were highly atypical; only one of the sixty respondents (plus women in 6.7 percent of the respondents' families) had inherited anything in this manner. Much more commonly, eldercare was supposed to be the province of the sons, and property dispensation was believed to reflect that responsibility, whether or not particular sons got property specifically as a result of eldercare.[78] Ritu and Vimla's husbands, for example, had both been the youngest sons and caretakers of their parents, and inherited the parents' residences by family consensus.[79] However, eldercare was not necessarily the only basis for distributing property in those families; Vimla's husband's brothers (and not his sisters) had received other property from their father. On the whole, all males were heirs and all females disinherited. As with many other families, one brother was responsible for the bulk of the caregiving, but all the males shared the property under the banner of sons undertaking eldercare. Among the kin of the SN women, it was very common for a parent to be living with one of the sons in the village, while other sons gave some crops or cash but were clearly not the primary caretakers; however, all males expected equal shares of land. Lakshmi's family dispute narrated on page 147 is a vivid case in point showing that, while some property awards may have been related to eldercare, shares of property were rarely distributed in proportion to the amount of caregiving.

The persistent trope of the daughter's emotional and financial severance from her natal family upon marriage and the son's continuing responsibilities to and privileges from that family strongly affect women's refusals of property, viz. the belief that women have no claims if they do not assume any corresponding responsibilities. Brothers' sole right to property is often seen by sisters themselves as a justifiable return for all the duties that are habitually assigned to the sons. As Kiran, a relatively newly married woman with an infant son living in the husband's "joint" family, said:

> My brother is the one who is going to be useful to my father and be with him in his times of joy or sorrow, so that is why he should have it [property]. We are away in our own homes. If my father runs into any problems, my brother is the one who will have to worry about it. We can maybe go there, but we can't help if they need money.[80]

Kiran's comment was typical of many women who implied that they *should* forfeit property because they were unable to help their parents, due to lack of financial resources, residential patterns, and most strongly, ideological restrictions. Kiran explained, "Among us the 'duties' have been fixed. We can worry about them [parents], if they really need help we could think about helping them in the time of trouble, but we are supposed to be 'attached' to our *own* [i.e., affinal] homes first." Suman also pointed out that her natal family had recently had many crises involving divorce, illness, and so forth, and although she was worried, she had not felt able to leave her allegedly primary responsibilities—her tasks in the nuclear family—to be with her parents in another city. However, her brothers had had to go, since their presence was expected in hard times.[81]

As a parent receiving assistance, Seema felt that her son ought to be rewarded and encouraged not just for physical and emotional support, but also as financial compensation for his assets that were diminished by helping the parents.[82] Her son had contributed large sums to the renovations of their house (which he would inherit, thus protecting his own assets) but also to his sister's and his own weddings. Thus, she felt that "since the son helps the parents with everything, and the daughter is in her own home not doing anything and saving on their [sic] own, while the son could also be saving on his own and could put aside a lot, I think that gives him slightly more rights." Here, the expenditure of time, energy, money, and even loss of the "freedom" to look after one's nuclear unit solely was sought to be compensated by property.

What is unfair in this customary division of duties is not that those who do actually expend resources are duly compensated, but that daughters are not permitted to share in eldercare (and hence property) per ideological proscriptions. In many cases this ban was framed in terms of the Hindu wedding ritual of kanyadan, translated as "gift of a virgin[83] daughter," in which the giving away of the daughter constitutes a high holy act for the father.[84] This is supposed to be the supreme selfless gift, to which the bulk of other material gifts are merely supplementary. As I learned from some of the middle-class women (21.4 percent of KE and 31.3 percent of KC respondents), the act was interpreted in their families as one in which the daughter is given away along with the dowry with no rights retained in her, and so parents accept nothing from her—stark symbols of woman-as-property.[85] In the strictest form, parents do not even drink water at their daughter's marital home; the "modern adaptation" of this is to eat a piece of fruit or drink a cup of tea, and usually leave a payment for large meals or extended stays, even if the stay is for an emergency in the daughter's home and at her request.[86] Women from families observing this practice made an explicit connection between kanyadan customs, eldercare responsibilities, and property inheritance. Bina said, "If we don't even eat at our daughters' homes then why do we have to give them things? . . . The son is doing all the work for us and we have given the daughters what we wanted already, so why bring them into the remainder that we haven't given?"[87] Both the privileges and responsibilities of eldercare were thus blocked by the act of a Hindu woman's marriage itself.

It appears quite significant that no women from SN brought up notions of kanyadan and the resultant blocking of any help from daughters. No similar taboos were ever mentioned; in fact, there were several instances where married women gave their families ongoing financial and other help. In contrast to KE where no cases of helping natal families were mentioned, and KC where two women narrated instances of sisters helping with family weddings and other financial crises and one woman gave her parents some financial support, there were several kinds of help proffered by the SN women. Among 13.3 percent of thirty respondents and in many other households in the neighborhood, the woman's parent, brother, or sister lived in her nuclear family. In 10 percent of cases, women paid for natal family funerals, debts, and legal expenses out of their own earnings; Medha described her motivation in doing this as wanting to be by her brother's side helping him through troubled times, an act of love and support.[88] Besides financial help, other assistance was provided by Deepa and her sister who would take turns staying with their father in the village a few months at a time, doing the cooking and domestic work because there were no women in their natal household.[89] There were clearly no cultural proscriptions against the women's natal family members staying or eating.

Although there were fewer restrictions on sources of help among SN families, no women had been given shares of immoveable property despite their assistance. Also, a much smaller percentage of SN women as compared to KC women (only 10 percent as compared to 25 percent, Table 4.2) believed that eldercare should play a role in the dispensation of property. The conclusion may be drawn that in this group, eldercare was a matter of assisting one's natal family based on social and affectional ties and not on financial considerations. Several women who had helped their families professed to believe in equal love and equal duties of sons and daughters, but also cited numerous barriers to claiming their own natal inheritance; for example, potential rifts with brothers. Thus, their own support was not necessarily tied to a calculated consideration of property. Even among the women from KE and KC who had helped natal families, there were only two instances of women wanting to claim natal property, including one brotherless woman. Here, too, eldercare was generally not undertaken in expectation of receiving property (except in the case of sonless property, where eldercare *was* seen as a necessary duty).

Although relatively few respondents mentioned the ideological relevance of eldercare in delineating how property should be distributed, several instances of actual inheritance showed that women did inherit property in dramatically unusual ways as a result of caregiving. However, because of strong ideological proscriptions women did not usually provide eldercare and did not typically expect inheritance in return when they did so. While only some of the sons (and daughters-in-law) actually did the caregiving in most cases, the rights of *all* male heirs to inheritance were nevertheless proclaimed to be connected to eldercare. The issue of eldercare thereby functioned as a screen for disentitling women from property; that is, sons inherited more in accordance with ideological prescriptions about sons undertaking the bulk of eldercare, whether or not they actually did any caregiving.

### Medha's Case: Complex Negotiations

Women's feelings about natal property revealed a complex mix of fears and strengths, pragmatic indifference and generous assistance, love and alienation. A detailed analysis of one response— Medha's attitude to taking natal property[90]—provides one of the most vivid illustrations of the discursive complexity over property. It shows that women's refusal of natal resources is not necessarily a mark of their consciousness being consumed by hegemonic norms, while also revealing the difficulty of structuring lives free from the deep hold of patriarchal power relations.

Unlike most Indian girls in rural areas, Medha had grown up with dreams of opportunity. Her grandfather, who owned a large amount of rural property, had indulged her as a child, often saying playfully that she could stay at her parents' all her life, could study instead of getting married, and work as a nurse or teacher. Not surprisingly, this had not come to pass, and she had married and borne three daughters by the time she was twenty-one. However, she still cherished those visions of independence, and valued the experiences provided by her job. Having passed her matriculate (school-leaving) examination, she was the most educated woman at SN (though low on the educational scale compared to KE and KC), one of the few SN women with formal employment, and an enthusiastic community worker.

A strong believer in the importance of women having property/ assets of their own, Medha had been trying to get a jhuggi in her own name, had her own bank account, and had also used some

savings to buy jewelry for herself and her daughters. Her apprecia-
tion of her need to be economically self-sufficient was further en-
hanced by the scant reliance she could place on marital and affinal
assets; her wages were crucial for the nuclear family because her
husband stopped giving her food money when he went on drinking
and gambling binges, and although they expected to inherit some
farmland presently joint between her husbands' brothers, she did
not trust her brother-in-law who had cheated her out of her wedding jewelry and also pocketed the cash dowry. She also felt a
strong affection and responsibility toward her natal family, to the
extent that she kept her full income secret from her husband, being
committed to certain expenses he did not approve of, such as helping her natal family with legal or funeral expenses.

Thus, Medha was completely aware of the value of financial
resources, had few illusions about getting control over any property
through her husband or in-laws, and had a strong responsibility
toward her natal family, showing herself to be a woman who did
not passively accept notions of women's access to financial resources
mediated through husbands, nor support notions of women's severance from the natal family upon marriage. Yet she did not believe
that daughters stood to gain by taking equal property shares. As
she formulated it:

> It might be good if people gave completely equal shares of
> money to all their children, but I think that one should not
> take equal shares from the brother. The brother has to make
> a living from that small area, and why should the sister take
> an equal share when she has a right to a part of her in-laws'
> property too? I also think that if I take a smaller share then
> he will look after me with more care. For example, if five
> shares are made of the property they will be very small shares,
> but instead if three shares are made for three brothers, the
> fourth is shared by sisters and the fifth is redistributed among
> the three brothers, then the sisters will have rights over all
> three brothers. She can stay with any of them and they might
> all look after her.

It appears from these words that Medha was unable to conceive of
a system of property distribution in which each couple could get
property from both sides of the family, or visualize a gender-neu-

tral world in which women could have equal economic power and responsibility and would not need looking after. Or rather, she could not realistically see this happening, and thus her plan was to choose the most empowering avenue in the present scenario.

As she planned it, she could take advantage of some natal family property, while giving up some to secure brotherly insurance, thereby simultaneously raising the living standard of her own nuclear unit and not causing her natal home to be visibly impoverished. To this end, she contemplated asking her eldest brother to give her and her husband two shops on a strip of land he was planning to develop commercially. These shops would be quite valuable and would certainly assure them a materially better life than they had now, but would be a very small portion of her father's total assets. Even to do this she would have to contend with her brother, who was more willing to give them less valuable agricultural land, and also with her husband, who wanted her to claim ownership over a larger portion because her family was wealthier than his.

Medha preferred to have use rights over the shops so that they could make a good living, and not to accept the other land with less profit potential; but also not to take so much that she lost her brother's support or gave her in-laws a reason to deprive her husband of his/their share. This conceptualization of property rights for women hovered between acceptance of customary patriarchal notions, such as women "getting" property through affinal families or women getting lifelong help rather than dowry, and active negotiations to maximize immediately profitable assets as well as long-term insurance. Her vision of property distribution vividly shows how women may be practically or emotionally unable to be free of constitutive ideology, yet able to negotiate solutions that optimize their needs rather than becoming passive martyrs of custom.

As Merry contends in her analysis of the contemporary significance of law, the very notion of individual resistance to regimes of power is double edged, often harming the resister in the very act of opposition, but also "disrupt[ing] those modes of conceptualizing and categorizing the world which lie at the heart of modern processes of power" (1995, 18). Medha's strategy, while contrary to her own maximal financial gain, nevertheless represents a keen evaluation of the structures of power governing her life, a "reshap[ing of] the way communities and identities are understood" (Merry

1995, 23). In that sense, her negotiations of property, which altered customary patterns only in minimal ways, were nonetheless acts of ideological contestation.

## Conclusion: Multiple Positions, Optimal Compromises

It seems evident that responses to property division are predominantly "negotiated" readings of culture as Hall (1987) would put it.[91] In delineating how property should be divided, some women echoed the patriarchal ideology that seemed contrary to their material interests, but often revealed their own dissociation from such beliefs, while underlining their socioeconomic powerlessness. Furthermore, in naming connections between inheritance and factors like eldercare, dowry, or long-term financial help, women demonstrated a process of cultural sensemaking in which they weighed their realistic possibilities of intervention against financial options. Without a broader change in socioeconomic relations, it would be difficult for women to proffer substantial help to the natal family and get property in return, and thus dowry from the natal home along with the "protection" supposedly offered through marriage was the safest economic route, whereas radically different actions could leave them too vulnerable. Most remarkably, the images used by these women, particularly images of love from and toward parents, demarcated a realm of feeling escaping from and indeed contrary to dominant discourse, a construction of entitlements very different from and yet at least as powerful as the notion of individual jural rights. Thus, what might appear to be a jumble of deluded attitudes from women toward refusing property were often complex attempts at optimizing material survival and bridging emotional alienation within a system giving them limited agency and subjectivity; as Moors puts it, "women may well see advantages in 'giving up property,' for property does not necessarily mean power" (1995, 256).

In celebrating the spaces of discursive leakage, however, it would be troublesome to forget the resilience of hegemonic discourse. The backdrop to women's negotiations of property divisions discussed here is, after all, the depressing portrait of how little property or substantial economic assets they actually owned, and how that limited their opportunities and aided their impoverishment and dependence. In that light, the rationales for refusing property that were optimized tradeoffs in women's minds could be seen as justifications of inertia, having little transformative momentum, at best covert acts of resistance from agents locked in fundamental economic dependence. Under this form of patriarchy, women maximized their short-term priorities at the cost of undermining their long-term material interests, and feelings of love and loyalty toward parents and the natal family were enacted in ways that bolstered male privilege. Despite exceptional cases of women receiving family property and subtle negotiations by women to retain natal ties, patriarchal principles of inheritance remain both ubiquitous and markedly stable.

# 5

## Knowing Themselves

### Women's Attitudes toward Wealth and Well-Being

How important *is* property to women's lives? To measure women's resources through the lens of property owner ship (as the previous chapters have been doing) is to put faith in conventional economic indicators of well-being; to measure women's wealth in accordance with "customary" law based on religious texts, however, is to foreground realms of timeless custom in a world of late capitalist relations. Each of these perspectives is a partial view of the sociocultural nexus because women do not live entirely by either market rules or scriptural prescriptions; rather, these are factors in a process of cultural sensemaking. Within this study that explores the myths and realities of property, this chapter describes some of the concepts women themselves prioritized in evaluating their sociocultural options: what women considered to be their most valuable resources; the toughest obstacles to progress; and the best solutions to these troubles. While it cannot be claimed that these views are the "most authentic" means of explicating the social nexus, they are important complements to women's decisions and sensibilities related to property.

The focus of this chapter is women's priorities, the value that they assign to various issues relating to their lives. The first topic explored is one that begs the question in light of the discussion in previous chapters, which focused on hegemonic constructions of property transmission: What does property mean to *women*? What do women consider to be the most important financial resources? According to them, how useful are land, housing, or traditional women's wealth like jewelry? The importance of the property question is judged in the light of factors women identify as the most pressing problems for women in society. The uses of the legal realm for bringing about social change, an important query in this project, is then explored in the context of evaluating these important problems and perceived solutions, as well as by examining women's attitudes to and actual encounters with the law. The significance of property is analyzed in the context of ideologies of wealth and power as understood and critiqued by the women.

## Reconceptualizing Stridhan (Women's Wealth)

Contrary to the popular image of the jewelry-bedecked Indian woman who values gold and is befuddled about money, this chapter shows that women were far from ignorant about the most valuable investments in current times, viz. banking, investing in financial schemes, buying property or running businesses. Only a minority of women from this sample found the customary female heritage of jewelry to be of value, and few considered this a prime asset. This conclusion is important in contesting perceptions that women are given what they really value—jewelry rather than property—in the property-dowry split between brothers and sisters, and that women live in a different financial realm as compared to men. Despite their refusals of natal property, women were not at all unaware of the advantages of owning property, nor naive about the personal and social benefits of having financial resources.

In the Hindu scheme of entitlements, women were not supposed to be entirely resourceless; while the bulk of property passed through males, women could have usufructuary/maintenance rights usually in the affinal family (or else in the natal family if single or separated), plus their own fund called stridhan, or women's wealth, typically in the form of jewelry or other domestic valuables like utensils. In most Indian Muslim and Christian communities with patriarchal inheritance practices, similarly, natal wealth was supposed to come to the woman through that portion of the dowry that consisted of her personal valuables. The jewelry given to the bride by the in-laws also became part of her individual wealth. In addition, she could add to this wealth through inheritance of jewelry or other valuables from mothers and mothers-in-law.

If one could envisage an economic system where gold (or other metals for making jewelry) was equal in worth to land, and an equitable bulk of the two was distributed among male and female siblings, then stridhan could indeed be counted as a fair share of property for women. In contemporary India, however, while the price of gold has risen at extremely high rates and made old jewelry correspondingly valuable, this is nothing compared to the explosion in property values. Most couples do acquire some jewelry upon marriage and rarely get property until later in life, but other modes of saving are counted as being far more important: savings accounts, fixed deposits (similar to certificates of deposit), nonbank-based investment schemes, or stocks and shares, depending on the amount of extra cash available and knowledge of these systems.

However, the perception that women should get property *only* in the form of jewelry or stridhan still dominates ideologically. The women in this study who said that women got dowry or gifts instead of natal family property were echoing this belief (Table 4.1). This notion is also a principal jurisprudential theme in the Indian postcolonial debate about Hindu women getting equal shares of property: the Second Hindu Law Committee's draft of a succession bill (1947) supported the first Committee's suggestion that daughters be given half of sons' shares of an intestate father's property, and claimed to balance the equation by giving daughters double of sons' shares of a mother's property (Parashar 1992, 123-25).[1] Notwithstanding that mothers' shares were highly unlikely to be equal or even close in value to fathers' resources, completely equal divisions of fathers' property were seen to be *unfair to men* on these grounds. Interestingly, while women's inheritance of land through the natal family was legally limited in this way, they have been able to get somewhat greater access over marital property by claiming certain kinds of wedding prestations as personal stridhan and not joint property.[2] But on the whole, stridhan seems to restrict women's wealth by inscribing them within an allegedly ancient system of entitlements that is markedly distant from contemporary women's notions about premium resources.

As Table 5.1 shows, within the world-system of capitalist relations, banks and other investment opportunities have clearly become prime resources to women. A comment from Asha (a sixty-year-old widow with a couple of years of schooling, living with

**Table 5.1**  Respondents' Attitudes about How a Woman Could Best Use Savings or Surplus Resources (in Percentages)

| HOW A WOMAN COULD BEST USE SAVINGS OR SURPLUS RESOURCES[1] | KE N=14 | KC N=16 | SN N=30 | TOTAL N=60 |
|---|---|---|---|---|
| **Save in a Bank/Investment Scheme** | | | | |
| Because they increase the most there | 71.4 | 75 | 40 | 56.7 |
| Because they do not get used up | 14.3 | 0 | 30 | 18.3 |
| Because they do not get stolen | 0 | 0 | 23.3 | 11.7 |
| Because withdrawal is easy | 7.1 | 6.3 | 13.3 | 10 |
| **Invest in a business** | | | | |
| If a woman has the talent for it | 28.6 | 37.5 | 20 | 26.7 |
| Because it makes the most profit | 7.1 | 12.5 | 13.3 | 11.7 |
| **Invest in land/property** | 35.7 | 31.3 | 3.3 | 18.3 |
| **Save as Jewelry** | | | | |
| Because it increases in value | 14.3 | 6.3 | 13.3 | 11.7 |
| Because it can be pawned easily | 7.1 | 6.3 | 13.3 | 10 |
| Because it can be used later for children's weddings | 0 | 6.3 | 10 | 6.7 |
| Because it is nice to wear | 0 | 0 | 10 | 5 |
| **Spend** | | | | |
| On living expenses/weddings | 21.4 | 37.5 | 23.3 | 26.7 |
| On self | 21.4 | 31.3 | 3.3 | 15 |
| **Save money at home** | 0 | 0 | 6.7 | 3.3 |
| **Do not know** | 7.1 | 0 | 3.3 | 3.3 |

[1]Percentages show frequency of responses in particular categories; since some answers could be multiple, the percentages do not add up to 100.

**Table 5.2**  Respondents' Attitudes about the Benefits of Women
Owning Property (in Percentages)

| BENEFITS OF WOMEN OWNING LAND/PROPERTY[1] | KE N=14 | KC N=16 | SN N=30 | TOTAL N=60 |
|---|---|---|---|---|
| Helps divorced/widowed/ vulnerable women | 28.6 | 25 | 26.7 | 26.7 |
| Generally useful, gives one strength | 50 | 31.3 | 10 | 25 |
| Beneficial for one's own maintenance | 14.3 | 12.5 | 23.3 | 18.3 |
| Beneficial for children's care/weddings | 0 | 6.3 | 30 | 16.7 |
| Gives independence/confidence/ freedom/pleasure | 14.3 | 31.3 | 6.7 | 15 |
| Beneficial for family, helps husband | 0 | 18.8 | 16.7 | 13.3 |
| Beneficial in old age because people help out of greed | 0 | 12.5 | 20 | 13.3 |
| Beneficial in old age, generally | 7.1 | 12.5 | 13.3 | 11.7 |
| Husband cannot sell it when drunk or angry | 0 | 0 | 23.3 | 11.7 |
| Beneficial for children's inheritance | 7.1 | 0 | 16.7 | 10 |
| Beneficial to own a residence | 14.3 | 6.3 | 3.3 | 6.7 |
| Depends on kind of land and its use | 7.1 | 0 | 3.3 | 3.3 |
| Makes no difference to women to have property | 7.1 | 6.3 | 6.7 | 6.7 |
| Not beneficial to have property | 0 | 0 | 6.7 | 3.3 |
| Do not know | 7.1 | 6.3 | 0 | 3.3 |

[1]Percentages show frequency of responses in particular categories; since
some answers could be multiple, the percentages do not add up to 100.

**Table 5.3**   Respondents' Attitudes toward the Importance/
Nonimportance of Jewelry as an Asset for Women (in Percentages)

| IMPORTANCE/NONIMPORTANCE OF JEWELRY AS AN ASSET FOR WOMEN[1] | KE N=14 | KC N=16 | SN N=30 | TOTAL N=60 |
|---|---|---|---|---|
| **Not Important Because** | | | | |
| Has to be left in bank vault/ Not safe to keep around | 35.7 | 50 | 20 | 31.7 |
| Market price of gold fluctuates | 7.1 | 12.5 | 30 | 20 |
| Value of gold is lost in repeat sales | 21.4 | 6.3 | 10 | 11.7 |
| Cannot be sold easily | 21.4 | 12.5 | 6.7 | 11.7 |
| Can be taken away from a woman by force | 0 | 0 | 13.3 | 6.7 |
| Not important, generally | 14.3 | 18.8 | 20 | 18.3 |
| **Important Because** | | | | |
| Can be pawned/sold quickly when necessary | 14.3 | 25 | 26.7 | 23.3 |
| Can be given to children later | 7.1 | 18.8 | 23.3 | 18.3 |
| Increases in value | 21.4 | 12.5 | 13.3 | 15 |
| It is nice to wear | 0 | 12.5 | 13.3 | 10 |
| One then has something of one's own | 7.1 | 12.5 | 0 | 5 |
| Only when there is a lot of spare money | 7.1 | 6.3 | 3.3 | 5 |

[1]Percentages show frequency of responses in particular categories; since some answers could be multiple, the percentages do not add up to 100.

her son's family), "if anything is needed in the house then one should try to take care of that; if nothing more is needed, then one can put it in the bank, what else could one do?"[3] represents the ubiquity of banks as financial reservoirs. The women's responses showed that this was true not just among the middle class, who were more solidly placed within the formal economy and supposed to have a more sophisticated view of finance, but also for those from rural backgrounds whose families had mainly agricultural resources. 76.6 percent of women from the middle-income group and 80 percent of women from the low-income group named this as one of the optimal means of saving.[4] For 35.7 percent women from

KE, 18.7 percent from KC and 36.7 percent from SN, these were the *only* forms of savings contemplated. Apart from the poorest, like Champa (with a maximum family income of about Rs. 700) who had no conception whatsoever of how one might save, and others like Mamta (with an erratic family income of around Rs. 1350 at best) who said that though saving was theoretically good, "I have never been able to save anything, so I don't know the most advantageous way,"[5] women even at the lowest income range voiced the importance of putting money in the bank.

However, some of the differences between the middle-income and low-income groups were in the kinds of financial investments and the uses associated with banks. While middle-income urban families were routinely paid through direct deposits to banks, having a bank account was specifically important to many SN women because this represented improved security, given their futile experiences of saving at home. Ideas of putting away money in a bank to prevent it being used up at home were also more commonly voiced from SN, while in the other areas surplus income usually always existed.

A significant distinction was also in the forms of investment contemplated; while the "multiplication" of money in the form of accrued interest was the primary attraction for most, women from SN found bank accounts per se beneficial, with only two women naming "fixed deposit" accounts and a few others referring to the advantages of bank schemes like those giving loans against savings. On the other hand, KE and KC women frequently preferred financial schemes with much higher returns than basic accounts, including investment packages. As Kavita, a twenty-five-year-old, married dance teacher with a household income of Rs. 6000, said: "If she [a woman] is quite intelligent she is going to invest it somewhere because the profit would be more, at the bank she would only get two percent to three percent but outside, in the *kitties*[6] I was telling you about she could get a lot more, it would be all profit and no loss."[7] Poorer families were likely to have less savings and may have counted on the entirety of banked money as emergency fallback, while those with higher incomes could afford to have extra money for investments. This difference, as well as possibly greater knowledge of investments among the middle class, leads to an ever-greater gap in resources between classes; the savings of the poor, already less in amount, further make substantially lower interest because the savings of the wealthy are invested more profitably. Thus, women's apparently similar goals of saving money through banks may have had markedly different motivations and consequences.

A significant number of women from various income groups pointed to the profitability of starting businesses with savings (Table 5.1). 43 percent of women from the middle-income group and 30 percent of women from the low-income group cited the potential usefulness of businesses. However, of these only one woman from KC and one from SN named businesses as the sole optimal means of saving; the majority referred to banking one's savings along with investing in businesses, with a few adding on jewelry and property in addition to banks. Thus, investing in a business was clearly regarded as being extra and supplementary for the most part, mostly a means of extending savings in the bank at a higher rate of profit.

In addition to preferring businesses for optimum profit, a significant corollary cited in naming businesses as a favored means of investment for *women* was the notion that this was possible only for particular kinds of women, those who were sharp and aware *(hunshiyar)* enough and those who were perceived to have a "knack" or talent for businesses. For such women, numerous opportunities and advantages were named: the chance to run a home-based business and bring in money without deserting the domestic arena; contrarily, the chance to leave home for part of the day; the ability to get goods and cash to support one's family or for one's personal use; and significantly, grounds of empowerment beyond financial reasons: "because it makes a woman feel she is able to do something if she can manage that herself" (Bindu, who ran a small tea shop in SN[8]). Having a business was frequently seen as an avenue for women to enter the capitalist market whatever their education or professional qualifications, a space to earn a living but not a full-time job with the resultant domestic stress.

Owning property in the form of land, residences, or shops was also named as one of the lucrative avenues for women to make money (Table 5.1). However, while 33.3 percent women from the middle-income group brought up this option, only one woman from SN (3.3 percent) did so. The women who found this method favorable mentioned the way this asset "generated" money through rent or produce and increased in value, with little scope of attrition because it was not used for daily needs, and also the security of owning one's home. The absence of SN women's responses in this category appears particularly discordant because, as seen in chapter 3, owning large amounts of land, especially in rural areas, was most prevalent and desirable among the SN families. One way to explain the discrepancy may be to follow the logic propounded by Madhu (a twenty-six-year-old, single woman earning Rs. 4000 a month), that it was only possible to envisage property as an option when there were enough savings: "If I have a lakh or two lakh rupees, I may even buy a piece of land, but if I have Rs. 10,000 or 15,000 then I'll just keep it in the bank."[9] Savings put aside by the SN women, who seldom had paid jobs and earned far less than women in the other groups when they did, were likely to be much smaller in amount; this could partly explain the difference. However, men from these families owned and often bought land though they too earned comparatively less than the middle-income groups. Thus, it might be that women's routine disinheritance from family land, along with the meager savings, played a significant part in placing ownership of property even beyond the bounds of hypothetical possibility.

The supposition that women from SN did not name property as a lucrative resource because they mostly had no realistic avenues to acquire any is confirmed by responses to the direct question about women's advantages of owning property (Table 5.2), where only 10 percent of the women claimed that property is not beneficial or makes no difference to one's well-being (though slightly more women from SN, 13.3 percent, did claim this as compared to 6.7 percent from the other groups). Arguably the most crucial difference in how benefits of property ownership were visualized by the different groups was in the uses of property; from KE and KC, the responses were clustered around issues of esteem and individuation, that is, symbolic status coming from wealth, while the SN women were far more concerned with basic maintenance issues, for example, a woman's primary responsibility for feeding and caring for her family and her insurance against violence and neglect. Thus, from KC and KE there were responses like "It gives a woman some 'freedom,' she can do what she likes with that, it's a very different situation from sharing the husband's property,"[10] "It's good to have some property in her name because she would have strength,"[11] "Land gives them financial security and confidence,"[12] and "Of course they should have land, women are also a part of society, they're not second-rate citizens."[13] In contrast, from SN there were frequent reactions like "it could be beneficial because if the husband couldn't make a living the woman could work on it and make a living for herself, she could feed and clothe her children well and fulfil her own wishes to get nice things for herself;"[14] and "if the husband beats her or drives her out or dies, then she can earn her own living and eat off that, or give it to hired labor and get money to raise the children."[15] Women from the middle class often formulated responses in terms of individual rights in land as a path to independence and strength, while immediate living concerns weighed much more heavily on the poorer women.

However, it is important to mark the similarities between the groups, especially in terms of women's overwhelming fear of financial survival without husbands. Because security and well-being were typically associated with a husband's income and assets, one of the principal uses of property was as a stand-in for husbands "in case something happens"—for example, marital breakups, untimely widowhood, and also the helplessness of old age (26.7 percent of total responses, Table 5.2). Several women also cynically pointed to the uses of property in arousing greed and thus ensuring care in their old age (13.3 percent). Significantly, the contrast between the large number of women who declined individual property available through the natal family and the many who could immediately cite numerous benefits of having property underscores that women were not naively unaware of the differences in power and capabilities brought about by having property, but were restrained by other social and ideological limitations. Even those like Shabnam, who with three children and a husband who often found no work as a daily wage laborer, had difficulty imagining how women might best save their resources, had no problem envisaging that property could be theoretically beneficial "because she could keep her children going and have peace and happiness her whole life."[16]

In contrast to the overwhelming preference for banks and investment, and even businesses or property, relatively few women found jewelry to be the optimum resource (Table 5.1). Only 16.7 percent of the thirty middle-income women named it as one of the preferred ways of saving, and none of them referred to it as the sole means. On the other hand, a third of the thirty respondents from SN named this as an important savings option, though only two of these women (6.7 percent) thought of jewelry as the only means of savings. The higher response from the lower-income area may indicate that jewelry was a more important resource for this group because women could more realistically acquire and save some, and store and exchange it in a relatively flexible way, while their restricted mobility and little education made it more difficult to deal with the other options individually, however lucrative they may have seemed.

Interestingly, attitudes to jewelry appeared more varied when the women were specifically asked about its usefulness, as Table 5.3 shows. 57 percent of KE women, 31 percent of KC women (total 43.3 percent from the middle-income groups) and 40 percent of SN women found it relatively unimportant for various reasons. 23.3 percent of women from the middle-income group and 33.3 percent from the poorer group claimed it as an important resource overall. A more mixed reaction, naming both positive and negative uses, came from only 14.3 percent of the women from KE, but 43.8 percent of women from KC and 26.7 percent of women from SN. Compared with the numbers in the previous paragraph, the number of women preferring jewelry as a significant resource remained identical except for a slight increase from KC. In KE, the wealthier of the two middle-income groups, where many more women were in paid work and more educated and mobile, there appeared to be a strong consensus that other financial resources were relatively more flexible and profitable. But one of the most striking distinctions to emerge was the ambiguity about the value of jewelry in the lower of the middle-income groups, KC; although storing savings as jewelry was said to be inadvisable mostly on the grounds of security combined with lack of easy accessibility of bank lockers and difficulty in trading, there was still a strong tendency to value gold as something women could individually trade, wear, and pass on to children. Even though banking and investing were seen as prime opportunities in line with the times, it seemed harder for the women to dismiss the values associated with jewelry.

Despite a certain ambivalence about jewelry, however, it seems generally very clear that gold was not women's premium resource of choice, and that other forms of saving and investment were regarded as safer, and more flexible and profitable alternatives. This conclusion has important implications for the widespread cultural notion that stridhan consists of jewelry, the form of wealth preferred by/for women under a certain construction of feminine nature, and hence given to them as part of the dowry in lieu of other kinds of assets. Women themselves rarely appeared to have any such illusions, and their customary acceptance of jewelry from their natal and affinal families may be better regarded as acquiescence of the only culturally sanctioned assets for women, rather than a claim over preferred resources. Hence, the idea that women have no desire or ambition for property/resources may be effectively counteracted by pointing to the figures in this section. They also help to dispel notions that women's entitlements should be based on a long-gone or mythically ancient socioeconomic system (when jewelry was apparently as valued as other resources, at least by women), while resource distribution between males remains entirely in tune with the pulse of the current political economy. Refusal of property may be grounded in numerous cultural rationales, but women's apathy and naivete about financial assets cannot be counted among them.

### Crucial Problems, Imagined Solutions

> A woman can never become independent, whatever "rank" [class?] she may belong to. This cannot be solved; perhaps all women could learn kung-fu and karate and become strong and learn to live by themselves; but even after they can do this, there are some things they cannot do. We have a Punjabi saying that people are afraid when they see even a man's slipper outside a house, whereas ten women in a house doesn't scare anybody. Even if women start thinking about their lives, society won't let them change. (Rani, a forty-six-year-old Punjabi woman living with her husband, two sons and daughter-in-law.)[17]

> This is the problem: If the husband is nice, then the woman doesn't have anything to worry about if he can take good care of the household. But if the husband is bad (*bura*) then she has a lot of misery and her life becomes unbearable, because for a bite of food she has to feel the man's shoe upon her back and hear his verbal curses, while she has to be responsible for the children. (Parvati, a fifty-year-old Nepali widowed head of household living with a brother, three sons, and a daughter-in-law.)[18]

Rani and Parvati's attitudes typify some of the themes that were perceived to be the greatest social problems for women. On one dimension, these statements represent the most frequently voiced opinions from their respective neighborhoods—the first a problem of women not getting equal status in society, the latter a fundamental economic problem of women's primary responsibility for and difficulty in providing for their families' needs in the context of ever-present violence. However, it is also significant that these two views, along with other cited problems like inferior educational and occupational opportunities, disproportionate responsibility for the domestic realm, economic dependence, and family control, together demarcated various strands of patriarchal domination delineated in feminist theories, viz. the realms of home, work, sexuality, violence, representation. Women named their prioritized problems depending on their own sociocultural standpoints, but when taken together these appeared to describe the ingredients of a particular patriarchal formation.

A large "Danger" sign does need to be flagged here. Despite the explanatory lure of conspiracy theories, looking for and finding patriarchal relations within disparate responses smacks too closely of "discovering" my own a priori assumptions in the results, and the imposition of a prefabricated "feminist" sensibility on the respondents. *Is* it possible to project the operations of "Patriarchy" here? Hennessy argues that, despite the current critical emphasis on relations of domination at a local level and within micropractices, metadiscursive constructs like patriarchy are still analytically valuable for examining broad connections between apparently distinct social phenomena:

> [M]aterialist feminist attention to patriarchy as an organizing social arrangement, however, is aimed precisely at shifting from this limited notion of power as rights and liberties to a more pervasive concept of the operation of power across economic, political and ideological arrangements." (1993, 25)

While not attempting to interpret the following responses about problems and solutions through a pregiven checklist of "patriarchal relations" or read nascent "feminist" consciousness into the respondents, I would still argue that the range of the women's responses pointed to some prime mechanisms of patriarchal control: violence, constructed economic dependence, and the backdrop of symbolic notions about gender. In terms of micropractices, each woman foregrounded that which affected her most deeply, providing an analysis of specific dimensions of domination, many (though not all) of which were grounded in gendered constraints.

While the principal problems described touched on various dimensions of patriarchal relations, the corresponding solutions envisaged did not challenge the fundamental roots of patriarchy or place women within a radically altered cultural context. Rather, the focus was on individual women changing their situations, or relying on social relations to take a turn for the better. Thus, analysis of a problem did not necessarily lead to the corresponding logical solution, but rather to answers that were, for the most part, small enough in scope to handle and based on existent realities. The noticeably absent mention of property relations in this context is a vivid example of bypassing solutions that could drastically transform social relations.

A significant number of middle-class women (Table 5.4, 64.3 percent of women from KE and 25 percent from KC, across various age groups and educational levels) located the central problem to be the persistence of ideas about gendered roles and capabilities despite changes in women's educational and employment patterns.[19] As Rani's response at the beginning of this section indicates, the difficulty was seen to lie not in women's absolute inferiority of strength or lack of independence, but in the cultural resilience of that belief.[20] Even if women made themselves physically strong, it was likely that they would still be judged by hegemonic ideas of female weakness, whereas men's symbolic strength was vividly represented by the footless "male" shoe, an object arbitrarily signifying gender (as a *male* shoe) and connoting physical power, inviolability, and resistance in the emptiness resonant with the absent phallic presence.

Within this category, women articulated different aspects of the problem. The oldest woman in my sample, seventy-seven-year-old Sonal who had been principal of a school in Pakistan, described the problem as lack of sufficient "respect" (*izzat*) for women in society:

> The real thing is that a woman is not just an object to be consumed/enjoyed (*bhogbastu*). She gives birth to the children, takes care of them, educates them, she makes so many sacrifices for them, and so she should get more respect than males. Our scriptures say that mothers should get eleven times as much respect as fathers.[21]

**Table 5.4** Principal Social Problems for Women as Perceived by Respondents (in Percentages)

| PRINCIPAL SOCIAL PROBLEMS FOR WOMEN AS PERCEIVED BY RESPONDENTS[1] | KE N=14 | KC N=16 | SN N=30 | TOTAL N=60 |
|---|---|---|---|---|
| Difficulty procuring food/ clothes/medicine | 0 | 0 | 46.7 | 23.3 |
| Women do not have equality/ equal strength/freedom/ enough respect/are too dominated | 64.3 | 25 | 0 | 21.7 |
| Double burden of domestic and paid work | 28.6 | 31.3 | 0 | 15 |
| Troubles with joint family life/with in-laws | 14.3 | 18.8 | 10 | 13.3 |
| Troubles with husband: alcohol, beatings | 0 | 0 | 23.3 | 11.7 |
| Hard life if one has no husband | 7.1 | 0 | 20 | 11.7 |
| Problems with working outside the home | 0 | 25 | 6.7 | 10 |
| Lack of mobility | 0 | 18.8 | 6.7 | 8.3 |
| Lack of education | 21.4 | 12.5 | 0 | 8.3 |
| Feeling unwell/Physical problems | 0 | 0 | 16.7 | 8.3 |
| Problems finding work/ Unequal wages | 14.3 | 0 | 6.7 | 6.7 |
| Worries about getting children married | 0 | 6.3 | 3.3 | 3.3 |
| Childlessness/Too many children | 0 | 0 | 6.7 | 3.3 |
| Vulnerability in old age | 0 | 6.3 | 3.3 | 3.3 |
| Dowry related troubles | 0 | 6.3 | 0 | 1.7 |
| No problems | 21.4 | 18.8 | 16.7 | 18.3 |

[1]Percentages show frequency of responses in particular categories; since some answers could be multiple, the percentages do not add up to 100.

**Table 5.5** Solutions to Principal Social Problems for Women as Perceived by Respondents (in Percentages)

| SOLUTIONS TO PRINCIPAL SOCIAL PROBLEMS FOR WOMEN AS PERCEIVED BY RESPONDENTS[1] | KE N=14 | KC N=16 | SN N=30 | TOTAL N=60 |
|---|---|---|---|---|
| Women getting a business/ a job/paid work | 14.3 | 31.3 | 20 | 21.7 |
| Educating women | 35.7 | 25 | 10 | 20 |
| Women's own self-reliance and strength | 21.4 | 18.8 | 13.3 | 16.7 |
| Explaining to husband/ in-laws reasonably | 21.4 | 0 | 16.7 | 13.3 |
| Women having enough financial resources | 7.1 | 6.3 | 16.7 | 11.7 |
| Hoping society will change eventually | 14.3 | 6.3 | 0 | 5 |
| Getting help from women's organizations | 0 | 6.3 | 3.3 | 3.3 |
| No possible solutions | 21.4 | 6.3 | 13.3 | 13.3 |
| Do not know/Inapplicable/ Other | 14.3 | 37.5 | 30 | 28.3 |

[1]Percentages show frequency of responses in particular categories; since some answers could be multiple, the percentages do not add up to 100.

To Sonal, the problem was linked to a widespread crisis of faith manifested in sexualization of women, and could be corrected by a return to scriptural precepts. To Shivani, who had just finished college and was job hunting, double standards in hiring appeared to be the most egregious aspect; to Sharmila, who had worked as a private yoga tutor in Calcutta before marriage, the restriction upon "independence" associated with curtailed mobility for married women was most irksome.[22]

Others like Ritu, Suman, or Parminder, all married women between thirty-five and thirty-seven, named the problem explicitly as the domination of a "male" society, of keeping women unequal by will rather than on the basis of any essential difference.[23] Suman commented:

The social problem is that the woman is kept completely under control, she's not allowed to progress in any area. . . . As far as the difference between "men" and "women" goes, Indian society believes that the woman is below us, in many kinds of work they consider that she won't be able to do this but we will. . . . Indian traditional society wants to keep women down.

Of note here is the realization of women's (and hence her own) subjugation coupled with the use of the first person plural *we* to designate "society." Although apparently an attempt to speak in the persona of the society of males, it can also be read in terms of women's own imbrication within systems that dominate them, of women's subjectivity constituted within and through patriarchal positions.

Several women did make more explicit references to their own complicity, by pointing out that the root of the problem and the mechanism of perpetuation was the socialization of girls and boys. As Madhu, being single at twenty-six and hence perceived to have more leeway to make social critiques, liked to point out, the distinction could be as seemingly innocuous as "the mother saying to the daughter 'could you make tea for the guests?' and to the son 'could you go to the market and get this for the guests?'"[24] Yet what starts out as a simple and comparable division of labor eventually translates into a substantial difference in education, income, and resources, through all of which gender difference becomes ever more entrenched and essentialized. Uma felt that the trend for urban women such as herself to be highly educated had not really transformed the norm that men were to receive education and become breadwinners; although she herself was atypically employed, women's education was usually a way for them to bide time before the inevitable marriage and assumption of the domestic role.[25]

Such realizations about the deep roots of socialization seemed to produce hopelessness, because the apparent progress in education, paid work, or social valuation of the girl child could then be seen as superficial dents in a system where the sexual division of roles and labor resiliently reproduced a system of domination. Bina's comment in this context brilliantly captured the frustration of her own childrearing, and the operation of patriarchal relations as a metadiscourse over various realms of social behavior: "It seems that we are only able to rear our boys as boys and our girls as girls despite all the changes in society."[26] Seemingly "progressive" trends were thus minor makeovers, and the transcendence of gendered identity (and hence rank) remained insurmountable.

The world of work also figured prominently among perceived problems (Table 5.4), but significantly, different aspects of the exploitation and hardship of labor were highlighted by women from different groups. From KE and KC, 30 percent of the women, including single women who had just started jobs, married women who were or had been in paid work or had never held jobs, and older women with married children, expressed strong opinions about the excessive strain upon women who worked outside the home. For instance, Vimal, a schoolteacher whose household included her mother-in-law, claimed that despite her husband's occasional help, the primary domestic responsibility was hers alone, and having had to keep an eye on her children even while they studied or played, she had no time to further her education for future promotions.[27] Some women felt that the double burden was aggravated for those who lived within a joint family; according to Bharti (not herself in an extended household), families expected all daughters-in-law to behave and work as they did a couple of generations ago even though women were now earning money to support their families, and so women with jobs felt like they lived in two worlds that were decades apart.[28] Even Bina as a mother-in-law pointed to this problem, though she confessed her inability to solve it as her sons and daughters had already been raised.[29] In these cases, one of the greatest sources of unhappiness was indeed the notion of women's double burden.

Notably, in the poorer area there were no complaints at all on this issue, even though women who did income-generating work still bore the major responsibility for the domestic realm. The major crisis here (Table 5.4, for 46.7 percent of the SN women) was formulated as one of procuring enough money for the survival of the family, particularly the children.[30] Because this job fell on the women whether or not the men gave them enough money, their primary focus was on doing anything and everything to garner enough resources, including potentially breaking the law. Thus, the disproportionate volume of women's work was an inevitable fact that they did not even comment upon. Rather, several women from SN expressed concerns about not being able to find sufficiently good jobs, and social constraints about women going out to work, while also pointing to the extreme hardship of women with no men to support them (Table 5.4).

In the other neighborhoods, particularly KE, far more women worked, and often had substantial incomes, whereas in SN, even the few women who had formal jobs additionally depended on other sources of income based in the informal sector. Whether they had paid jobs or not, they had to compensate for husbands who sometimes failed to give any household expenses. Moreover, they usually undertook all the domestic work, which was typically far more work than in middle-class households that were more likely to have gadgets or domestic helpers. Thus, complaining about the double burden or asking for men to share domestic chores may have seemed pointless; the biggest worry was making enough money for the family's survival, with overwork for women being a given.

Unlike Rani's metaphor of the footless show signifying symbolic male power, Parvati's comment prefacing this section visualized the shoe as having a powerful corporeal effect, being an everyday instrument of assault. This was one of the few references to violence, the big dirty secret of systems of domination, even at SN where it was at least mentioned as one of the problems faced by women (Table 5.4, by 23.3 percent of the SN respondents). Yet even women who brought it up were careful to name domestic violence as a general problem for women in the neighborhood and to distance themselves individually from it.

In areas like SN where individual households had little privacy and women were less isolated from the larger community than a middle-class area of apartments with more space between them, the secret of violence was not very well preserved. My first tangible encounter (besides the stories from the women who came to the community organization for help) was in the midst of my conversation with Protima, an episode preserved in muffled echoes on tape. In the late afternoon, her elder brother-in-law, his voice thick with drunkenness, threatened her—"Daughter of a whore, fuck your mother, I'll fuck you all"—ostensibly angered because she left her home and spent the night at her sister-in-law's to avoid her husband's drunken rage. Protima was one of the most financially desperate women in the neighborhood with several small children, no formal job, no financial support from her husband, no connections with her natal family, suffering regular near-public physical and verbal abuse. Yet her answer to the question about problems

for women was "I don't know, maybe problems with the body (illness), I don't have the intelligence (*dimak*) to answer this question,"[31] completely blocking out questions of violence or domination.
Thus, no correlation can be drawn between the responses that named
violence as a problem and the experiences of those respondents;
those who mentioned it could have been directly unaffected, while
those most affected could have been too frightened, mortified, or
mentally distanced from the phenomenon to bring it up.

It must be noted that the silence on this issue from KE and KC
should also be read in terms of the above untraceability. There
were no specific references to the issue in response to this question
or other discussions. The only traces of violent behavior revealed to
me were a canceled appointment at Harjinder's because her daughter-in-law had temporarily run away as a result of domestic trouble,
a reference by Poonam to beatings in the early days of her marriage when her husband drank a lot and reacted to his mother's
complaints about Poonam, and a plea by Rama to end the interview quickly so that her in-laws did not get upset. I am unwilling
to impose narratives without concrete evidence, but neither can the
absence of violence be proclaimed when the propensity of middle-
class and wealthy areas to keep domestic violence private and pin
it upon the poor and uneducated is well recorded.[32]

Solutions suggested for the above problems (Table 5.5) were, on
the whole, limited and pragmatic, even pessimistic for the most part.
A large number of women (41.7 percent, including those who said
they could not think of any problems) indicated simply that they
could not conceive of or did not know enough to formulate solutions.
The other avenues commonly named were: getting paid work or
financial resources, education, self-reliance, gradual social change,
reasonable discussion. Thus, the focus was on change at the micro
level, on the individual woman improving her own circumstances
through education, work, strength of will or at the very least, keeping things calm by negotiating the status quo only very gently.

Naturally, there was a certain degree of matchup between problems outlined and solutions proposed. For example, many of the
23.3 percent women (including 46.7 percent of SN respondents)
who suggested solutions for problems of basic sustenance looked
toward women getting jobs or being able to acquire sufficient financial resources (21.7 percent overall, 20 percent among SN respondents). Among those who pointed to the pain of husbands' alcoholism

and physical abuse, all but two (i.e., 16.7 percent of 23.3 percent SN respondents) foresaw the only "solution" to be explaining matters to husbands reasonably and hoping for transformation. (The other two suggested getting independent financial resources and legal help.) Given that domestic violence is an exercise of power often grounded in the economic dependence of the abused upon the abuser, laying hope in this sort of transformation seems especially tragic because it reinforces the power dynamic without improving material conditions.

Perhaps most idealistic was the notion expressed by 20 percent of the respondents that educating women would go a long way toward changing societal attitudes of gender equality. Education was the most important solution for KE women (35.7 percent), who were also the most educated group. Yet highly educated women had themselves already analyzed that gendered constructs of women's worth and roles did not alter despite women's education and placement in the work force. As for those who looked toward women's employment as a major solution (21.7 percent overall), they were, not surprisingly, those who had pointed to the discrimination against women in the labor market and social constraints about women in the workforce. However, the silences from employed women on this score, along with the widespread realization of the stresses of the double burden, indicate that paid work in itself is unlikely to solve problems of gender equality without a transformation in notions of the gender division of labor.

In contrast both to ideas of placation and changing men, which were largely passive and reinforced the status quo, and of education and employment, which were associated with at least some degree of positive empowerment for the individual, variations on the prevalent theme that the solution was for "women to be strong and self-reliant" (expressed by 16.7 percent respondents) were double edged. On the one hand this could imply women resisting subordination by demonstrating their equal capabilities, as in Renu's hope that "if the woman worked and brought her earnings into the home . . . she wouldn't have to listen to being put down by anyone . . . women should make themselves advance, they should stand on their own feet, they should fight for themselves."[33] Renu herself was a fifty-three-year-old married woman who had worked as a secretary long ago, before her marriage; she strongly supported women empowering themselves through their own paid work and believed they should be independent enough to disdain family property. Parminder's conception was simple and powerful—"It is essential that women become proud of themselves"—with a focus on emotional strength altering current socialization;[34] while Suman, Hema, and Pushpa (of them, only Hema was the main economic support of the family) went back to the idea of economic strength, of deriving pride and resilience against criticism by working hard and being able to raise one's children well through that work, or of becoming wise in legal and financial matters through education and employment.[35] Jaya, who was married but owned a shop and hut of her own and supported women owning separate property and resources so that they had options beyond their husbands' whims, emphasized *both* economic strength and socializing women to be strong; she regretted that her parents had not given her enough education for her to get an office job, and said she planned to take her daughters to various locales to give them diverse experiences and options.[36]

However, the rationale of "women's self-reliance and strength" was also sometimes a call for women to internalize their resilience, to call upon their power not in order to be able to transform their lives but to be able to bear their lot better. Thus, Vimal proclaimed that women should be self-confident and try to solve their own problems without hiding behind a weak image, attaching as an illustration the story of her niece-in-law being harassed by husband and in-laws for dowry, to whom they had said that she should learn to handle household disputes rather than running to the natal family for solutions.[37] This tale of a woman's mortal danger is a significant example of the ways in which notions of women's strength can be co-opted against them, with strength being reduced to the coping device that will pull a woman through, rather than any material transformations or protests against inequity. However, in 60 percent of the ten responses in this category, education or employment or financial resources were mentioned as a *means* of achieving self-reliance. Even though these supplements usually do not by themselves alter widespread attitudes, they could aid individual empowerment and decrease vulnerability, and certainly offer alternatives beyond stoic resilience.

Have we forgotten completely that the subject at hand is property? The resounding silence on this topic with regard to important problems and solutions seemed to indicate that the issue was more an intellectual exercise for the researcher than an urgent concern for respondents.[38] I would argue that the very silence combined with the cited problems and solutions pointed to the importance of property relations. The most important problems described (persistence of cultural ideas about women's inequality, economic hardship, and dependence on the husband), the most favored solutions (women gaining jobs, financial resources, education, or self-reliance and strength) together with the overwhelming vote for the benefits of property discussed in the previous section all point to the uses of financial assets like property for addressing women's most urgent concerns. Yet property is viewed as such a distant entitlement for women that it is placed beyond the bounds of speculation, despite its potential for change.

Women made no direct references to property in pondering problems, but their disparate responses revealed that property relations were a sealed box that they would not approach in their solutions. A vivid instance of this evasion is revealed in comparing the responses to the uses of property with the responses about primary problems. From KE and KC, a majority of answers (Table 5.2) indicated that property is useful because it gives women strength (40 percent), independence, confidence, and so on (23.3 percent), while a large number of women also said that one of the principal problems for women was that they were not credited with having enough strength, independence, and so on (Table 5.4, 43.3 percent). Similarly, many responses from SN (Table 5.2) pointed to the usefulness of property in women sustaining themselves (23.3 percent) or their children (30 percent) or helping the husband defray family expenses (16.7 percent), while numerous women described problems with providing adequately for their families (Table 5.4, 46.7 percent). Yet the solutions women named covered means of betterment like education or employment and cultural strategies of empowerment, that even they knew to be feeble, completely bypassing how equal distribution of family assets *would* be a symbol of changes in socialization and cultural norms, *and* a pathway to less dependence on husbands' resources and a means of economic sustenance. The notion of property thus functioned yet again as a specter whose presence no one would acknowledge, because admitting its corporeality or attempting to exorcize it might point to a change in work and entitlements far more radical than individual women were willing to take on.

## The Shadow of the Legal Realm

Although this study set out to probe the intersection between property and law with respect to gender, there were few findings about
legal cases being waged. Few women had direct knowledge or experience about legal encounters; and by all accounts, families tended
to avoid litigation even at the cost of incurring substantial losses.
Legal remedies were rarely resorted to as a means of solving critical problems; rather, legal strategies were used by and against
women narrowly, in response to particular cultural transgressions
(see chapter 2, pp. 69–74). Like property, law also functioned as a
specter in the sense that it was an overdetermined fetish, both its
benevolence and its burden being overvalued in some contexts. For
many women, the legal realm connoted empathy and advantage,
yet they also realized its frustrations, social costs, and inefficacy in
altering social relations.

While the interviews yielded relatively little information about
legal skirmishes, questions of law followed me, as I would be pulled
into houses for hushed conversations with families I was not planning to visit for interviews. People knew I was not a lawyer, but
interested in legal encounters for my research, and the knowledge
that this was presumed to require appeared to place me in a somewhat informed state, despite my many disclaimers. Perhaps this
was a way for the families to mull over legal strategy without
taking the formal step of a legal appointment. In SN, a young
married woman visiting her mother's house with her infant daughter intercepted me one morning before I got to the neighborhood,
telling me about the tension, violence, and poverty at her in-laws
and asking me about the ways in which one could get a divorce. We
talked about the logistics of divorce, but also the socioeconomic
aftermath, which might have been even harsher than the existing
one, especially since her natal family also thought that she ought
to go back and be more accommodating while asking her husband
to behave a little better. However, in just a few days she went back
after her husband came to get her, with no apparent change in
situation in the affinal home. Similarly, from other areas, I got
numerous queries about property and inheritance (chapter 1, p. 1–
2). In none of these situations, were legal steps actually taken (at
least in the short term); at best, the empowering possibilities of
legal action were pondered for future usage. Nevertheless, these

instances reflect some patterns about use of the law: the predominance of marriage and property as subjects of dispute; the optimism of thinking about law as a safeguard against one's worries; and the seemingly contrary horror of being engaged in endless litigation.

Marriage breakdowns were one of the areas where litigation could rarely be avoided. Among KE and KC families, irreconcilable marital differences were inevitably resolved through legal divorces (eleven divorces mentioned, and only one informal separation as a form of marriage resolution). Of these divorces, there were six cases (54.5 percent) where maintenance was also asked for by the woman, and one custody dispute (9 percent). As for dowry return, no formal cases were reported from these areas, although there was in fact a certain amount of exchange after a marriage ended, each side usually reclaiming the jewelry they had invested, with other items like furniture or appliances being more contested. The nature of marital and dowry disputes from these areas indicates that in the middle-class areas, legal resolution of marriage was the most important thing, and marital relations could not be left ambivalent, particularly because of concerns over inheritance or children's alleged legitimacy. Suits for maintenance or custody were attached only in special circumstances—for example, great differences in wealth, punishment for perceived "fault," and the like.

Maintenance was usually sought from particularly wealthy families, although the circumstances of women who were themselves from wealthy families filing maintenance suits is significant in the context of property relations. As Suman narrated, her brother-in-law was having to pay maintenance because his ex-wife's brothers, though having plenty of family money, had submitted an affidavit that they would not support their mentally handicapped sister.[39] Thus, although the marriage was potentially fraudulent because the affinal family was not apprised of the bride's mental condition, the affidavit implied that the wedding ceremony itself transferred the right of economic sustenance to the husband and broke off any entitlements to natal family wealth.

In SN, legal marriage dissolutions were the exception rather than the rule, and usually occurred as an outcome of other issues. Only three of the twelve marital disputes mentioned by these women (25 percent) had been resolved by formal divorces in court, and these had not come about as a result of pleas to end the marriage but in conjunction with maintenance, dowry return, and custody suits. In Parvati's case, for example, the judge gave a formal divorce while deciding a custody suit in her favor, even though she had not formally sought divorce in response to her husband's bigamy.[40] When Hema's niece was sent back by her in-laws, her family filed the requisite police case for getting their dowry back, and the legal outcome was both an order for the goods to be returned and a divorce.[41] Thus in these cases, divorces were secondary to other issues more urgent for the plaintiffs, often property as in the latter case.

Most families in SN preferred to end marriages by coming to an agreement at a community meeting, for example, village councils (*panchayats*), or by settlement between families. Maya, who at the time that I met her had trouble with both her sons' marriages, described how the cases would probably be resolved if the women did not come back.[42] They would ask for the arbitration of the village council (*panch faisla*), probably at the bride's village, and each side would bring two relatives who had been present at the wedding. In the presence of the council and those relatives, they would draw up a document that stated the woman was not willing to come back and that each partner was now free to marry. The bride's family would probably get back the jewelry, utensils, and so forth, but the groom's family would "deduct" the approximate amount they had spent on wedding expenses. Maya's family intended to pay maintenance expenses to the daughter-in-laws' families only if the women came back—that is, as recompense to the women's natal families for looking after "their" women. The families did not want to go formally to the courts because they dreaded both the expense and the prolonged involvement; they wanted to resolve matters as cleanly and quickly as possible. In families with rural connections, such methods of negotiation were much more common, and served the families most efficiently. But in the urban or suburban milieu there was no equivalent community-level dispute resolution structure, and hence more of an imperative to formalize matters in law.

The other major area of discord was dispute over land, a subject whose prevalence and coexistence with coercion and violence has become a common metaphor for antagonistic class relations, gang strongholds, and bureaucratic corruption in India. The disputes reported reflected common problems: disagreement over land boundaries; forcible occupation of land/houses by gangs or tenants; fraudulent land sales; resentment between siblings over property shares. There was as much trouble reported in the rural areas as there were disputes over urban land, but a high degree of passivity toward formal litigation in both cases. Only one of the nine reported land problems (11.1 percent, not involving daughters'/wives' rights to property) from KE and KC ended up as a legal case; this was in Sharmila's family where her father and uncles were fighting their stepbrothers for shares of rooms in the ancestral home.[43] Even here, her father's side gave up because they could not make the time to go to court or pursue lawyers, and opted to take a much smaller share.

Even in instances where the violations seemed legally straightforward, people with an apparent advantage preferred to lose substantial property resources rather than enter into legal skirmishes, which they ultimately viewed as more wasteful and ineffective. Kavita's mother-in-law used most of her jewelry to buy a plot of land in Delhi that a group of alleged gangsters then seized for a club. Kalpana and family bought their flat in KC with the little money they got as "compensation" after losing their previous house, which the owner had presold to someone else.[44] They preferred to live with their losses rather than venture into court.

In SN, too, of eleven cases of property dispute (not involving daughters' or wives' shares), there were only three cases (27.3 percent) being fought in the courts, (including the case against the city filed by a large number of SN families charging destruction of huts and crops on squatter land without adequate notice). In many other instances, people preferred to take their problems to either a designated head of the village (*pradhan* or *mukhiya*) or beyond that to the village council, rather than get into complicated legal procedures. While this appeared to be an acceptable form of adjudication to them, its degree of justice should also be critically regarded by remembering that in the two *legal* cases being fought, both in Medha's family, the matter had been taken to court because the parties felt that village heads took bribes and ruled accordingly.[45] Thus, local bodies were likely to have their own problems with corruption and a bias toward influential people, but could be trumped by a "higher" justice sought in the formal legal arena (also potentially corrupt, but where the disempowered got a theoretically neutral hearing).

In most cases, people from SN decided to settle privately, or simply accept the situation, rather than getting into any form of adjudication. When Bindu's husband's five bighas got sold by a person who forged his signature and procured a copy of the title, or when Reena's father's land got occupied by a neighboring farmer (also a cousin), these men did not start any proceedings even though they lost the majority of their resources.[46] Bindu's husband felt that he did not have the money to pay lawyers and keep going back to the village for the many years he would be required to, nor any guarantee of winning; Reena reported that her father simply felt he was not sharp (chalak) enough to fight or win a case and preferred not to antagonize his cousins.

Given this widespread apathy and even revulsion for legal solutions, it is all the more striking that where women's property was concerned, families seem to have had little hesitation in going to court to challenge wills or orders (viz. cases discussed in chapter 2), even though their chances of winning these cases were not very high. In every reported case where a woman was getting property in a noncustomary fashion, for example, a share for daughters, a reward to the eldercaregiver, or equal rights of female heirs in cases of intestate succession to personal property, male heirs mounted a legal challenge, but all outcomes were reported to be either in the woman's favor or appeared to be going her way. These legal cases, in the background of prevalent passivity to litigation, thus indicate examples of cultural transgressions outrageous enough to warrant extreme solutions. Litigation was usually also a last resort when efforts to manipulate women ideologically had failed; the courts were seen as an area where women, thought to be relatively less conversant with the public realm, could finally be defeated. As Table 5.6 indicates, gender-based taboos on going to court do exist; women who are seen in court may be thought to be morally corrupt, greedy, and immodest. Thus, threatening to start a case against a woman had the power to affect her social and moral standing, which may have been as (or more) important to her as the property contested. Hence litigation itself may be a substantive threat whether or not the woman has the resources or persistence to fight and even win.

Paradoxically, the results reflected the limited benefits that women could get within the formal legal arena where customary entitlements to property were technically invalid. Legally, it appeared to be a losing battle to try to stop women from getting legitimate shares, but because this seemed to be territory which male relatives could not concede without formal contest, cases were fought in these areas with limited or no success against women, while many blatantly criminal violations in other areas went unchallenged for fear of prolonged litigation.

Women's attitudes toward turning to the law for solutions mirrored this duality of apathy and advantage (Tables 5.6 and 5.7). On the one hand, their silence about the legal realm in pondering

**Table 5.6**  Respondents' Attitudes about whether Courts/Laws Can Help Women (in Percentages)

| RESPONDENTS' ATTITUDES ABOUT WHETHER COURTS/ LAWS CAN HELP WOMEN[1] | KE N=14 | KC N=16 | SN N=30 | TOTAL N=60 |
|---|---|---|---|---|
| Yes, women can seek redress there | 7.1 | 18.8 | 13.3 | 13.3 |
| Yes, women can get financial help there | 0 | 0 | 23.3 | 11.7 |
| Yes, they can be a last resort | 7.1 | 6.3 | 6.7 | 6.7 |
| No, there are enough laws, but poor enforcement of laws | 35.7 | 50 | 16.7 | 30 |
| No, laws do not change people's behavior | 35.7 | 43.8 | 6.7 | 23.3 |
| No, legal solutions take too long | 21.4 | 0 | 3.3 | 6.7 |
| No, laws are for weak, women should be strong | 0 | 0 | 13.3 | 6.7 |
| No, bribes are needed to win in court | 0 | 12.5 | 3.3 | 5 |
| No, other forms of arbitration are better | 7.1 | 0 | 3.3 | 3.3 |
| No, legal solutions increase problems | 7.1 | 0 | 3.3 | 3.3 |
| No, other | 0 | 0 | 16.7 | 8.3 |
| Do now know | 21.4 | 6.3 | 13.3 | 13.3 |

[1]Percentages show frequency of responses in particular categories; since some answers could be multiple, the percentages do not add up to 100.

**Table 5.7**   Respondents' Attitudes about whether Women Will Be
Treated Fairly in the Courts (in Percentages)

| RESPONDENTS' ATTITUDES ABOUT WHETHER WOMEN WILL BE TREATED FAIRLY IN THE COURTS[1] | KE N=14 | KC N=16 | SN N=30 | TOTAL N=60 |
|---|---|---|---|---|
| Yes, treatment is/ought to be equal | 14.3 | 43.8 | 53.3 | 41.7 |
| Yes, generally | 28.6 | 0 | 0 | 6.7 |
| Yes, if go with someone familiar with the system | 0 | 6.3 | 7.1 | 3.3 |
| No, because women going to court are regarded poorly | 14.3 | 18.8 | 20 | 18.3 |
| No, because the poor are treated badly | 14.3 | 18.8 | 6.7 | 11.7 |
| No, because bribes determine outcomes | 0 | 6.1 | 0 | 1.7 |
| Cannot answer, because I have no knowledge of this | 21.4 | 25 | 16.7 | 20 |
| Do not know | 28.6 | 0 | 10 | 11.7 |

[1]Percentages show frequency of responses in particular categories; since
some answers could be multiple, the percentages do not add up to 100.

solutions to critical problems (Table 5.5), and their perceptions of
the limited usefulness of law when asked specifically about whether
laws or courts could help women (Table 5.6), reflected the general
social disenchantment with litigation. The inefficacy of law in altering social behavior and the lack of enforcement of numerous
laws already on the books were said to be particularly egregious.
Yet a large number of women were surprisingly optimistic about
using the courts (48.3 percent, Table 5.7), believing that they would
be given a fair hearing, that the legal system would "listen" to
them.[47] Even some of those who believed that one could win in
courts only through bribery, or that women lost social standing by
entering courts, believed that in spite of these, women would in
general receive justice.

Those who refrained from litigation were hardly exaggerating
the time, money, and complications involved in cases, and women

did lose a certain social-moral advantage by fighting in court. But still, this faith in litigation may not have been misplaced. First, there is the evidence about actual cases where women did win when they sought property (even though many of the women who felt optimistic about using the courts had not heard any such accounts). This evidence is strengthened by taking into account the fact that the few women who had been to court also concurred that judges had listened to what women had to say and taken their situations into account in making decisions (although one of them believed that *currently* bribery might rule the courts). That women's successful encounters described in these few cases were not entirely a coincidence is also borne out by statistics based on actual legal cases in chapter 6, where women often won when they went to court. These positive outcomes confirm the contentions of scholars who argue that women stand to benefit more as individual jural subjects before the law rather than when they rely on customary entitlements.[48]

However, women's hope of a fair reception in the courts did also reflect a rosy expectation of care and protection for women from the state. For example, there was frequently a fascinating play between possibility and moral expectation in envisaging women's treatment in the courts, in the play on "will" and "should": "Of course they will be treated fairly, why shouldn't they be?" being a popular answer. This indicated a *faith* in jural equality, rather than a response informed by other women's (or their own) experiences, and downplayed the law's hegemonic allegiances by emphasizing its alleged protective functions. Such trust might be cause for disillusionment for women when it is recalled that the inscription of women's needs within systems of law is often less than satisfactory, even though more women may triumph in terms of absolute numbers (see chapter 6).

Thus, women's attitudes toward law reflected both a potentially exaggerated optimism and a seemingly contrary indifference toward using law as a tool. While the formidable resources required to fight cases or the loss in social status for women should not be underestimated, and the reluctance to view law as a vanguard of deep social change motivated the indifference to legal solutions, women's perceptions about the odds of winning a case by insisting upon their legal rights seemed realistically favorable if they persisted in court. At least for those problems to which there may be satisfactory short-term solutions, and where cultural constraints do not outweigh the advantages of legal wins, women may be able to use law as a favorable catalyst for altering the status quo.

## Conclusion: The Limits of Critical Analysis

The exploration of women's priorities in this chapter reveals the limits of theories of "false consciousness" which claim that the "oppressed" are unaware of the structure of privileges within their society, and have no perceptions of the conditions of their exploitation or visions of change. Among these women, who shared some gendered restrictions/"oppressions," although their privileges by age, education, employment, or religion varied, there was a succinct analysis of patriarchal relations, with no naivete about profitable financial resources or risks that endangered their material status quo. They could relate to the frustrations of court battles, but often understood too that as women they might benefit from protection under law. Thus, they realized how gender affected their lives unfavorably and favorably; they did not live in a nonmonetized or altruism-propelled world. If the conditions for change they suggested made only moderate, individual alterations in the system, this may be read not as an inability to visualize alternatives from within an "oppressed" position but as a realistic acknowledgment of their currently limited options and their economic and cultural dependence upon, and constitution within, existent social locations.

# 6

## Protecting Property

### Gendered Identity
### in the Indian Higher Courts

I n recent years, some Indian women's encounters with the legal
system have precipitated crises of nation; simultaneously,
women's bodies and gendered entitlements have been the sites
of mythmaking about "national character" in an allegedly democratic secular state. Alongside the legal victories of Shah Bano and
Mary Roy,[1] which have pointed to emancipatory spaces within law,
gender has also routinely been reinvented more unobtrusively in
other courtrooms, through the pronouncements of judges who theo-
rize "nature" and "culture" in the process of dividing shares and
deciding family entitlements. These pronouncements point to the
benefits of hailing the rhetoric of liberty and modernity in seeking
greater social equality, while also revealing the complex ways in
which religion or class or gender are negotiated in legal settings.
The figure of Woman is refracted in numerous competing and contradictory ways within the legal system; individual women get
represented as empowered agents, invisible presences, signifiers
of sexual, family, and property relations, while law in its relation
to women gets coded as arbitration, protection, conservation, or
liberation.

It has been well documented that the rationale of gender equality was frequently used in colonial regimes to justify legal change,
to replace systems of customary law with "Western" law predicated
on individual rights and liberties, as a way to demarcate relations
of rule.[2] Such change was often bitterly contested by native (male)
elites resisting the potential loss of hegemonic space, which led to

191

the final form of legislation incorporating concessions to the ancien regime. As Nair argues, "one of the colonial state's preferred modes of seeking collaborators amongst Indians was to support and buttress Indian patriarchies" (1996, 42), and domestic authority was legally accorded to males to balance the supreme authority of the colonial state in other matters related to property and person (Singha 1996; Chowdhry 1994, 102–11). Tanika Sarkar contends that it is crucial to mark these moments of collusion, to remember the ways in which "colonial structures of power compromised with, indeed learnt much from indigenous patriarchy and upper caste norms and practices," in order to resist histories that denote colonialism as the primary source of exploitation (1993, 1869).

Lawmaking similarly served to establish a new authority and legitimacy for those who took on the reins of power in postcolonial regimes, and here too, the redefinition of women's rights that served the image of a modern new nation was an infallible tool for cementing control.[3] While the predominant motive may have been political manipulation, scholars have contended that the effects have been generally advantageous for individual women, who often stand to gain from invoking rights discourse and need no longer be completely vulnerable to familial authority or the invocation of custom and religion (Starr 1984; Lazarus-Black 1992). However, protection by the legal system also needs to be regarded with profound wariness, because the modern state in turn becomes the powerful arbiter of destinies, typically instituting narrow legal meanings of family and sexuality, such that any benefits to women are confined to a heavily patrolled zone with rigid interpellations of femininity, that reinforce existent hegemonies of class, religion and sexuality.[4] Moreover, "the law" is administered by judges whose very notions of logic, fairness, and justice are embedded within their discursive universes, and hence their interpretations reinforce cultural biases in the very act of attempting to transcend them through law. This relationship of patronage and policing centrally marks the legal system's inscription of women, as the following analysis of contemporary family law cases in India shows.

In this chapter, a map of Indian women's recent encounters with the law relating to property (inheritance and succession) is traced; this history of the public realm is meant to complement women's perceptions of legal entitlements explored in the previous chapters. These cases may be read as negotiations between the postcolonial state's lawmaking processes and the life later assumed by laws translated into court cases: not only does the encoding of laws by the legislature and their decoding in the courts constantly involve the invocation of utopian ideas of equality alongside the preservation of traditional privileges, but some laws also acquire dimensions and interpretations that are either absent or veiled in the encoding process.

The interplay between this chapter and the preceding ones occurs on several registers, dealing with questions of class, women's entitlements to property under customary law, and the efficacy of legal solutions. This chapter profiles women who persisted in claiming family property, in stark contrast with the interview respondents who largely avoided this (chapters 2 and 4), fearing family wrath; the accusations and strategies used by family members in cases discussed here show the manifestations of such wrath and the unusual strength required to withstand the pressure. Furthermore, property cases discussed here invoke the rationales of eldercare, dowry in lieu of property, and women's right to affinal rather than natal wealth that came up in the interviews (chapter 4), showing that these are not simply excuses from women justifying their decisions, but are actually used by judges themselves to stretch legal boundaries.

As for the apathy toward litigation combined with optimism for women's "protection" within the court system voiced by many of the interview respondents (chapter 5), this overview of legal process shows that their feelings may be substantially justified; it was simultaneously true that cases could last years (even decades for many property cases) with little hope of a fair outcome, but individual women also generally fared well when they brought cases to court (even when gender issues got framed in ideologically disturbing ways). But while preceding chapters showed that women's socioeconomic circumstances were related to their property ownership (chapter 2) and to their attitudes about pressing social problems and prized financial assets (chapter 5) the significance of class in the legal realm seen in this chapter is more ambiguous. In general, substantial resources are required to persevere in the legal arena, explaining the widespread disinclination of families to engage in litigation. However, despite contentions that Indian women are usually far removed from state institutions and that only middle-class women benefit from legal reform (Rai 1995, 407; R. Kumar

1993, 4), notable instances like that of Shah Bano and Vera Aranha (discussed later in this chapter), as well as many of the cases discussed in the following sections, show that amounts of property were not necessarily very large when women laid claim to shares, and that some women with minimal resources met with surprising success. Subsequently, such unusual successes have often been recuperated as glowing icons of the legal protection of women, masking numerous other inequities, or have had their radical potential undone by subversive social or political action. But the potential spaces of empowerment within law are immensely significant nonetheless.

Family law is a crucial site for examining the detailed workings of "heteropatriarchy" (Alexander 1997), for studying what Patricia Uberoi calls "judicial ethnosexology," the ways in which "a set of widely shared cultural assumptions" inform the substance of legal decisions (1996, 185). As Kapur and Cossman have argued in their extensive analysis of women and law in post-Independence India, "the legal regulation of women is informed by and serves to reinscribe familial ideology," where "familial ideology" is defined as "a set of norms, values, and assumptions about the way family life is and should be organized; a set of ideas that have been so naturalized and universalized that they have come to dominate common sense thinking about the family" (1996, 13).

Issues of inheritance and succession within family law showcase the tussle between postcolonial legal change and the persistence of privileges particularly well. Property laws are a vivid example of inert and merely cosmetic legal reform. What maintains women's disenfranchisement is not legal barriers but cultural constructions of gendered entitlements on the part of both male and female heirs as well as on the part of judges. Extrajudicial ideas of family responsibility (who does eldercare? who supports the family?), resource distribution (what really constitutes dowry and how does it measure against total family resources?), and meanings of access to property (what does it mean for women to "have" affinal family property?) determine how property gets divided. The realm of inheritance is thus particularly appropriate for examining how cultural constructions of gender, family, religion, and nation saturate the allegedly impartial milieu of legal decision making in India.

The following section offers an overview of the ways in which gender has been inscribed within Indian law in recent history, showing how women's rights signify both cultural heritage and emancipatory progress. A brief account of wins and losses by women in cases dealing with property follows, alongside detailed analysis of recurrent judicial tropes. These readings reveal not only the images used to characterize contemporary Indian women in various settings, but also demonstrate how meanings of nation and religion are reconfigured in considering women's entitlements. The central concern is with law as a site of deep ambivalence, a space of potential revolution that never becomes one.

### Mise-en-scène: The Legislative Construction of Women's Property Rights

Contemporary Indian law, while purporting to extend rights and opportunities to all who would be enfolded within its new nationhood, is still strongly marked by the shadow of its colonial origins. Within this body of law, gender difference and, particularly, women's bodies, stand out as the space where each of these discourses—ancient customs that are claimed as the new nation's unique history, egalitarian rhetoric invoking Enlightenment philosophy, and elite/colonial control of subaltern/colonized groups—seek to brand themselves.

As many historians have argued, colonial lawmakers' inscription of the (Indian) female body as a site of reform was a mechanism of social control.[5] A combination of "rationalist" sensibility and the selective interpretation of chosen "ancient" texts by certain British-picked Indian scholars was used to proclaim the "natural justice" and "real" Indian spirit of British-made laws. Yet the very opposition of concepts such as "native" Indian law versus "modern, Western" law is falsely constructed. In what Spivak names as the "epistemic violence of the legal project," much of the colonial legal intervention in India consisted of rereading a polymorphic and ambivalent religiolegal system into a nexus of binary codes compatible with British conceptions (1988, 281; also R. Kumar 1993, 14). Attempts to "weld the host of disparate practices that went in the name of Hindu law into a single legal code" was claimed by the British "as part of their civilising mission" (Nair 1996, 24), resulting in measures such as the creation of "schools" of Hindu law similar to schools of Islamic law (Nair 1996, 28), the aggressive transformation of the laws of matrilineal Hindu communities (Nair 1996, 33; Chhachhi 1991, 159), and a "Brahmanization" of customary laws (Nair 1996, 41; Chakravarti 1993, 579). Thus, pre-British "Hindu" law that used multiple layers of interpretation and had diverse local/regional manifestations was reduced to unitary meanings and binary schemes that were expedient to the relations of rule.

Islamic law, which had functioned as the overriding state law in most parts of India in the centuries immediately preceding British occupation, had also been open-ended in practice. It had incorporated heterogeneous sources of religio-legal authority, based on sources divided according to their use of memory and interpretation (Parashar 1992, 54). Although it became more rigidly codified around the tenth century with great emphasis on the principles of *shariat* in matters of family law, it is widely believed by scholars that Hindu subjects could seek justice under Hindu law except for criminal matters, and that disputes were frequently settled by local landlords and councils (Parashar 1992, 54–60). Hence the general application of the *shariat* was not coterminous with rigid ecclesiastical jurisprudence.

Such a diversity of dispute resolution systems was only superficially maintained by the British; administrative, financial, and criminal laws were made universally applicable, but people (only Hindus and Muslims) were supposedly governed by "personal" law in other matters. Most importantly, the British did in fact frequently codify and criminalize "personal" laws in the process of maintaining hegemonic control. Macaulay's remark expresses the spirit of their transformative "nonintervention" perfectly: "We do not mean that all the people of India should live under the same law. Our principle is simply this—uniformity where you can have it, diversity where you must have it—but in all cases certainty" (quoted in Parashar 1992, 67). Hence came the move to seek unilateral, "authentic" meanings from ancient texts to fit the "rational" and "universal" spirit of post-Enlightenment Western law.

While the British project of legal codification was used as a means to contest native elites' hold on discourse, Indians themselves were implicated in the project in complex ways. To add "authenticity" to this "epistemic violence," it was usually Indian scholars who were authors of textual reinterpretation. Ideas of the nation-state and the rights of the bourgeois individual also propelled some

Western-educated nationalists into declaring the Indian past as mired in ignorance, superstition, and tyranny. As Chakrabarty puts it, the subject positions of elite Indian nationalists often swung between "the two poles of the homologous sets of oppositions, despotic/constitutional, medieval/modern, feudal/capitalist. Within this narrative shared between imperialist and nationalist imaginations, the 'Indian' was always a figure of lack (1992, 339)."

Yet, alongside this alienation and cultural angst was also the contradictory presence of resistant cultural areas that were designated as being uniquely "Indian," areas that were to become representative of the cultural "authenticity" of the new Indian state (T. Sarkar 1993). Chakrabarty contends that the most significant opposition was against "two fundamental tenets underlying the idea of 'modernity': the nuclear family based on companionate marriage and the secular, historical construction of time" (1992, 343). The centrality of the woman question, affected both by delineation of family roles and by the persistence of ineffable "tradition," marked these crucial spaces of resistance to the ideology of modernity. Male authority in the domestic sphere was designated as being critical to the preservation of Hindu culture, a sacrosanct zone where British intrusion would be the worst form of violation (Singha 1996; T. Sarkar 1993). The privileges and pleasures of the joint family, founded upon women's socioeconomic subordination and the erasure of their sexual self-determination, were retained despite the alleged virtues of the "modern" nuclear household. According to these Indian proponents of modernity, the exceptional place occupied by women was the last precious bulwark of "Indian" history and tradition.

This fractured colonial subject, protective of a sacred realm for women and supportive of abstract egalitarianism, was not only an enduring figure in the postcolonial era of lawmaking, but even survives within the contemporary legislature and judiciary (Sathe 1992). The lawmaking process for the newly independent Indian state exemplifies this conflict.[6] On the one hand, the cohorts (largely upper- and middle-class, upper-caste Hindu and male) who took on the reins of government in the executive and legislative arenas had invested in learning the allegedly modern British legal system, and campaigned strongly to retain it. In fact, the British legal system was regarded among many lawyers as the prime positive legacy of the colonial regime (Galanter 1989, 41), and was at the heart of access to discursive and political power for certain groups in the new nation. Yet on the other hand, this power could only be negotiated by incorporating demands for certain "ancient traditions," which were not genuinely old, authentic, or scripturally central so much as they were optimal justifications for a skewed distribution of resources. Thus, the apparent debate between inclusion of modern/"civilized" versus traditional/"Indian" elements in law can be read as an always contemporary contest between various groups seeking public space or advantages.[7]

This contest is exemplified par excellence in the Parliamentary debates over the laws for the new nation. The gender card was played repeatedly, the aim being not a radical transformation within the born-again social structure, but the self-conscious construction of a "progressive" national imaginary that would reject regressive practices but retain certain "traditional" customs (and women's circumscribed role within them). While the question of greater equality for women provided definite leverage for reforming some laws in line with political and developmental initiatives presented to a world audience, the process of reform was markedly piecemeal, with little comprehensive socioeconomic change to make the legal provisions viable.

The most prominent example of this contradictory approach to gender equality is in the aborted Hindu Code bill (resubmitted in the form of several bills that now constitute the Acts of Hindu "personal" law),[8] presented as being in accordance with the spirit of the new Constitution. In the bill, the Hindu Marriage and Divorce section was said to represent "an essential aspect of national development, namely social progress," adoption laws for Hindus were brought in line with Constitutional principles stressing that "the unit of society was the individual," and Hindu succession was made far more uniform (Parashar 1992, 87–88). This was a dramatic change from British days when personal laws were regarded as relatively sacrosanct; change could be undertaken now as being necessary for "modernizing" the nation.

In fact, some remarkable reforms such as the right of nonmarried women to adopt children, the legal invalidation of all forms of customary divorce in favor of court-sanctioned divorces, and the equal division of self-acquired property among all children, passed despite stiff opposition because the justification of timely social reform was used effectively. Women's rights to property became markedly more stable because of the new provision that widows would get absolute ownership (as opposed to usufructuary rights) of the land they had been given in lieu of maintenance from their husbands' family estates; both the discourse of women's equality in a modern nation and the view propounded by certain ancient scholars that women could own property were used to justify this change to the legislature.

Yet, in many cases it was all too apparent that the agenda of development[9] was an exercise in public relations and not a move toward substantive gender equality; as Nair puts it, this was a "reform process where the input of women themselves was marginalized, and in which the rights of women were subordinated to the modernizing impulse of the Indian State" (1996, 226). One of the most blatant examples of this double-talk was around the question of daughters' succession. The first Hindu Law Committee recommended that daughters be simultaneous heirs along with wives and sons of Hindu males who had died intestate, and refused to distinguish between married, unmarried, and widowed daughters' shares. Despite a huge opposition to the law based on the claim that the committee ignored sons' financial responsibilities and spiritual duties linked to owning property and allowed outsiders (i.e., sons-in-law!) into the joint family, this initiative made it through Parliament by relying both on alleged scriptural authority and constitutional directives. However, the superficiality of this reform was revealed when it came to the *quantum* of the daughter's share; the second Hindu Law Committee gave daughters only a half share as compared to sons,[10] righteously claiming that this was double the quarter share recommended in the *smritis*, and that daughters would get double the sons' shares in the mother's property (Parashar 1992, 124).

Even the then Law Minister, who had been the prime proponent of the Hindu Code and who resigned in protest of it failing to pass in the original comprehensive form, revealed the limits of his reformist vision: when the Select Committee of the Constituent Assembly suggested that daughters and sons be treated as equal with respect to the quantum of inheritance for intestate succession, "Ambedkar, the great champion of Hindu law reform, described this alteration as an effort by his enemies to make the entire reform process appear ridiculous, and thereby cause the entire reform process to be abandoned" (Parashar 1992, 124). In response to suggestions that the Mitakshara coparcenary be drastically reformed, the Law Minister also claimed that this could perturb many families, promising that subsequent legal reform would target the coparcenary (which has not happened to date). He opined that "it would not be proper 'in the name of doing justice to women' that action should be taken to alter such transactions" (Parashar 1992, 127). Those who wanted to retain male privilege in joint family property were thus reassured that legal loopholes had been left to ensure that the status quo would not be unduly disturbed, and that wills could be written to disinherit women if so desired (Parashar 1992, 128).

While the reform of Hindu law was propelled by using the tropes of modernity, individual rights, and the egalitarian nature of the nation-state, the nonreform of inequalities in other personal laws was justified through the language of noninterference and freedom of religion. The official line of the government was that it could not interfere with religious laws unless requested by the community (although this had not prevented the transformation of Hindu law without "permission"), but the substantial electoral banks represented by the minority population and the need to placate the influential elites within these communities were important factors in the nonintervention. The lack of reform perpetuated a system of family law with widely varying provisions for divorce or custody, and even greater gender inequality than in Hindu law.[11]

However, even here the issue of women's rights provided grounds for some limited reform. The Shariat Act of 1937, which brought the principles of the shariat formally within Indian Muslim law, was presented as legislation safeguarding women's rights. It ostensibly prevented Muslim males from claiming that disinheriting daughters was local practice, because under the shariat they would become subject to Islamic and not customary law. However, because agricultural land was exempted from this law and women got only a half share compared to their siblings as per Islamic law, the act merely cemented Islamicization of Muslim people's lives rather than achieving uniformity (Parashar 1992, 147–50).

Because of this two-step move, whereby Hindu law appeared to be have been "modernized" in the new nation while other laws were left untouched, Hindu law gets portrayed as progressive and equitable, the hegemonically valued ideal law trumping others in crossover cases,[12] while the truth about scant change in fundamental hierarchies remains concealed. Simultaneously, the laws of other

communities, particularly Muslim law, can be represented as the
space of the primitive Other where women cannot be given equitable rights because of intransigent religious obstacles, a myth
maintained despite better provisions for Muslim women in areas
such as property.[13] Hence Hindu law is interpellated as secular,
national law and the Indian/Hindu State characterized as feminist
in commitment, with the privileges of male Hindu middle-class
elites written into legal practice as commonsense ideology.

One of the most notable legal cases in recent history, the "Shah
Bano case," reconfirmed such ideological inscriptions while also
transforming Indian women's relation to law. Shah Bano, a septua-
genarian Muslim woman, asked for minimum maintenance from
her wealthy lawyer husband of forty-three years who was divorcing
her to avoid paying for support, persisted with her claim through
the courts, and won in the Supreme Court in a case that seized the
public imagination with historic consequences.[14] The situation
brought about the fiercest postindependence Hindu-Muslim tension, throwing up virulent anti-Muslim strains in Hindu discourse,
as well as a vocal pro-Islam lobby where the preservation of minority culture got equated with Muslim women's subordination according to alleged textual mandates. The issue became framed in terms
of "interfering" in Islamic guidelines about maintenance versus
allowing autonomy within religious personal laws, rather than the
crucial question of equitable and updated laws for women of all
religions. Despite constitutional provisions for a uniform civil code,
the national government's solution, strongly guided by looming
elections, was to pass the "Muslim Women's (Protection of Rights
on Divorce) Act" (1986) which aimed to deprive divorced Muslim
women of legal remedies against penury, remedies that are available to all other Indian men and women. While placating powerful
Muslim leaders, this measure reinforced the "progressive" (Hindu)
state versus "primitive minorities" dualism, and fueled communal
tension.[15]

Yet despite this legislative setback, Shah Bano's win marked
women's jural presence within law and their recourse to the egalitarian rhetoric of "modernity" in irreversible ways, snowballing a
series of cases from other women who faced blatant legal inequities
in their own personal laws. Mary Roy won her challenge to the
Travancore Christian Succession Act's (1916) unequal division of
property among siblings.[16] Vera Aranha demanded maintenance

from her husband in a case with strong echoes of Shah Bano.[17] Representatives of the journal *Manushi* filed a public interest litigation suit on behalf of Maki Bui for Ho widows' rights to family land (Kishwar 1994b, 11–22). Although some women were defeated and many continue to struggle within the legal system, there were some radical victories, and most tellingly, the effects of these legal challenges showed in the perturbation of communities. A telling example is that of Indian churches, worried about retaining their substantial tithes in the wake of the Mary Roy decision, who are scurrying to sponsor legal programs that can help parishioners with will-writing strategies for effectively preventing daughters from claiming land.[18]

## Patterns of Authority

In recognizing that legal authority comes from sociopolitical standpoints rather than from a subjectless distillation of universal truths, legal scholars have come to recognize the contingent and situated nature of legal axioms.[19] It is crucial to mark the basis and source of authority, to consider the question of "who can speak for whom" and how the authority to speak "on behalf of" is related to sociolegal hierarchies and experience-based identities. One of the most useful formulations in this context is Spivak's elaboration of the Marxist terminology for representation: the distinction between the two meanings of "representation" revealed in the two German words for it, *Vertreten* and *Darstellen*, meaning respectively "representation as 'speaking for,' as in politics, and representation as 're-presentation,' as in art or philosophy" (1988, 275). This goes to the very heart of judicial authority in representations of gender because, while judges are nominated to act on behalf of people and supposedly in their best interests, their powerful roles in legitimizing discourse allows them to portray those interests according to their own ideologies. Thus, the representatives of justice could be re-presenting people's motivations, needs, and subjectivities. In the following cases, for instance, women who won their suits may have done so because judges inscribed female nature or women's rights in distinctly patriarchal ways, and created easy legal remedies at the cost of ideological disempowerment for women.

The Indian courts have dispensed with the jury system, making judges' evaluations of evidence and pronouncements all-important for determining legislative outcomes. While this autonomy as well as other tools like public interest litigation have been interpreted as having the potential for radical activism and direct intervention,[20] the obverse result is also the unfettered extent of power that rests in judges' hands. In this chapter, the discursive authority of the judgments highlights the ways in which legal decisions, proceeding from particular sources and contexts, acquire the power to delineate broad cultural meanings.

In the following sections, cases dealing with property/succession are analyzed for their constructions of gendered subjects, the postcolonial state, and legal entitlements and responsibilities. Within these areas of discourse, some themes recurred in judicial rhetoric, illustrating the continuing presence of the tropes of women's "sacred" realm versus women's rights as a symbol of "modernization," as well as illuminating judges' beliefs about the range and depth of their legal authority. These included:

Reinterpretation of social or political theory and judges' tendency to generalize across historical periods or political economies in applying the theory.

Religious interpretation by judicial authorities, with speculation on the "true nature" and "essential characteristics" of various religions, often translating religious texts into legal logic.

The characterization of contemporary social life and its development with respect to the (distant or immediate) past.

The needs, roles, and expectations of people within a joint family versus a nuclear family.

Essentialist depictions of "woman" and references to differences in intelligence, agency, motivation, and need between women depending on their education, social class, and urban or rural residence.

National historiography, especially the construction of "ancient" history and alleged postcolonial transformations.

Metajurisprudence: Judges' comments on the unique characteristics of Indian jurisprudence and the particular wisdom of framers of the Indian Constitution, especially in comparison with "the West," and the recurrent tendency to read the "social welfare" or "intent" behind certain pieces of legislation as if they were transparent.

The analysis in this chapter is based on cases dealing with disputes over property,[21] published in the *All India Reporter* journal[22] between 1988 and 1991.[23] A surprisingly large proportion of the cases studied *did* involve either gendered questions or include women as participants (although sometimes only among long lists of codefendants with no directly active role). Of a total of 159 succession and inheritance cases, I considered 27 (16.9 percent) to have no relevance to gender issues or women, plus 13 to have minimal relevance, thus 119 or 74.8 percent cases were finally considered for delineations of gender.

Of the 159 cases studied, 22 percent dealt with the validity of wills, 16.4 percent with the quantum of shares and partitions, 15.7 percent with dispensation of "self-acquired" versus "joint family" property, 11.3 percent with widows' property in lieu of maintenance, 9.4 percent with questions of probate, 5.6 percent with gifts related to Muslim law, 5 percent with adoption issues, 5 percent with topics pertaining to guardianship, custody, and valid marriages, 3.1 percent to other questions of women's property, 1.9 percent with property of Christians, and 4.4 percent with other miscellaneous issues. While the above cases were tabulated to reflect the single most crucial issue and were not counted in multiple categories, each case often dealt with several topics, and the juxtaposition of certain subjects provided clues to the most urgently contested legal arenas. For instance, cases of valid wills, shares from partitioned land, and the issue of particular estates being "joint family" (and hence having limited alienability especially for women) versus "self-acquired" often overlapped, indicating that these legal avenues provided the most fertile grounds of challenge.

The total number of wins for women in this selection of cases was impressive: 66.4 percent wins in 119 cases, 29.4 percent losses, and 4.2 percent cases where women both gained and lost something. However, despite an overall positive picture, the map of successes and failures for women in the following sections is best understood through a crucial contradiction; women seemed to have an advantage when overall numbers were considered, but closer attention to the details of judgments revealed a pattern of superficial victories and deeply troublesome characterizations of women's nature and of gendered rights.

## Different Spaces for Daughters, Sons, and Wives

Judgments of property cases showcase numerous routes of deploying gender difference and justifying differential rights. They show judges' invocation of women's helplessness and yet their belief in women's economic dependence and entitlement to lesser resources than men (Kapur and Cossman 1996, 136). Moreover, judges frequently use culturally prevalent ideologies about women's rights and responsibilities to justify women's widespread disentitlement from family property, such as property being a reward for eldercaregiving by sons, dowry being a form of property, or daughters' entitlement being confined to affinal family property only, despite the irrelevance of these standards in "reformed" law.

In many cases, judges depicted themselves as being sympathetic to women raising property concerns in court. Notably, however, such women were interpellated as being morally righteous, unretaliating, simple, or helpless—that is, constructed as deserving "feminine" candidates of patronage. Thus, in *Joti Dadu Navale vs. Monikabai Kashinath Mohite*[24] the judge openly rebuked a brother for trying to oust his sister from their parents' property: "The defendant has not succeeded in painting a very glorious picture of himself before the Court. On his own showing, he is a grabber. He has no regard for the rights of his own sister; that she wants only a quarter share but he was not inclined to give even that pittance." The moralistic tone here clearly spilled beyond legal boundaries. By referring to the potential illegality and manipulative intent of the brother's adoption as an adult, his sister's plea for less than her fair share, and his attempt to carry out a legal ouster to deprive her entirely, the judge portrayed the defendant as someone grasping the wealth of his adoptive family all for himself. By not having demonstrated any token attempts to support the sister with her wedding expenses or otherwise, the defendant had done nothing to show that he had balanced his privilege of a greater share of inheritance (as a male heir) with the corresponding symbolic responsibility (as a man) of taking care of those who inherited less, and thus had no favorable ideological excuse that the judge could use to justify his legal claims.

Similarly, some widows were depicted as deserving the court's extra protection because of their age or their lack of legal knowledge, while their opponents' attempts to maneuver them out of their property was treated harshly. In *A. Venkappa Bhatta vs. Gangamma*,[25] the widow who sought a share from the brothers-in-law controlling joint family wealth was described as: "an old lady in late sixties and literate, not well versed in the ways of the world . . . leading the sheltered life of a widow in an orthodox family. . . . very much under the influence of the first defendant, *kartha*[26] of the family and brother of her late husband. She had no sons or support to look to." Again, the court assumed the favored garb of protector of the most vulnerable. It is no coincidence that the lack of sons was added to her sources of weakness (she had two daughters), because the judge assumed that sons are invariably responsible for the financial and social support of parents. A similar role for daughters, who were presumably virilocally married and retained no interest in property, was not even brought up, and a conclusion that the mother had "no support" was drawn.

In a similar example (*Mathew vs. Devassy Kutty*[27]), the presence of daughters who were viewed as being just as vulnerable as the widowed woman was used to buttress the image of helplessness. In finding that a will where the elder son had no share of property was valid, the judge focused on the father's responsibilities to all his children, including one deaf-mute daughter and one daughter who was a nun. Yet even while showing obvious contempt for the son—"ungratefully, the defendant questions the generosity of his father"—the judge gave serious consideration to the son's contention that disinheritance of the elder son was in itself a mark of the father's mental incapacity, and could finally justify the will only by bringing up the gifts already made to this son in lieu of property. Despite the son's getting nothing in this case, the "natural" property rights of sons were legally emphasized, whereas the disinheritance of daughters is so routine that it would be unlikely to raise similar questions about the mental capacity of a father.

Women's perceived helplessness and weakness could thus be a strong ground for judicial support for them. That is, in such decisions women got judicial approval for successfully matching a hegemonically favorable image of Woman, representing an ineffable ahistorical "Indianness" that could be comfortably championed through law. This ideal of passivity could be deliberately invoked, such as in *Parnam Balaji vs. Bathina Venkataramayya*,[28] where a sale made several years previously by a woman whose husband had appointed her as her sons' guardian was claimed as invalid by the family *including the woman*. They alleged that she had no right to sell because under prevailing Hindu law women did not have the right to be appointed as legal guardians who could make financial decisions. The judge did not invalidate the sale, finding that the woman had acted under the implicit authority of her husband, the official kartha, but investigated the profound legal questions of whether women could be guardians of their children, surrogate karthas of the family with the husbands' permission, and even whether they were "adult members of the family" (as karthas needed to be) under Hindu law. In finding that women could not legally occupy those roles, the fundamental alienation and secondariness of women within "reformed" Hindu law were underlined. While the woman in this case could not win by calling upon her innate legal paralysis within contemporary law, the judgment made it clear that it was the firmness of her surrogate contract that was the determining factor, and that she did not in fact have rights to adult status or guardianship within the Hindu joint family.

Decisions dealing with property distributed on the basis of eldercare received more mixed reactions from judges, with support swinging between the validation of strong inequities in Hindu property law on the one hand, and an understanding of inheritance as a reward for caregiving on the other. In *Sushila Bala Saha vs. Saraswati Mondal*,[29] the judge declared the validity of a will where a mother left her property to one daughter (out of two daughters and a son); it was decided that the distribution was not unnatural as alleged, because the daughter had resided with the mother and "looked after her comforts," whereas the son had not only failed in his "bounded duty" to maintain his mother but had also stolen from her, tried to defraud her and forced her to leave her home in fear of her life. The judge clearly supported eldercare as a possible basis of property division rather than gendered rights. Yet even here, the trace of entitlement patterns differentiated by gender was seen in the reference to the *son's* duties to maintain the parent and thereby deserve a share of property, although the reward in this case was deflected because of the son's neglect and criminality.

In *Ram Piari vs. Bhagwant*,[30] where a will was contested by one of two daughters, the judge used the grounds of eldercare to decide that the will was valid even though the sons of only one of the daughters were the heirs. Here neither daughter had bad relations with the father, but the judges in the lower and High Courts had interpreted the exclusive bequest by emphasizing the gift to the children of the daughter with whom the man lived (i.e., an eldercare reward), the special closeness with these grandchildren due to greater proximity, and the "happy marriage" of the disinherited daughter. Other reasons given by the High Court were that provision had to be made for "the lesser fortunate" and that property must not be allowed to "pass out of the family." Differences in wealth between the daughters was hinted at as being the rationale for property division; thus, "happy marriage" was a euphemism for the disinherited daughter's affinal prosperity, although the wealth in question was presumably the son-in-law's, and sons are rarely disinherited for having individual wealth or rich spouses. Even more importantly, the judge's reference to keeping wealth within "the family" nodded to the *male* line of inheritance created by the bequest, to what appeared to be the only grandsons, thereby giving legal support to one of the customary forms of property division in sonless families despite the absence of such principles in law.[31]

In other cases, such as *Paramma vs. Chikarangappa*,[32] male entitlements to property were even more blatantly protected. Here, the father made a gift of one acre of land to the daughter he was living with (he had two daughters), calling the sons "lazy and vagabond." Because this land was part of the joint family estate and the daughter did not have a direct share to it, one of the few ways he could give it to her was by claiming that it was a "gift for pious purposes." The sons claimed that the gifted land was the most productive portion of the joint family estate of six to seven acres and hence that their father was depriving them of the means of livelihood, pointing also to his obvious contempt for them and throwing in allegations about his having had a concubine. The court focused on the jointness of property and held that the gift was too large and was thus unjustifiable.

This case is a vivid example of the persistent obstacles to women's getting family property despite their attempts to overcome gender roles which rationalize their disentitlement. Whether or not women maintained ties with the natal family and assumed responsibilities like eldercare that were customarily undertaken by sons partly in lieu of property, the persistence of the *legal* notion of the joint family to which only males had property rights by birth prevented the parent from rewarding daughters for help or from changing the gendered nature of inheritance despite the sons' ill treatment. The court's support of the idea that only sons were permitted to derive a livelihood from "joint family property" and hence that daughters should only draw on individual or affinal resources, while reflective of the letter of the law, showed the paralysis of the judiciary in the inability to apportion property according to paths of affection or reward, and bowed to the patrilineal model that excluded women from sharing their natal families' wealth.

On the one hand, judges were obviously enamored of "progressive" changes made in Indian law as a result of postcolonial legislation, which mirrored a modern image of their adjudication. For example, in *Babu Nigappa Yalgundri vs. Arunkumar alias Basappa*,[33] the Hindu Adoptions and Maintenance Act (1956) was praised as being "revolutionary" because it allowed a widow to alter all coparcenary shares of joint family property by her power of adoption. Several cases dealing with section 14 of the Hindu Succession Act (1956) elicited profuse praise from judges about the "ameliorative social reform" (e.g., *Kamini Bewa vs. Srimati Dei*[34]). In *Narsimhulu vs. Manemma*,[35] while ruling that a widow's alleged "unchastity" would not stand in the way of her receiving maintenance from her husband's property, the judge praised the broad intent of the Hindu Succession Act (1956) and claimed that "the Legislature felt the need most acute to remove many a disability under which the Hindu women are reeling from [*sic*] in matters of inheritance." Such decisions reflected well on the progressive, rational identity in which judges liked to garb Indian jurisprudence.

Yet at other times, the judiciary put the weight of its authority behind extralegal ideologies about property and family roles that appear to run counter to the spirit of such legislation, making legal reform appear merely cosmetic. In justifying a will where a man left property to his nephew and only maintenance rights to his wife as being not unnatural (*Chandania vs. Gyan Chand*),[36] the judge argued strongly that "he appears to have decided to keep the property within *his family*. . . . There was apprehension in the mind of the testator that after his death his brothers-in-law would usurp the immovable property" [emphasis mine]. The judge appeared to accept the lawyer's contention that

> among the Hindus it is not uncommon that if the owner of the property has no issues [children] he wills his immovable property in favor of some member of his family in whom he has implicit confidence, so as to prevent the property being passed on by his widow to the members of her own family.

On the judge's part, there was no criticism that such Hindu customs were presumably overridden by the new legislation. Nor was there any recognition that the property in question, apparently self-acquired, could well be regarded as being as much the wife's as the husband's because of her lifelong contribution through labor and savings, and hence she could have had the right to inherit and bequeath it as she wished. The idea that women have no ongoing responsibilities to their natal families and can only be thankful recipients rather than cosharers of marital property was thereby reinforced by the court.

In several other cases too (*Ajit Kumar Maulik vs. Mukunda Lal Maulik, Bhagwan Kaur vs. Chetan Singh, Dharam Singh vs. Aso*,[37]) the disinheritance of daughters was seen as a mark of "natural" dispensation of property, as evidence of mental stability demonstrated through adherence to custom. The marriage of daughters was regarded even by the judges as an event bringing about a disentitlement to property and being equivalent to sons having self-supporting incomes.[38] In *Khusbir Singh vs. The State*,[39] the court claimed that a man's will made out to the son and excluding a daughter of a second marriage was quite rational because he "may well have wanted to solemnize his daughter's marriage during his lifetime and that may have led him to disinherit her," and quoted a previous judgment saying that "the two currents of natural affection and settlement of properties can flow in distinct channels, and that the change in the course of one need not necessarily have any effect on the direction of the other." The court thus lent weight to the notion that dowry or marriage expenses can be regarded as equivalent to property shares, and fed the assumption that giving dowry was a legitimate ground for disinheritance, even though the son here got a house and a business and the daughter could at best have got some money in the bank, that is, a far smaller share, if she had been given a dowry. The further justification of "channels of affection" provided gratuitous support for ideologies of women's disentitlement from property, implying that property distribution must follow predetermined cultural routes, changes in law notwithstanding, and could not be affected by emotions or needs.

Especially notable in these cases is the ease with which customary social practices predating the laws came to be viewed as "natural behavior" motivating the dispensation of property, such as the idea that daughters with sons should be viewed preferentially because male heirs "kept" property within the "family." Often, blatant forms of gender discrimination were naturalized through judicial authority by being depicted as immutable essential "facts" about Hindu practices, while the equality lauded in postcolonial laws simply faded away in that context. As Kapur and Cossman point out, legal judgments actively contribute to women's economic subordination: "Women are not simply assumed to be economically dependent, but rather, the assumptions that inform the law continue to constitute women as economically dependent" (1996, 136). Thus, the preservation of ineffable "Indian" traditions of love and caring validates the distribution of material resources.

### Defining Religion, Faith, and Custom

In the absence of a uniform civil code in India, gendered rights to property vary by religion. Hence, defendants need to construct or claim a particular religious identity in order to ask for property, and judges further this process of interpellation, determining the religion of legal subjects in terms of seemingly transparent markers. The legal reasoning involved in negotiating such identities reveals the arbitrary social parameters used to denote religion.

A vivid example is K. Devabalan vs. M. Vijayakumari,[40] where the case hinged upon whether the property at issue belonged to a Hindu or Christian man. The sons in this case questioned their late father's right to bequeath a piece of land to one of his daughters as part of her dowry, claiming they were a Hindu joint family and that the father as kartha could only alienate land in the best interests of the other coparceners (males). On the other hand, this daughter claimed that her mother was Christian and her father had converted upon marriage, making the property personal and not part of the joint family, his to dispose off at will. The implications were that religion could be read off from choice of spouse or possible conversion, and could posthumously alter the effect of one's financial decisions or multigenerational contracts about property.

In this case, "proof" of religious identity came not from specific faith-related icons or choice of deity but from extraneous signifiers associated with religion: the alleged religiosity of the names "Adichan Nadar" (connoted as Hindu) versus "Yesudas" (signifying Christian), and their appearance in school, marriage or business records, determined religion, and hence property decisions. On the basis of the conclusion that Adichan Nadar remained Hindu, the judge then debated whether the marriage with a Christian woman was valid, and if so, "whether a son born to a Hindu in marriage with a Christian woman *could be considered as a member of the family*" [emphasis mine]. The family in question was, of course, the Hindu coparcenary, but in terms of the legal debate it was the only relevant one because it brought membership to property.

Most significant of all was the erasure of the daughter's claim as a necessary component of Hindu identity. A reevaluation of the sales was ordered by the High Court, with the rights of sons proclaimed to be firmly predominant within Hindu law. The gift to the daughter, rather than being a simple transfer of resources at the time of marriage, was explained as a "compensation" for the "difficult" job of marrying a woman who had once been abducted. Thus, the woman's subject position with regard to property was multiply violated: the idea that she was "devalued" through abduction assumed a patriarchal ownership of women's sexuality; this "devaluation" was "compensated" to her husband rather than to her; and the gift was further contested by the brothers who resented alienation of "their" property, that is natal property to which she seemed to have little entitlement.

While in the above case proof of Hinduism was associated with barring property gifts to women, in the following cases Hindu law was appealed to as the surest avenue for women to claim natal property. The irony of Hindu law being a partial guarantor of women's property rights can be explained by the existence of multiple personal laws and the hegemonic Hindu nature of the Indian legal system. Because customary laws of other religious communities (in these cases "tribal" laws of *Bhumijs* and *Santhals*) had not been recodified in any way, supposedly to keep those groups appeased, women's "reformed" if inadequate rights under Hindu law could appear as the only refuge. Significantly, however, women making such pleas could only camouflage their claims in the alleged haven of Hinduism by transliterating their rights to natal property into their wifely rights.

In *Ashok Kumar Hembrom vs. Rani Hembrom*,[41] Rani Hembrom, a Santhal woman, sought to get *her* father's land (which she had been cultivating for many years) for herself and her sons (no daughters are mentioned), but could make no direct claim because women were barred from inheriting land under Santhal Tribal law. By asserting that she had got married to Anand Tudu in a *Gharjamai* (uxorilocal)[42] form of marriage, however, she could claim that a share of property ought to come to her through him. According to this argument, by marrying her Anand was in the position of an adoptive son of her father, and ought to have inherited in the same way that a predeceased adopted son did under the Hindu Adoptions and Maintenance Act (1956), daughters' direct rights to Hindu *family* property being minimal. In granting her case and acquiescing that the Hindu law could override the conflict with customary law, the court thus cast Hindu "personal" law as having ultimate veto and being applicable to all Indians, instead of voicing concern about the absence of uniform civil rights that could give substantive equality to women of all religions.

Ironically, as Mitra points out (1989, 223–27), among Santhals the Gharjamai form of marriage is meant to give the married *daughter* the traditional rights and responsibilities of a son in the areas of property and maintenance, while the presence of the "at-home" son-in-law is merely a mechanism for the daughter to have the cultural respectability of marriage. Despite the overall patriarchal bias in Santhal law, this device is a means for women to inherit property directly. Yet the framing of issues and the judgment in Rani Hembrom's case implies that such spaces for more balanced rights in non-Hindu systems were invisible within the Hindu hegemony of the legal structure. Only the dominant patriarchal aspects of other religions were found to be textually acceptable, and these other religions were monolithically read as having "primitive" attitudes toward women compared to the allegedly reformed nature of Hindu law. Furthermore, the blatant biases against women in the *Hindu* Adoptions and Maintenance Act (1956) remained unstated as the convoluted paths for Rani Hembrom to get natal property under the patronage of Hindu law were portrayed as the sole haven guarding women's entitlements.

While Rani's case involved a clear abduction of Santhal law and a judicial extension of the alleged benevolence of Hindu law, the case of *Gopal Singh Bhumij vs. Ginibala Bhumij*[43] portrayed a much clearer plea to claim actual Hindu *identity* as a way for a woman to secure property. Here, the daughter Ginibala wanted to inherit her parents' property, but could do so only if she proved that her family was "Hindu enough" for Hindu laws to be applied to them. The judge claimed to be using the principle that "[i]t is possible that aboriginals of non-Hindu origin can become sufficiently Hinduised so that in matter of inheritance and succession they are governed by the Hindu Law, except so far as any custom at variance with such law is proved." Thus, Ginibala would have to "show that the family and/or other Bhumijs of the village and/or neighboring villages have adopted Hindu religion and have been following all the rites and customs normally followed by Hindus." Because the law is rigidly segmented according to religious identity, a distinct polarization between religions had to be set up, and the fluidity and overlap seen in the articulation of religious practices could not be accommodated within legal discourse.

Ginibala's claim that she was Hindu was based on factors such as the fact that she spoke Bengali and that a festival for the Hindu goddess Saraswati had been arranged at their school. Yet language cannot necessarily be equated with religious practice (the large number of Bengali Muslims and Christians being an obvious refutation), nor is the religious affiliation of one's educational institution a clue to individual faith. On the other hand, Ginibala's opponents, her male cousins, based their claims of being non-Hindus, *Adivasis* (literally First Peoples, part of the so-called Scheduled Tribes) and *Bhumij* by caste, on other arbitrary markers of religious identity. According to them, the fact of Ginibala's mother having given her away in a Kanyadan ceremony had an unhindulike connotation because Hindu widows, being "inauspicious" in strict Hindu scriptural terms, did not usually participate in such rituals. The persistence of burial of the dead in their family rather than cremation (as common among Hindus) was seen as further evidence, as were the *Sarhul* and *Buruhil* festivals in Ginibala's family and the absence of Siva temples or religious "idol" worship in their village.

While Ginibala may well have called upon Hindu identity merely as a convenient device to secure property, the court's methods of testing "Hinduisation" reveal shortsighted definitions of Hindu identity. For example, despite their equation of Hinduism with idol worship, only certain versions of Hinduism embrace idol worship, and many sects like the *Brahmos* scorn it in favor of belief in a formless spiritual entity. If Ginibala's community were indeed in a transitional Hindu stage, it would be extremely likely that they would continue many of their original religious practices (viz. burial rituals or particular festivals), while incorporating other elements of the dominant religion. This characterization of religion in divided terms reflects the binary logic followed in legal reasoning, but runs contrary to the realities in India where religious practice is often unidentifiably diffuse, and people layer customs from various religions into their spiritual practices.[44] For example, communities including Hindus and Muslims frequently worship both (Hindu) *sadhus* or (Muslim) *pirs* (hermits or persons regarded as holy) who may be locally revered. Like the ambivalent boundaries between Hindu and Sikh identity, and as the existence of matrilineal Indian Muslims indicates (Agarwal 1994, 131–32), religious affiliations often fail to be singular and practices show distinct regional adaptations rather than textual adherence. Thus the very question of trying to ascertain religious identity is likely to be moot.

Most egregious of all in this "test" of Hindu practice was the claim by Ginibala's cousins that they were not Hindus because married daughters had not received shares of natal property in their families, although they were supposed to under Hindu law. In accepting this as a valid rationale characterizing Hindu culture, the judge clearly ignored the *social* reality of Hindu women's succession to property, choosing to focus instead on the relatively rosy picture of Hindu women's access to property ensconced in *law*. If Ambedkar's promises to leave loopholes for preventing female inheritance and maintaining the status quo with regard to land in the context of passing this "reform" in law are remembered (p. 199), the judge's actions reveal not only a hypocritically superior view of Hindu law, but also the propagation of a myth about Hindu women's lives. Such a myth both hampers the claims of non-Hindu women by false logic, and also depicts Hindu women as having more rights and resources than they actually do, veiling the fundamental inequality of the rights as well as their continual curtailment through legal and ideological maneuvers.

## Conclusion: "Spoilt Darlings" and "Patient Packhorses"?

The above appellations are credited to Lord Justice Denning in the context of comments on English family law reform in the 1950s and 1960s (Smart 1984, 29). His complaint is that law in the modern state is strongly biased in favor of women and willing to pamper them with legal rewards, whereas men are treated harshly, being expected to be primary breadwinners while receiving few traditional domestic privileges in return. The contemptuous tone toward women in Denning's description belies the support for "reform," as men's alleged stoicism and uncomplaining labor is contrasted with a slothful and petulant image of women culled from the stereotype of a wealthy Victorian woman confined to the home. Such contentions are relevant here because they echo an attitude common among the very people entrusted to make the law more egalitarian, that jurists not only care keenly about gender justice and address it within jurisprudence, but also that they are currently in danger of leaning too far toward favoring women.[45]

Denning's notion of the benevolent patronage extended to women by the courts in the modern state is also echoed in statements such as the testimony of an African witness to the Native Economic Commission in Natal in 1931, who complained that "the court is the husband of the wife," that white courts in the colonial era had undermined the "traditional" authority of husbands, fathers, and elders (McClendon 1995, 538–39). The grievance is representative of the unease of privileged groups anticipating a loss of customary privileges, and underlines the centrality of invoking women's legal rights to delineate relations of rule in colonial and postcolonial states. The evocative metaphor implies that the courts have indeed assumed the traditional husbandly function of being the ultimate protector and arbiter of destinies, usurping the role from the realm of familial control; women need no longer confine themselves to the absolute authority of the home. But the richness of the metaphor lies also in the control and implicit violence inherent in notions of husbandly power and the persistent ambivalence in ideas of protection. Thus, the courts are "husbandly" also in the sense of having transparent sanction to control women's sexual/social behavior, extending benevolent protection for pliable female behavior and unleashing authoritarian wrath against those who transgress from the rigid boundaries of femininity. In this aspect, they reinforce and validate the patriarchal power of husbands, of the family and household, thereby mitigating the usurpation of power in other domains by the state machinery in the modern state.

Women's complex and brittle inscription within the legal system in contemporary India gives the lie to such assertions of favoritism toward women in the courts. As the history of jurisprudence in the new Indian nation as well as the profile of contemporary property cases has shown, women are far from being treated with universal favor and leniency in the courts. Yet comments in the spirit of Denning's statements still echo among legislators and judges, betraying a self-indulgent rereading of the emancipatory reaches of legislation, and a blankness about remaining biases or the ignominious political origins of laws founded on the consolidation of patriarchal wealth.

Among the cases studied, women's rights to property within Hindu, Muslim, or Christian law were broadly recognized and supported by the courts, indicating that the legal realm was not entirely inhospitable to women pursuing legal claims. However, these not unfavorable hearings occurred at the appellate or Supreme Court level, indicating that there was a higher chance for women to get expansive or sympathetic treatment when they had the time or resources to persist with cases. With no available data about the majority of cases that never get to become case law, or even reach the appellate courts, the typical hearing received by an average woman can only be a matter of conjecture.

Furthermore, some of the most supportive hearings for women involved the judges' portrayal of themselves as wise patrons of helpless, blameless women, or "secular" proponents of a national ethos represented by "reformed" Hinduism, thus enforcing gender and religious hierarchies in the very act of "protecting" women through law. Even with those professed sympathies, there were persistent male privileges that had survived reform, and moreover the judges included in their calculations customary practices of property division meant to be overridden by the new laws. The worst obstacles for women remained the intransigent sexist bases of "reformed" legislation, with the list arguably headed by the survival of the Hindu Mitakshara coparcenary where married women get minimal rights to natal land while men get shares equal to their fathers at birth. Non-Hindu women's inability to get equal shares of property on the grounds of adherence to religious texts or "custom" was another major cul de sac.

Regimes of power such as law can thus be sought out for greater gender equality only with much ambivalence. As Carol Smart argues, "law is never a stable ally, indeed it is hardly an ally at all. . . . We should recognize that law is more a part of the problem (in the way that it genders, sexes, and sexualizes the male and female body) than part of the solution" (1995, 52). In the clear-cut blockages within law identified above, for example, the Hindu coparcenary, or the uneven operation of rights across religions, the tasks seem relatively straightforward: asking for legal changes, closely monitoring the legislative process, seeking practical ways to make changes in law realistic, and advocating broad socioeconomic reform to make a greater empowerment of the legal subject possible. However, as the aftermath of recent amendments to the Dowry Prohibition (Amendment) Act (1986) and the fate of seeking an end to sex-determination tests show (Kishwar 1994a, Mahila Dakshata Samiti 1988), even narrowly targeted legal change can be an impossibly difficult goal because of the translations and negotiations that take place between "feminist" campaigns for laws and their eventual sociopolitical shape. Moreover, because family law is the space where the remnants of kinship-based privileges, often based on patriarchal notions of family, duty, and labor, are most jealously safeguarded within the "modern" state, these may be among the transformations that are hardest to achieve.

However, these formidable obstacles still appear light when the difficulties of exercising vigilance over judicial inscription are confronted, viz. monitoring the characterizations of gender, entitlement, and justice operating in the cultural realm and saturating the legal framework. The opinions of judges are constituted through the very discourse that guides other property decisions. Here, the strict level of scrutiny required to eliminate or track gender bias in judicial decisions seems practically unenforceable, not least because a majority of favorable legal avenues and positive outcomes for women would need to be critiqued if the mixed rewards of "protection" were deconstructed.

And yet, entirely avoiding the realm of law would leave women even more defenseless in the modern state where jural rights are of supreme importance. In debating this crisis, scholars of feminist jurisprudence have emphasized the need to remember the shortcomings of law but also to recognize its power. Smart contends that despite "inadequate interventions" of law in transforming feminist policy, "achievements, opportunities and possible developments" are also associated with the legal realm, and recommends an active feminist engagement with the law, a "commitment to treating law as the site of struggle" (1995, 125). Other solutions involve a strategic yet critical approach to the workings of law: Nair advocates being conscious of the limitations of law and working within them (1996, 6); Gottell suggests making the "complexities and conflict" evident by revealing "that legal arguments are always the products of politics and normative assertion" (1995, 123); Ahmed puts forward a model combining a deconstructive technique that works by "destabilizing, complicating or bringing out the paradoxes of values" with pragmatic challenges that query who benefits from certain laws (1995, 60–61). Kapur and Cossman indicate that feminist engagements with law may be viewed as a "discursive struggle, where feminists seek to displace ideas of women's roles and identities" (1996, 15), and to cede it would be to make room for fundamentalist forces (1996, 285). Thus, the critique and debate over lacunae in law may in fact be of greater significance than perfect resolutions.

As the cases discussed in this chapter show, law has sometimes been able to function as a strategic ally; while the impact of changes in property law is unlikely to be widespread in the absence of changes in the labor market and constructions of kinship, post-independence reform has opened up spaces of possibility. Despite the formidable tasks of maintaining surveillance over legal rhetoric, it is important to use law as a potential mode of change and a site of negotiation with dominant ideologies.

# 7

## Conclusion

### Property and Propriety

The specters filling this study, ideological tropes about gender and property, possess immense power to coerce and terrify. They play a definitive part in determining the distribution of social resources, even though the effects of these discourses are differentially felt depending on socioeconomic factors such as class, age, and rural-urban affiliation. As Jameson reflects while visualizing Marx's ghost haunting the sites of current critical theory (1995, 85), specters are fundamentally about inscribing the present in terms of a deliberately constructed past, about justifying future actions by creating a reading of the past. In this case, women's circumscribed access to family resources is haunted not so much by the return of the colonial repressed as by the negotiations between structures of privilege within the postcolonial order.

If Woolf's ghost can be said to haunt the ground of research on women and property, the specter of Marx is not absent from there either; alongside feminist concerns about women's access to space and resources are ever-present worries about the nature of agency or possibilities for resistance that can create that access. Reflecting a time of disillusion with socialism, racial and ethnic crises, and cyber-identities, studies of resistance/struggle have recently tended to focus on individual contestations of ideology rather than collective action, paralyzing though that seems as a basis for transforming social relations (Merry 1995). Yet, in delineating the power of intransigent systems of privilege like property, the challenge lies not just in unpacking layers of discourse, but in finding ways to undo the privileges.

Within the capitalist world system, the significance of property or economic resources cannot be over emphasized. Access to meager amounts of assets does little to alter exploitative class relations, but in the absence of a radical transformation of social hierarchies, women's independent access to property is crucial for ensuring their material well-being, safety, and empowerment. As discussed in chapters 2, 4, and 5, women often acquired or wanted to get property as a safeguard against the financial unreliability or coercion of husbands, as insurance for getting care in old age, and as a symbol of strength and self-respect. In naming what they perceived to be the most fundamental problems and possible solutions for women (chapter 5), the importance of raising women's social status and of having enough resources to support their families, they also indirectly pointed to the potential significance of acquiring property. Despite the appearance of women's aversion to property as seen in their refusals of natal inheritance, property was in fact extremely important for women in addressing their worries and dreams.

These findings reiterate the conclusions drawn by Agarwal (1994, 27–42) on the significance of property for women. Agarwal argues that it would be extremely beneficial for individual as well as social development if women received their legitimate shares of land. The advantages she names are: (a) welfare: assisting in better nutrition and quality of life for women as well as children by providing resources, because these responsibilities are usually ultimately borne by women; (b) efficiency: formal access to land or property allows women to seek agricultural improvements or credit to increase their assets directly, and takes advantage of women's allegedly superior ecological responsibilities, agricultural productivity and debt repayment rates; and (c) equality and empowerment: gender equality can be said to be a measure of an egalitarian society, and land rights not only give women economic empowerment but strengthen their position in dealing with other social injustices. These factors are relevant not just in class-specific ways but pertain to women in varying situations, and certainly do not ignore the vast majority of women with sparse family resources.

Recent instances of land reform in India (both state initiated and products of grassroots activism) that made women's needs central to the redistribution of resources and power show the radical political empowerment that accompanies women's ownership of the most meager of property shares. For example, while other Indian states have shown only minimal progress and have even backslid in their commitment to land reform (Haque and Parthasarathy 1992), Kerala's Marxist government has stringently pursued policies enabling the poor to own the land their homes stood on, and achieved a marked improvement in living standards, including a substantial rise in rates of women's literacy and paid employment (Haque and Parthasarathy 1992; Jeffrey 1993). Jeffrey (1993, 184) points out that while class differences have not been disturbed, and poverty has not diminished despite a fair standard for wages being set, women report a feeling of security and pride in ownership after having got residential property of their own.

The most dramatic instances of land reform in India have involved grassroots activism, where women's claims for land/housing in their names have been part of larger movements where they have realized the conditions for exploitation of their labor and the lopsided process of "development," campaigned for better working and living conditions, and assumed leadership positions within the social movement (Agarwal 1994, 444–52; Bapat and Patel 1993; Guha 1989). On the one hand, property rights "given" to women seem to empower them in various aspects of their lives as delineated by Agarwal (1994), and are a redistribution of state power in some small measure; on the other hand, women often seem to come upon the significance of property while radically critiquing the multiple systems of power governing their lives, and their demand for property becomes a cornerstone for self-empowerment and challenges to their numerous oppressors, viz. the state, contractors, landlords, husbands, and parents.

Unfortunately, the results of my study provide little support for the widespread presence of such radical reformulations. While the respondents did not passively echo the ideologies on which their disentitlement to property was based, they reacted with mild negotiations of the current order and much fear about losing the familiar comforts of their known worlds if they brought up questions of property. Despite the benefits for themselves and their families that they could visualize, the fear of being turned into the haklenewali, the social stigma of being grasping and greedy, and worst of all, the apprehension of losing the symbolic space of love represented by the natal family, often made women decline natal property in favor of a dubious dependence on marital and affinal resources—that is, the investment of staying married.

Various socioeconomic parameters reinforced women's reliance on marriage as the path to acquiring economic assets. Women's unequal wage status in the labor market (the gap being even higher in non-"white-collar" jobs), and lower rates of workforce participation in the formal sector (Banerjee 1991), made it much more difficult for most women to acquire substantial savings or property independently. As they rarely got any property from their natal families, they could not rely on inheritance for building up their fund of resources either. Furthermore, despite lip-service to the idea of families being responsible for husbandless daughters, single or divorced women were at best grudgingly given small portions of family property and more often expected to make their own way and support themselves through wages (chapter 4). On the other hand, the most favorable paths for them to become either de jure or de facto property owners, as seen in chapter 2, was either as widows or as contributory spouses, that is, through marriage. While paths to property mediated through marriage did not address some of the crucial needs for property, in most cases they nonetheless ensured a superior material standard of living as compared to nonmarried women's struggles to survive without the financial resources of males.

Thus, as Sharma contends in her study of North Indian hamlets (1980, 198), the heart of women's dependence and vulnerability is in male control of productive resources; assertions of ideology or custom being responsible for the current distribution of assets are screens veiling that control. For instance, alleged alternative pathways for women to acquire property, such as rewards for eldercare and shares for daughters in sonless families, were seen to be modes which constructed women as surrogate and temporary owners in the place of male heirs, and affirmed fundamental male entitlements to property (chapter 4).

The idea of marriedness as the prime form of women's property is buttressed by two popular notions of ways in which women get property: the phantom equivalence of dowry with inheritance, and the idea that women "get" affinal property. As the tabulation of marriage payments shows (chapter 3), the primary aim of wedding prestations was not to build up a resource fund or stridhan for the woman, but to strengthen kinship relations and to display the status of both families. In wealthier families, sons' weddings tended to be lavish, yet had no proportionate effect on property division. When the brides' families did spend more, they tried to ensure that their affines would be satisfied enough to make no further demands, and that brides themselves would feel too obligated by the repeated expenditures to bring up yet another transmission of resources in the form of property, thereby reserving the property fund for male heirs. Thus, dowry served to deflect the demand for inheritance, falsely representing itself as the synecdochal part for the whole of inheritance.

Yet simultaneously, dowry did represent one of the few assets transferred by natal families to women. The typical gifts of clothing and jewelry for the bride were largely a display of status rather than a parallel fund of wealth, but appeared to be accepted enthusiastically by women even though they were fully aware of its symbolic nature and were under no illusion that such presents represented the best or most useful form of financial resources (chapter 5). Their acquiescence and even enjoyment of "dowry" can be read in terms of what these gifts actually represented: the only substantial expenditure from natal families for female children, the only culturally acceptable female entitlement to the fund of natal wealth. Given women's profound desires to stay connected with and feel loved by their natal families (chapter 4), wedding and postwedding prestations were also an important emotional acknowledgment of their natal family connections.

Based on such ideas of dowry as sole transfer of assets to women, scholars such as Kishwar (1989b) have claimed that banning dowry can disadvantage women even further if equal inheritance laws are not simultaneously enforced. Such "which comes first—dowry or inheritance?" conjectures can be replayed in infinite circles, leading to an impasse where nothing can be changed in the absence of radical transformation. However, it *is* true that if women's structural subordination remains constant, strict legislative attempts to either ban dowry or enforce equal inheritance are likely to increase women's vulnerability and dowry-related violence against them. On the one hand, removing dowry entirely in the absence of guarantees of inheritance (wills, gifts, etc., being common strategies to bypass legal directives about equal inheritance, chapter 2) deprives women of the few natal resources they garner and value. On the other hand, emphasizing inheritance for women without being able to stem the custom of wedding prestations leaves open possibilities for harassing women and their families for years over property, while dowry expenses are not curtailed in any way, and there is no return flow of resources in the form of eldercare or other financial help. For women to be truly empowered by changes in sociolegal norms of dowry and inheritance, they have to have access and control over independent *financial* resources (acquired through the labor market on equal terms with men and through inheritance), accompanied by changes in the ideologies that assign them to powerless positions in the household as brides/junior women, deny them reproductive freedom, or overburden them with domestic labor, affecting their productivity in the paid labor market and their status as equals.

Women's reliance on marriage as the path to property and on dowry as a natal inheritance reflects their understanding of the stronghold of structures of privilege, of the conflation between hegemonic ideas and the economic status quo. However, while women did not overtly resist the customary distribution of resources, they did not internalize the ideological construction of their needs either; rather, they made room for some of their needs and desires by negotiating the meanings of those ideologies. For example, while most women were unable to do anything to alter extant property relations, they strongly contested dominant notions that marriage ended their ties with the natal family, both by helping and taking help from their families in some cases, and more prevalently, by claiming to forego property shares in order to keep the natal connection alive.

In spite of kanyadan-related proscriptions in some middle-class Hindu families, married daughters (and their spouses) helped the woman's natal family in cases where it was necessary (chapter 4). Among the poorer families with a rural base, the level of help proffered was much higher, and the idea of severance was discursively absent, with married women also seeking extensive help *from* natal families, living with them for months in lean seasons. Those daughters who could give help did so in the form of medical, legal, funeral, or wedding expenses, or gifts of time through contributions of domestic work or physical caregiving. Yet contrary to the ideology that eldercare went to those children who helped their parents with various crises, men rather than women reaped the benefits of property, whatever their role in eldercare.

The notion that women declined natal property shares in order to maintain more profound ties with their natal families involves a more problematic conception of ideological contestation. Many women claimed to have refused property in order to help the natal home prosper, to prevent angering their brothers and sisters-in-law, and to preserve the natal home as a space of emotional wealth contrasting with the quotidian realm of work, duty, and abnegation in married life (chapter 4). Because this symbolic enrichment was achieved at the cost of their individual material impoverishment (through forfeiting property), and against their own overwhelming preference for distributing property equally between sons and daughters in an ideal situation (Table 4.2), it is harder to portray such gestures as beneficial cultural bargains. If this were to be denoted as resistance, it consists of women renaming their affinities and duties and being cognizant of how systems of power operate, but doing so by implicitly supporting the notion of brothers' anger against property-seeking women. However, knowing that this anger would be far from illusory (as the legal cases in chapter 2 show) left them few other satisfactory options.

While gender is an ubiquitous standard separating owners from nonowners of property in all classes, class also affects the form of property ownership substantially. In this study, differences in access to property were further exacerbated by social class, complementing the research showing the consolidation of class interests through elite women's acquisition of property.[1] As seen in chapter 2, many middle-class women were sole owners of flats, which had risen substantially in value over the decades and which were often the only or most valued piece of property owned by that family. However, being sidelined from natal wealth had begun to have more significant consequences for middle-class women, as few young couples could afford to buy urban property given the inflation in real estate values, making inheritance all the more crucial for getting any property, and lowering women's chances of being direct owners of the nuclear family residence.

In contrast, poorer women who were "property owners" had the dubious honor of "owning" only shacks, property with little legal standing or monetary value. Their impoverishment in the context of the total wealth of their families was even greater, because they had no share in the substantial amounts or rural land bought or inherited by men in their families, which formed the prime asset in those families (while the shacks were often regarded as temporary living quarters). Thus, poorer women who needed economic resources most urgently for supporting their families (chapter 5), and who were often openly skeptical about regular financial support from husbands and affines, were also in the most vulnerable position with regard to financial assets.

While poor women were the most disadvantaged in terms of access to productive assets, middle-class urban women did reap some economic benefits from their class position regardless of their marital status, viz. access to education and white-collar or professional occupations. These were connected to a prime consolidation of wealth. That is, women from KE and KC owned far less immovable property than the males in their families, and their social vulnerability was related to that disparity, but access to and chance to avail themselves of good educational and employment opportunities gave them important economic resources for survival, for improving their standard of living or that of their nuclear families (plus, they shared the benefits of their spouses' superior financial resources if married). Although not all women derived the full benefit from such assets, this form of property was potentially one of the most profitable ways (other than inheritance) of building wealth within contemporary relations of production.

In this sense, "middle-class" women had an important advantage over the men from rural areas living in squatter colonies; despite the fact that those men often owned substantial rural land, they were unable to acquire the social capital necessary to access prime urban jobs or run large urban businesses. Middle-class women's social assets thus contributed to the perpetuation of the urban underclass. Women from the poorer areas and often with rural backgrounds were the worst off, without educational assets, good opportunities for formal employment, or much chance of getting family land, making an independent existence most difficult. They were usually left with an unreliable dependence on men who were themselves disempowered in the urban milieu.

The formal realm of law occupies an ambivalent place both limiting and supportive of women's equitable participation in the socioeconomic realm. As the legal cases described by the respondents (chapters 2 and 5) and the appellate cases analyzed in chapter 6 show, women fared quite well within the legal process. Given the length of litigation and rampant corruption, it was easier for women with substantial financial assets to take on the risk of court battles, but even those who had few assets achieved some victories.

However, these wins are circumscribed by substantial limits; women could only benefit from gender equity within narrow areas of law, and judicial "reform" was confined to those corners. Moreover, judges frequently betrayed the androcentric biases of legal logic/rationality, welcoming women's claims involving vulnerability and the need for protection, but often echoing as examples of "human nature" the very rationales of patriarchal customary law that post-independence legislation attempted to undo. The absence of uniform civil rights combined with the hegemonic domination of Hindu law made the legal rights of non-Hindu women particularly limited and erratic.

But while there was some hope for property claims for women in the legal arena, where individual jural rights and notions of equity had some standing, families tended to stay away from legal solutions, and women themselves did not think that would be the optimal resolution for problems in their lives either (chapter 5). Taking cases to court tended to be a strategy to intimidate women seeking property and shame them into acquiescence, and threats to this effect from women's brothers were carried out even though families (usually men, as the property owners) chose not to challenge other clearly illegal acquisitions of property that did not involve women's rights to land. Despite the possibility of favorable resolutions for women, going to court was a mark of irreconcilable differences with the natal family, and hence associated with emotional losses that may not have compensated entirely for material gains.

The lessons for feminist jurisprudence here are that legislation cannot be the sole focus for social change, because the advantage of favorable laws can only be appreciated in the context of other socioeconomic empowerment (Parashar 1992; Rosen 1978). Moreover, the mere encoding of laws cannot effect changes in cultural practice substantially unless there is a concerted state effort to achieve widespread *legal* literacy, to explain the benefits of greater equity and address the fears of undoing customary privileges.[2] The terms under which women's rights get written into law and are subsequently invoked in judgments, for instance in terms of male patronage and female dependence, are also deeply troublesome concepts about which feminist jurists need to be vigilant.

As Manicom argues in delineating the evocation of gender within South African law, one of the most fundamental difficulties with turning to the state to inscribe women's equal entitlements within law is that state formation is often historically gendered, such that the bases of labor law, property, or concepts of race are founded on specific gendered notions (1992). If the state "be understood not as unitary or coherent but as institutionally diverse with different objects being taken up and produced as policy and practice" (1992, 465), then this profound gendering cannot be erased by piecemeal appeals to certain authorities. For example, while the sympathies of the contemporary democratic state appear to be somewhat more diffuse than that of the feudal one, the state still benefits from supporting the rights of property owners and will only transform property relations in marginal or contradictory ways (1992, 452). Thornton (1991, 466–68) argues similarly that because of "the central legitimating and ideological role played by law within the liberal state," hegemonic masculinity is naturalized in numerous contexts, and feminists must struggle hard to retain and reconstruct any spaces they have squeezed out.

Customary notions of property distribution continue to dominate in postcolonial India, establishing not an ancient or mythical social distribution of resources but cementing contemporary structures of gender and class privilege. Divisions evoking rationales of dowry as inheritance, virilocality determining caregiving, and the joint family living together off the land, depict a world where usufructuary rights seem reliable, wages in the marketplace have little effect on subsistence or assets, joint family residence is viable, and daughters married as infants to far-off places retain limited connections with families of origin. They are transliterated smoothly into a world of increasing nuclearization of families, immense reliance on wages and capital, regular contact with adult daughters, and awareness of domestic violence and the possibilities of divorce, with the distribution of property further enhancing vulnerabilities of gender and class in the urban milieu. These specters portray a shimmering past that diverts attention from current material conditions.

However, realizing the power of these specters is not in itself an act of exorcism. Rather, finding spaces of rupture or liberation within such structures is one way of undoing privilege. Law might provide occasional pockets of relief, but is unlikely to be the vehicle of choice for transforming fundamental structures of power that operate largely through familial units. Other researchers have found women's involvement in land reform movements to be a powerful way of beginning to undo such privilege, but in this sample there were very few instances of direct confrontation over property and little prospect for imminent change. The challenges to hegemonic domination primarily consisted of women's alternative and resistant constructions of ideology.

Yet radical spaces of rupture may lie within these small gestures. As Jameson (1995) and Merry (1995, 23–25) proclaim, one of the preeminent current crises of intellectual faith is an inability to find or trust revolutionary solutions, to put Marx's spirit to rest as it were. Rather, the favorite postmodern form of "resistance" seems to have become finding individual and seemingly ineffective moments of cultural negotiation. While these subtle and sometimes self-destructive gestures appear to have little transformative momentum, Merry contends that they have far more potential than we fully know. On the one hand, they leave one with a somewhat romantic hope in a noncompliant subject who does not subscribe to dominant ideologies. Even more importantly, it is impossible to predict how these individual moments can become the basis for collective action, because distinguishing collective movements from solitary gestures "is to deny agency, the extent to which institutions and structures . . . act in terms of common sense and everyday practices, and, as they develop competing images of the world, refuse to go along" (Merry 1995, 24).

While the system of property ownership uncovered in this study seemed depressingly stable, the mild ruptures in discourse that had no visible effect were not necessarily lost without trace. Although the disparity in interests and competition among social classes makes a cross-class coalition of women unlikely, there is no knowing where women's present realizations of jewelry being ineffective as a financial asset or their desires to include daughters in distributing their property will lead them over the years, and how they may ultimately challenge constructions of property and wealth. The effect of noncompliance may be felt among those who were not the original nay-sayers but were among their friends, neighbors, and relatives, and may not be realized in this generation. But processes of accumulated critique and mutual education and empowerment built from individual insights may have many unexpected effects.

Marx's ghost will have to be appeased by these fervent "maybe"s, as no mass mobilization among these atomized households, each concentrating on their own interests, seemed imminent. Meanwhile, the most urgent priorities for those who want to be involved with issues of women and property are to be engaged in deconstructive critiques that can reveal the consolidation and contradictions of power, along with practical attempts at legal literacy, calls for legal reform and political action, and most of all, broad-based attempts to redress property distribution by focusing on the entirety of socioeconomic relations.

# Appendix A

Demographic Profiles and Property Ownership
of Interview Respondents

Demographic Profiles and Property Ownership of Interview Respondents

| Interview # | Name Assigned | Area | Age | Marital/Household Position | Household Type | Religion | Education | Ethnicity/ State of Origin |
|---|---|---|---|---|---|---|---|---|
| I1 | Asha | KE | 60 | Widowed, Senior Woman (Mil) | Nuclear + In-Law | Hindu | 1–3 Yrs School | Punjab |
| I2 | Lata | KE | 67 | Married, Only Woman | Nuclear | Hindu | B.A. | Ex-West Pakistan |
| I3 | Rekha | KE | 55 | Widowed, Only Woman | Woman-headed-Household | Hindu | M.A. | Uttar Pradesh |
| I4 | Shivani | KE | 21 | Single, Junior Woman (D) | Joint | Hindu | B.A. ongoing | Punjab |
| I5 | Suman | KE | 37 | Married, Only Woman | Nuclear | Hindu | B.A. | Uttar Pradesh |
| I6 | Madhu | KE | 26 | Single, Junior Woman (D) | Woman-headed-Household | Hindu | M.A. | Himachal Pradesh |
| I7 | Bharti | KE | 27 | Married, Only Woman | Nuclear | Hindu | Ph.D. ongoing | Madhya Pradesh |
| I8 | Rama | KE | 24 | Married, Junior Woman (Dil) | Joint | Hindu | B.A. | Tamil Nadu |
| I9 | Rani | KE | 46 | Married, Middle Woman (Dil /Mil) | Joint | Hindu | B.A. | Punjab |
| I10 | Indira | KE | 42 | Married, Only Woman | Nuclear | Hindu | B.A. | West Bengal |
| I11 | Ritu | KE | 35 | Married, Only Woman | Nuclear | Sikh | Ll.B. | Uttar Pradesh |
| I12 | Kanta | KE | 27 | Single, Junior Woman (D) | Nuclear | Hindu | B.A. B.Ed. | Haryana |
| I13 | Kamla | KE | 59 | Married, Senior Woman (M) | Nuclear | Hindu | Matriculate | Ex-West Pakistan |
| I14 | Uma | KE | 27 | Married, Only Woman | Nuclear | Hindu | M.A. B.Ed. | Bihar |
| I21 | Bina | KC | 52 | Married, Senior Woman (M) | Nuclear | Hindu | Matriculate | Uttar Pradesh |
| I22 | Seema | KC | 49 | Married, Senior Woman (Mil) | Joint | Hindu | Matriculate | Punjab |
| I23 | Parminder | KC | 34 | Married, Only Woman | Nuclear | Sikh | B.A. | Delhi |
| I24 | Kalpana | KC | 45 | Married, Junior Woman (Dil) | Nuclear + In-Law | Hindu | B.A. | Delhi |
| I25 | Rehana | KC | 26 | Married, Only Woman | Nuclear | Muslim | Never in school | West Bengal |
| I26 | Kavita | KC | 25 | Married, Junior Woman (Dil) | Joint | Hindu | B.A. | Madhya Pradesh (Punjabi) |
| I27 | Shashi | KC | 55 | Widowed, Only Woman | Woman-headed-Household | Hindu | Never in school | Ex-West Pakistan |
| I28 | Kiran | KC | 23 | Married, Junior Woman (Dil) | Joint | Sikh | B.A. | Delhi |
| I29 | Sharmila | KC | 35 | Married, Only Woman | Nuclear | Hindu | B.A. | West Bengal |
| I210 | Harjinder | KC | 47 | Widowed, Senior Woman (Mil) | Nuclear + In-Law | Sikh | Matriculate | Ex-West Pakistan |
| I211 | Madhuri | KC | 20 | Single, Junior Woman (D) | Nuclear + In-Law | Hindu | B.A. ongoing | Rajasthan (Punjabi) |
| I212 | Renu | KC | 53 | Married, Only Woman | Nuclear | Sikh | HigherSecondary | Ex-West Pakistan |
| I213 | Vimla | KC | 36 | Married, Junior Woman (Dil) | Nuclear + In-Law | Hindu | M.A. B.Ed. | Haryana |
| I214 | Poonam | KC | 33 | Married, Only Woman | Nuclear | Sikh | HigherSecondary | Madhya Pradesh (Punjabi) |
| I215 | Sonal | KC | 77 | Married, Senior Woman (Mil) | Joint | Hindu | Matriculate | Ex-West Pakistan |
| I216 | Dolly | KC | 43 | Married, Only Woman | Nuclear | Hindu | B.A. | Punjab |

Demographic Profiles and Property Ownership of Interview Respondents (continued)

| Interview # | Paying Work Reported | Income (Rs.) | H's Occupation | Family Income (Rs.) | # Sons | # Daughters | # Brothers | # Sisters | Own Property |
|---|---|---|---|---|---|---|---|---|---|
| I1 | None | None | Service (Bank) | 4501 | 3 | 3 | 3 | 3 | 1 MIG Flat |
| I2 | Govt. Service (Retired) | 2000 | None | 2000 | 1 | 1 | 2 | 4 | 1 MIG Flat |
| I3 | Govt. Service (Retired) | 4000 | Doctor | 4000 | 2 | 0 | 3 | 3 | 1 MIG Flat |
| I4 | Student | None | N/A | 6000 | 0 | 0 | 1 | 0 | None |
| I5 | Home-Based Teaching | Not Known | Service | 3501 | 1 | 1 | 2 | 3 | None |
| I6 | Govt. Service | 4000 | N/A | 8000 | 0 | 0 | 0 | 1 | None |
| I7 | Professor | 3500 | Service (Engineer) | 10,000 | 0 | 1 | 2 | 1 | None |
| I8 | Accountant (Pre-marriage) | None | Service | 4000 | 0 | 0 | 2 | 4 | None |
| I9 | None | None | Govt. Service | 13,800 | 2 | 1 | 1 | 1 | None |
| I10 | Home-Based Teaching | Not Known | Service (Accountant) | 12,000 | 2 | 1 | 0 | 1 | 1 MIG Flat |
| I11 | Lawyer | 6000 | Govt. Service | 10,000 | 1 | 0 | 5 | 6 | Office Space |
| I12 | Laboratory Technician | 2500 | N/A | 10,000 | 0 | 0 | 2 | 5 | None |
| I13 | Teacher (Retired) | 850 | Govt. Service | 3500 | 2 | 1 | 2 | 2 | None |
| I14 | Service (Publisher) | 2000 | Service | 10,000 | 1 | 0 | 2 | 1 | None |
| I21 | Business | Not Known | Service + Business | 2800 | 1 | 3 | 1 | 2 | 1 LIG Flat, Shop P |
| I22 | None | None | Govt. Service | 11,000 | 1 | 1 | 2 | 1 | 1 LIG Flat |
| I23 | None | None | Shop | 4000 | 1 | 1 | 3 | 2 | None |
| I24 | Home-Based Teaching | Not Known | Shop | 3501 | 2 | 2 | 1 | 1 | 1 Shop P |
| I25 | None | None | Shop | 2501 | 1 | 2 | 4 | 3 | None |
| I26 | Dance Teacher | 1500 | Service | 6000 | 0 | 1 | 1 | 3 | None |
| I27 | Shop | 1500 | Business (Dairy) | 1500 | 1 | 3 | 3 | 3 | 1 LIG Flat, Shop T |
| I28 | None | None | Service | 6001 | 1 | 0 | 3 | 0 | None |
| I29 | Yoga Tutor (Pre-marriage) | None | Service | 3000 | 1 | 0 | 1 | 5 | None |
| I210 | None | None | Singer | 1001 | 1 | 1 | 2 | 5 | 1 LIG Flat |
| I211 | Student | None | N/A | 5500 | 0 | 0 | 1 | 2 | None |
| I212 | Secretary (Pre-marriage) | None | Govt. Service | 2500 | 2 | 1 | 3 | 5 | LIG Flat |
| I213 | Teacher | 4850 | Govt. Service | 9500 | 1 | 1 | 0 | 1 | None |
| I214 | None | None | Business | 2000 | 1 | 2 | 2 | 5 | None |
| I215 | Teacher (In West Pak) | None | Teacher | 5000 | 2 | 3 | 1 | 0 | None |
| I216 | None | None | Business | 4501 | 0 | 3 | 2 | 1 | None |

Demographic Profiles and Property Ownership of Interview Respondents (continued)

| Interview # | Couple's Property | In-laws' Property | Parents' Property | Abbreviations Used |
|---|---|---|---|---|
| I1 | N/A | None | Houses, Unspec U | R = Rural Property |
| I2 | 1 MIG Flat | None | 1 House, Unspec U | U = Urban Property |
| I3 | N/A | Unspec R | Unspec U | Sub-U = Suburban Property |
| I4 | N/A | N/A | 1 House | Unspec = Amount Unspecified |
| I5 | Rooms in a House | House, Unspec U | 1 House | LIG = Low-income Group |
| I6 | N/A | N/A | 1 House, Unspec U | MIG = Middle-income Group |
| I7 | 1 MIG Flat | 1 MIG Flat, Unspec U Jt. | 2 Houses | P = Permanent Stucture, Formal Business |
| I8 | None | 1 MIG Flat | None | T = Temporary Structure, Informal Business |
| I9 | 1 MIG Flat | None | Houses, Businesses | Jt. = Owned by Joint Family, Not Yet Separate |
| I10 | 1 MIG Flat | Unspec U | Businesses, Unspec U/R | |
| I11 | 1 MIG Flat | 1 MIG Flat | Shops P, Unspec U | |
| I12 | N/A | N/A | 1 MIG Flat | **Other Terms:** |
| I13 | 1 MIG Flat | None | 1 House | Jhuggi = Hut, Shack |
| I14 | None | Unspec R | Houses U/R | Bigha = 1/3 acre |
| II1 | 1 LIG Flat, 2 Shops P | 1 LIG Flat, 1 House | Houses, Shops P | |
| II2 | 1 LIG Flat | 2 Houses R | <1 bigha R | |
| II3 | 1 LIG Flat, 1 Shop P | 1 LIG Flat | Businesses, Unspec R | |
| II4 | 1 LIG Flat, 1 Shop P | 1 LIG Flat | 1 House | |
| II5 | None | 1 House R | Unspec R | |
| II6 | None | 1 LIG Flat, Unspec U | 1 House, Unspec U/R | |
| II7 | N/A | Unspec R | Unspec U | |
| II8 | None | 1 LIG Flat | 1 House Jt. | |
| II9 | None | 1 House Jt. | 1 House Jt. | |
| II10 | N/A | None | 2 Houses | |
| II11 | N/A | N/A | 2 MIG Flats | |
| II12 | 1 LIG Flat, <1 bigha U | 1 House | 1 House, 1 Shop T | |
| II13 | 1 LIG Flat | 1 LIG Flat, 1 MIG Flat, 1 House | 1 House, 1 Shop T | |
| II14 | 2 LIG Flats, 1 Shop P | 2 LIG Flats | 1 House | |
| II15 | 1 LIG Flat | 1 Shop P | 1 House, Shop P | |
| II16 | 1 LIG Flat, 1 Shop P | None | 1 House | |

Demographic Profiles and Property Ownership of Interview Respondents (continued)

| Interview # | Name Assigned | Area | Age | Marital/Household Position | Household Type | Religion | Education | Ethnicity/State of Origin |
|---|---|---|---|---|---|---|---|---|
| 31 | Jaya | SN | 30 | Married, Only Woman | Nuclear | Hindu | 1–3 Yrs. School | Bihar |
| 32 | Hema | SN | 42 | Widowed, Only Woman | Woman-headed Household | Hindu | 5th grade | Uttar Pradesh |
| 33 | Bindu | SN | 29 | Married, Only Woman | Nuclear | Hindu | 4th grade | Uttar Pradesh |
| 34 | Alka | SN | 19 | Married, Only Woman | Nuclear | Hindu | 5th grade | Uttar Pradesh |
| 35 | Gita | SN | 35 | Married, Only Woman | Nuclear | Hindu | Never in school | Bihar |
| 36 | Lakshmi | SN | 26 | Married, Only Woman | Nuclear | Hindu | Never in school | Bihar |
| 37 | Lalita | SN | 27 | Married, Only Woman | Nuclear | Hindu | Never in school | Bihar |
| 38 | Shabnam | SN | 20 | Married, Only Woman | Nuclear + In-Laws | Muslim | 1–3 Yrs. School | Bihar |
| 39 | Shobha | SN | 31 | Married, Only Woman | Nuclear | Hindu | Never in school | Uttar Pradesh |
| 310 | Mamta | SN | 35 | Married, Only Woman | Nuclear | Hindu | Never in school | Uttar Pradesh |
| 311 | Pushpa | SN | 37 | Married, Only Woman | Nuclear + In-Laws | Hindu | Never in school | Uttar Pradesh |
| 312 | Protima | SN | 25 | Married, Only Woman | Nuclear | Hindu | Never in school | West Bengal |
| 313 | Medha | SN | 21 | Married, Junior Woman (Dil) | Nuclear + In-Laws | Hindu | Matriculate | Bihar |
| 314 | Ganga | SN | 30 | Married, Only Woman | Nuclear | Hindu | Never in school | Punjab |
| 315 | Parvati | SN | 50 | Widowed, Senior Woman (Mil) | Woman-headed Household | Hindu | 10th grade | Nepal |
| 316 | Shanti | SN | 20 | Married, Only Woman | Nuclear + Brothers | Hindu | 5th grade | Bihar |
| 317 | Sushila | SN | 25 | Married, Only Woman | Nuclear + In-Laws | Hindu | 3rd grade | Bihar |
| 318 | Durga | SN | 28 | Married, Only Woman | Nuclear | Hindu | Never in school | West Bengal |
| 319 | Parveen | SN | 27 | Married, Junior Woman (D) | Joint (Uxorilocal) | Muslim | 5th grade | Uttar Pradesh |
| 320 | Pramila | SN | 33 | Married, Only Woman | Nuclear | Hindu | Never in school | Uttar Pradesh |
| 321 | Reena | SN | 18 | Single, Junior Woman (D) | Nuclear | Hindu | 3rd grade | Uttar Pradesh |
| 322 | Paro | SN | 33 | Married, Only Woman | Nuclear + Brothers | Hindu | 5th grade | Bihar |
| 323 | Shipra | SN | 25 | Married, Only Woman | Nuclear | Hindu | 1–3 Yrs. School | West Bengal |
| 324 | Champa | SN | 29 | Married, Only Woman | Nuclear | Hindu | Never in school | Uttar Pradesh |
| 325 | Deepa | SN | 20 | Married, Junior Woman (Dil) | Joint | Hindu | Never in school | Uttar Pradesh |
| 326 | Preeti | SN | 22 | Married, Junior Woman (Dil) | Nuclear + In-Laws | Hindu | Never in school | Uttar Pradesh |
| 327 | Radha | SN | 32 | Married, Only Woman | Nuclear | Hindu | Never in school | Uttar Pradesh |
| 328 | Meena | SN | 22 | Married, Only Woman | Nuclear | Hindu | Never in school | Bihar |
| 329 | Sushma | SN | 28 | Married, Only Woman | Nuclear | Hindu | 1-3 Yrs. School | Uttar Pradesh |
| 330 | Maya | SN | 45 | Married, Senior Woman (Mil) | Joint | Hindu | Never in school | Uttar Pradesh |

Demographic Profiles and Property Ownership of Interview Respondents (continued)

| Interview # | Paying Work Reported | Income (Rs.) | H's Occupation | Family Income (Rs.) | # Sons | # Daughters | # Brothers | # Sisters | Own Property |
|---|---|---|---|---|---|---|---|---|---|
| 31 | Shop | 400 | Vending | 2650 | 1 | 2 | 3 | 0 | 1 Jhuggi |
| 32 | Vending, Daily Labor | 1250 | Weaver | 1250 | 4 | 2 | 5 | 3 | 2 Jhuggis |
| 33 | Shop, Home-Based Sewing | Not Known | Shop, Transportation | 1200 | 4 | 1 | 3 | 2 | 2 Jhuggis |
| 34 | None | None | Shop | 2500 | 0 | 0 | 4 | 2 | None |
| 35 | Shop | 1350 | Construction | 3000 | 2 | 0 | 2 | 2 | 1 Jhuggi |
| 36 | None | None | Daily Labor | 1000 | 0 | 3 | 5 | 1 | None |
| 37 | None | None | Transportation | 1001 | 3 | 1 | 0 | 0 | 1 Jhuggi |
| 38 | None | None | Daily Labor | 2700 | 3 | 0 | 2 | 4 | None |
| 39 | Coal-selling | Not Known | Vending | 1800 | 2 | 3 | 4 | 2 | 1 Jhuggi |
| 310 | None | None | Daily Labor | 1350 | 3 | 1 | | | 1 Jhuggi, <1 bigha U |
| 311 | None | None | Service | 1001 | 2 | 2 | 2 | 3 | None |
| 312 | Coal-selling | Not Known | Vending | 1800 | 2 | 1 | 3 | 1 | None |
| 313 | Teacher/Community Worker | 900 | Transportation | 2800 | 0 | 3 | 3 | 1 | None |
| 314 | None | None | Politics, Community Work | 3000 | 2 | 4 | 1 | 3 | 1 Jhuggi |
| 315 | Agriculture/Community Worker | Not Known | Service | 3000 | 5 | 0 | 5 | 0 | 3 Jhuggis |
| 316 | None | None | Transportation | 3350 | 0 | 0 | 5 | 2 | 1 Jhuggi |
| 317 | None | None | Floor Polisher | 900 | 1 | 0 | 0 | 2 | None |
| 318 | None | None | Auto Repair | 1500 | 1 | 1 | 2 | 1 | 1 Jhuggi |
| 319 | Home-Based Sewing | Not Known | Vending | 1800 | 2 | 3 | 3 | 3 | None |
| 320 | None | None | Govt. Service | 2000 | 3 | 3 | 4 | 4 | None |
| 321 | Student | None | N/A | 900 | 0 | 0 | 2 | 2 | None |
| 322 | None | None | Transportation/None | 200 | 2 | 1 | 2 | 3 | 1 Jhuggi |
| 323 | Coal-selling | Not Known | Vending | 1000 | 0 | 2 | 1 | 2 | None |
| 324 | None | None | Factory Worker | 700 | 3 | 1 | 1 | 1 | None |
| 325 | None | None | Govt. Contractor/None | 2000 | 0 | 0 | 1 | 2 | None |
| 326 | None | None | Auto Repair | 2250 | 2 | 0 | 1 | 2 | None |
| 327 | None | None | Vending | 3501 | 3 | 1 | 4 | 1 | None |
| 328 | None | None | Transportation | 1501 | 0 | 2 | 0 | 2 | 2 bighas R |
| 329 | None | None | Service (Printing press) | 3000 | 2 | 1 | 2 | 1 | 1 LIG Flat |
| 330 | None | None | Govt. Service | 2100 | 2 | 1 | 1 | 0 | 1 Jhuggi |

Demographic Profiles and Property Ownership of Interview Respondents (continued)

| Interview # | Couple's Property | In-laws' Property | Parents' Property | Abbreviations Used |
|---|---|---|---|---|
| 31 | 1 House, 1 Jhuggi, 1 Shop T | Unspec R | 4 Houses R, Unspec R | R = Rural Property |
| 32 | N/A | Unspec R | <1 bigha R | U = Urban Property |
| 33 | 2 Jhuggis, 1 House R, 5 bighas R | Unspec R | None | Sub U = Suburban Property |
| 34 | 1 Jhuggi, 1 Shop T | 1 House R | 3 Houses R | Unspec = Amount Unspecified |
| 35 | 2 Jhuggis, ~2 bighas R, 1 Shop T | 8 bighas R Jt. | 15–20 bighas R | LIG = Low-income Group |
| 36 | None | 1 House R | <1 bigha R Jt. | MIG = Middle-income Group |
| 37 | 1 Jhuggi | 40 bighas R, 1 House R | None | P = Permanent Structure, Formal Business |
| 38 | 2 Jhuggis | 10 bighas R | 15 bighas R | T = Temporary Structure, Informal Business |
| 39 | 1 Jhuggi | 3 Jhuggis, 5 bighas R | 1 House R | Jt. = Owned by Joint Family, Not Yet Separate |
| 310 | 1 Jhuggi, <1 bigha U | 3 Jhuggis, 1 House R, Unspec R | None | **Other Terms:** |
| 311 | 1 Jhuggi, 1 LIG Flat | 20 bighas R | 10–12 bighas R, 1 House R | Jhuggi = Hut, Shack |
| 312 | 1 Jhuggi | ~2 bigahs R | None | Bigha = 1/3 acre |
| 313 | 1 Jhuggi, 6 bighas R | 25–30 bighas R | >100 bighas R | |
| 314 | 1 Jhuggi | 60 bighas sub-U, 150–200 bighas R | 9 bighas R, 1 House R | |
| 315 | N/A | 80 bighas sub-U | 500 bighas R | |
| 316 | 1 Jhuggi, Unspec U | Unspec sub-U/ R | Unspec R (lots) | |
| 317 | 1 Jhuggi | 2–3 bighas R | None | |
| 318 | 1 Jhuggi | 10 bighas R | 1 House R | |
| 319 | 1 Jhuggi | 8 bighas R | 2 Jhuggis, 3 LIG Flats, 5 bighas sub-U | |
| 320 | 1 Jhuggi, <1 bigha R | 5 bighas R | 8–10 bighas R | |
| 321 | N/A | N/A | 1 Jhuggi, Unspec sub-U | |
| 322 | 1 Jhuggi, 5 bighas R | 20–30 bighas R | Unspec R (lots) | |
| 323 | 1 Jhuggi | 40–50 bighas R | ~30 bighas R Jt. | |
| 324 | 1 Jhuggi | 20 bighas Jt. | 5 bighas R | |
| 325 | None | 5–6 jhuggis, <1 bigha R, 2 bighas sub-U | 3 bighas R | |
| 326 | 1 Jhuggi | 2 Jhuggis, 2 Houses, Unspec R | 1 House R, Unspec R | |
| 327 | 1 Jhuggi, 8 bighas R | None | 150 bighas R Jt. | |
| 328 | 1 Jhuggi, 3 bighas R | 10 bighas R | 5 bighas R | |
| 329 | 1 Jhuggi, 1 House, 1 LIG Flat | Unspec R (lots) | 20 bighas R | |
| 330 | 1 Jhuggi | 1 House R, 1 Shop P | None | |

# Appendix B

## Demographic Survey Questionnaire
## Interview Questionnaire

### Census Survey of Neighborhood:
### Preliminary Interview

Area: _____

Interview #: _____

1. Number of people in residence: _____
2. Ages of Residents: _____
3. Family Relationships Between Residents: _____
   _____
4. Marital Statuses of Residents: _____
   _____
5. Number of years in this house: _____
6. Number of years in New Delhi area: _____
7. Is this house rented/bought/inherited: _____
8. Education of residents: _____
   _____
   _____
9. Schools attended by children: _____
   _____
   _____
10. Jobs of employed family members/sources of income: _____
    _____
    _____

241

11. Income/Income range:
    a. Family Income: _____
    b. Women's Income: _____
    c. Inherited Income:_____
12. Women's natal family occupations:

    _____
13. Ethnic/state identity: _____

    _____
14. Religion:_____

    _____
15. Would you consent to a later interview? What would be a con-
    venient time? _____

    _____
16. Other comments: _____

    _____
    _____
    _____


### Interview Questionnaire

1. To start off, what do you see as the biggest problem facing
   women in our society today? How does it apply to you? _____

   _____

2. a. Who are the various people living in this household? _____

      _____

   b. For married members, when did they come into the house-
      hold? _____

      _____

   c. Did you have a ceremony for the purpose? What happens at
      the ceremony (i.e., duration and rituals)? _____

      _____
      _____

   d. Were there any negotiations between families before the
      marriage? What was negotiated? _____

      _____
      _____

   e. How are expenses covered? _____

      _____

f. Do you get or give any money or jewelry or land because of this union? Who is this handed to? Do you know how it is then used? _____

_____

g. For household members other than immediate family: How did they come to be part of your household? How did the family unit come to be constituted the way it is now? Who made the decision? _____

_____

3. a. Have any of the marriages of household members been unsuccessful or ended? _____
   b. How was the marriage ended? _____
   c. Did you have to return or redistribute any money, land, jewelry, etc., because of the marriage ending? _____

_____

   d. Did you have to go to courts to settle the end of the marriage or the redistribution? What happened in court? _____

_____

   e. Is the woman paid maintenance even after the marriage ends? If so, for how long after the end of the marriage? Are children paid maintenance or given gifts, etc.? _____

_____

   f. If there is any land or property to be inherited, will children still inherit from both sides? _____

4. a. Within your family, who owns what property?_____

_____

   b. How did it get distributed that way? Who made the decision about how it should be distributed? _____

_____

   c. What happened to your father's property/possessions? How is your father's/parents' property going to be distributed?

_____

   d. What did the women get of his property? Who made that decision? Were you told *why*? _____

_____

_____

e. What is your reaction to this distribution of property?____
_____

5. a. Do you have/are you going to have any property or wealth in your name? _____
   b. If not, what claims do you make upon what is owned by others in your family? _____
   _____
   c. Do you have access to it now? Can you spend it/use it if needed? _____
   _____

6. a. If you suddenly need a large sum of money (specify) at short notice for medical emergencies (or for children or financial/business reasons), how would you go about getting the money? Who would you ask first? Who are the different people you would eventually ask? _____
   _____
   _____
   b. Of these, whom would you need to repay? What would be the terms of repayment in the various cases? _____
   _____

7. a. Are you responsible for or did you inherit any debts? If you are not, who is responsible for your family debts? _____
   _____
   b. How did the debt come about? _____
   _____
   c. How did it come about that you were responsible for paying it? _____
   _____

8. a. Has the distribution of property by your father/mother/parents/in-laws ever been challenged by other family members?
   _____
   b. Has property ever been left directly to women and has that been challenged? _____
   c. Have the women ever challenged not being left an equal share? _____
   d. Has the distribution of debt been challenged? _____
   e. In what ways were the problems resolved or how are they being tackled? _____
   _____

f. Did you go to anyone outside the family who could mediate the dispute? _____

9. a. Have you ever gone to the courts over any property disputes?
   _____

   b. Who made the decision to go to the courts? How and when was the decision made? _____

   c. In what way were the women of your family involved in the dispute? What would they have gained by it? _____
   _____

   d. If you were actually in court, could you describe the experience, including the questions you were asked? _____
   _____

   e. How did your larger family or neighbors view the problem and how did they think it should have been resolved?____
   _____

   f. What did they think of you resorting to the law—how did they respond? _____

10. a. Was the decision given by the court ever fully enforced?
    _____

    b. If it was, did it resolve the initial problem satisfactorily?
    _____

11. a. How do you feel about women owning land? _____
    _____

    b. How should parents distribute their property? _____
    _____

    c. Do you feel that when women are divorced by their husbands they still have a right to the husband's property? Should they get maintenance? _____

    d. In case concrete information is cited about how distributions are supposed to occur, i.e. legal rules: Where did you get that information? How did you find out about it? _____
    _____
    _____

12. a. What should women do with money or products from their land? How can women use money of their own?_____

_____

b. Should they keep it in jewelry? Why is or isn't this a useful idea?_____

_____

13. a. Earlier you said that _____ was the biggest obstacle for women in our society—what do you see as the solutions?

_____

_____

_____

b. How can one make a start toward or go about solving the problems? _____

_____

_____

c. Can the courts help in solving the problem? Can they help the most? _____

_____

d. Does one's sex and class and religion make a difference in the way that one can be helped by the law? _____

# Notes

## Chapter 1. Introduction

1. Magu (1996); U. Sharma (1980); Hershman (1981); Agarwal (1994).

2. See chapter 6, pp. 1–2.

3. Interview 1.13, KE, 12/16/91.

4. Throughout this dissertation, I use "feminist" not in any particularized "Western" sense or with reference to a specific social movement but to mean, generally, a consciousness of women's oppression within varied patriarchal structures and a commitment to strive toward removing hegemonic, and particularly gender-based, inequalities.

5. United Nations. 1985. In *The State of the World's Women 1985*, 4. Nairobi: U.N.

6. *Subaltern* is used here and elsewhere in this document in the sense popularized by the Subaltern Studies historians (e.g. Guha and Spivak 1988), denoting a social positionality and consciousness invisible and inexpressible in the hegemonic discourse of a system.

7. Patricia Caplan's study of a Tanzanian island shows that men with more opportunities to earn cash and with the benefit of inheritance laws owned more lucrative resources like coconut trees, livestock, and boats, while women mainly had access to bush or meadow land for growing crops (1984, 25–29).

8. Fortman and Nabane on state forest land in Zimbabwe (1992, 2–10).

9. Croll on postrevolutionary China (1984, 53–57); Robertson and Berger on African women, pointing to the importance of taking both formal property ownership and access to/control over resources into account (1986, 9–10).

10. Starr on Aegean Turkey (1984, 104).

11. Diwan (1991, 397–412); Parashar (1992, 212–13). Because equity principles inspired the legislation but were ultimately overridden by alleged

247

Hindu constructs of sons' spiritual and familial duties and daughters' access to *stridhan* or "women's wealth," male control of productive resources saturates the principles of the Hindu Succession Act (1956).

12. Tenancy can include permanent tenure over land with heritable and transferable rights.

13. Fruzzetti and Ostor 1990, 98; I. Singh 1989, 21–46; Sethi and Sibia 1987; Rosen 1978, 24.

14. Finley 1993; R. West 1993; Majury 1991; Eisenstein 1989; Okin 1989; Mackinnon 1987, 63–69; Kirp et al. 1986; Scales 1986; Williams 1991; Crenshaw 1989; Dalton 1987–1988.

15. Frug 1992; Kapur and Cossman 1996; Das 1996.

16. Singha 1996, 310; Rai 1995, 390; Kapur and Cossman 1996, 12–13; Das 1996.

17. Toungara 1994; S. Moore 1992; Scaglion 1990; Fruzzetti and Ostor 1990; Merry 1986; Rodman 1985; Tiffany 1983.

18. L. Gill 1994; Gledhill 1988; McRobbie 1984; Radway 1984; Kapadia 1995.

19. Oldenberg 1991; Raheja and Gold 1994; Jeffery and Jeffery 1996.

20. Concepts such as "patriarchy" and "women's oppression" are not transparent and self-evident notions but need to be historicized and particularized (Mohanty 1991, 51–80). The exploration of women's subjectivity in this book is in tune with Mohanty's contention that rather than assuming that women are always already powerless victims within "patriarchy," feminist analyses should emphasize that "women are produced through these very relations as well as being implicated in forming these relations" (Mohanty 1991, 59).

21. See chapter 6 for a detailed description of the case.

22. The stratification of class in this study follows a revised Weberian approach, using not just household income but other measures of status— viz., kind of residence, use of amenities, general occupational profile or level of education—as markers of class distinction between neighborhoods. See Giddens (1973), Cottrell (1984, 93) and Crompton (1993, 207) for important revisions of Weberian thought which bring in notions of power, politics, and multiple socioeconomic levels and cultural practices affecting class categories based on "status affiliation."

23. For example, Delphy and Leonard 1986, Sanghera and Malhana 1984; Zetkin 1984.

24. I observed repeatedly that legal aid units of urban Indian women's organizations did not like to handle property claims, which were seen as much less crucial than divorce, dowry, or maintenance cases. Organizations thus claimed to choose not to put their energies into becoming a recovery agency for relatively wealthy women.

25. Because sample surveys were conducted by choosing certain neighborhoods according to their perceived "class," there was a certain homogenization of class despite there being some overlap in occupations, family resources, and even income between the neighborhoods. However, regardless of individual cases, the households did share certain living conditions that could be assimilated as social status and power differences, giving them a different "class" profile from those living in other kinds of neighborhoods.

26. The convention of deriving women's class position from their husbands' (Goldthorpe 1983; Parsons 1954) has been trenchantly critiqued by feminist scholars who point out that women's differential access to productive resources determines their de facto class position, that derivative notions of class assume a pooling of household resources contrary to cultural practices in many societies, that women's own waged work is also a determinant of their class position, and that unpaid domestic work has a distinct mode of production and should not be ignored (Szelenyi 1992; Robertson and Berger 1986, 9–13; Delphy 1984; Walby 1986; Whitehead 1984b; J. West 1978). As Crompton's summary of gender and class debates concludes, both women's individual occupation/property and their "household class" are important indicators of their class affiliations, and either can become relevant according to circumstances (1993, 93–97).

27. The methodology is based on probability sampling rather than judgment or opportunistic sampling; while conclusions drawn about the universe on the basis of the sample may thus have a more precise statistical grounding, they cannot be universalized unless the exact relation between the sample and the larger aggregate is known (Honigmann 1982, 87). The samples may also be more opportunistic than they appear, given that rapport with the researcher or experience in dealing with strangers affected consent to interviews.

28. See Jorgensen (1990) and Snow et al. (1986) for discussions of the field role, Ahmed-Ghosh (1991) and Gurney (1985) for the particular problems encountered by women researchers, and Bhavnani (1993), Shields and Devin (1993), Hale (1991), Minister (1991), Stacey (1991), Anderson et al. (1990), Devault (1990), and Oakley (1981) for the dilemmas of getting past hierarchical socioeconomic differences between interviewer and interviewee, including the exercise of power in the interview-for-research situation.

29. According to the World Development Report, India's mid-1992 population was 883.6 million (1994, 162); Bose reports an increase in 160 million people between 1981 and 1991, and a 1991 population density of 267 persons/sq. km (1991, 47). The 1992 per capita GNP is $310, eighteenth in ascending order among all nations, even though the 1992 GDP is a relatively hefty $214,598 million, twenty-first in descending order (World Development Report 1994, 162–66). The discrepancy is attributed to over-population and prominence of the agrarian sector in conventional economics, but Marxists and feminists have pointed to the unequal distribution of wealth and resources and the selective repressive underdevelopment of certain groups as causes of widespread poverty and deprivation. In terms of "quality of life" indicators considered important for research on gender, the 1991 sex ratio was 929 females to 1000 males, the 1991 female literacy rate was 39.42 percent as compared to a male rate of 63.86 percent (Bose 1991, 47), and the female share of the labor force in 1992 was 25 percent (World Development Report 1994, 218, not including informal sector labor). The imbalance in these figures indicates the possibility of the existence of strong patriarchal relations, although social class and urbanization may be the greatest barriers to equal opportunity.

30. Given the number of small businesses in this area with no fixed income, monthly income is also likely to be under reported.

31. Interview in New Delhi, January 1993.

32. Op. cit.

33. Several studies of women in squatter colonies in Delhi (Fernandes 1990; N. Sharma 1985; Karlekar 1982) show that women's work largely brings in subsistence wages and little class mobility, but that women have knowledge of civic, political, and legal rights. Urbanization for women is alternately portrayed as creating greater seclusion and alienation on the one hand, and as leading to a better standard of living including fewer restrictions on movement and veiling on the other.

34. The sociological entity known as the Indian "joint family" is multi-generational and with numerous branches, including married brothers, their wives, children, and parents (or some married brothers, etc., plus unmarried brothers and sisters) living in a common household. Customarily, within the joint family, males acquired rights to the common family property at birth, and distant relatives and dependents including widowed or single women had usufructuary or maintenance rights and were supposed to get financial and social "protection." However, as shown in chapter 4, nowadays common households where all brothers and their families live together, or pay maintenance for dependents, is quite rare, and the notion of the joint family is more of a legal and tax convenience for male

heirs (Diwan 1991, 322–85). Except for joint ownership of ancestral property, lineage-based alliances and ties are feeble, and the interests of the nuclear family are usually predominant. Some scholars have contended that because of the confusion between legal and sociological definitions of the "joint family," the multigenerational household unit should be more accurately called the "joint household" (Goody and Tambiah 1973, 75; Hershman 1981, 59–60).

35. As Hennessy warns in her review of feminist standpoint theory, claims to "women's" knowledge on the grounds of experience (based on biology or social positionality) are essentialist unless a materialist analysis is juxtaposed with identity-based epistemology (1993, 67–74).

## Chapter 2. Women and Property Inheritance

1. 1 bigha = approx. 1/3 acre = approx. 1613 sq. yards.

2. While many women claimed to have little idea of general property values, they had a much better sense of how much they had spent on buying and acquiring immediate (nuclear) family property (though less idea of how much their in-laws' or parents' property was worth).

3. Interview 1.9, KE, 12/10/91. In the new residential areas being developed in the now-suburbs, a three-bedroom flat in an upper middle-class area designated to be very "modern" was selling in 1994 at Rs. 3,000,000 (approx. $100,000 at the 1991–92 exchange rate).

4. Interview 2.2, KC, 2/4/92.

5. Interview 3.1, SN, 12/7/92. Several of those who were evicted from their *jhuggis* and given LIG flats had sold those flats (Pramila's flat sold for Rs. 35,000, and the sum was used to buy rural orchard land at about Rs. sixty thousand per bigha). Direct *monetary* compensation from the city for evictions was much less, at Rs. 500/unit.

6. The anthropological terms *virilocal, uxorilocal,* and *neolocal* refer to the site of a married couple's residence: couples residing virilocally live with the husband's family, those living uxorilocally live with the wife's family, and those living neolocally set up a new residence not connected to either family following marriage.

7. However, in the total sample, there is a moderately good correlation between age and ownership of property (correlation coefficient 0.38, p-value 0.0028); i.e., women's chances of owning property increased with age, regardless of class.

8. Interview 3.20, SN, 12/30/92.

9. Interview 1.2, KE, 12/3/91.

10. Interview 2.1, KC, 2/3/92.

11. Interview 2.12, KC, 2/17/92.

12. Interview 2.2, KC, 2/4/92.

13. Interview 1.3, KE, 12/4/91.

14. Interview 1.10, KE, 12/11/91.

15. Interview 3.29, SN, 1/8/93.

16. Interview 3.9, SN, 12/14/92; Interview 3.1, SN, 12/7/92.

17. Interview 3.28, SN, 1/7/93.

18. As Table 1.8 shows, a large number of KE women were in the paid labor force as teachers, doctors, lawyers, scientists, and designers.

19. Moors demonstrates how modes of property ownership vary substantially by socioeconomic status and have different consequences in times of social disruption. In her sample of Palestinian women, wealthier families often had more money invested in banks and shares than in land or gold, and could also obtain better jobs abroad by virtue of better education and professional experience, which made them far less vulnerable to political unrest (1995, 44).

20. McCauliff on medieval England (1992); Herlihy on medieval northern Europe (1985); Klapisch-Zuber on Renaissance Italy (1985). Crummey makes a similar case for the Ethiopian Amhara between 1750 and 1850 (1982).

21. Erickson's research on early modern England (1993); Spaulding (1982) and Crummey (1982) on the eighteenth- and nineteenth-century Sinnar and Amhara Ethiopian communities respectively.

22. Agarwal 1994, 146; Croll 1984, 52–53; Pinea-Cabral 1984, 81–84; Starr 1984, 101.

23. Hershman's (1981, 70–75) and U. Sharma's (1980, 47–74) research on Punjab and Himachal Pradesh also show that property was predominantly distributed among male kin, while daughters were usually asked to sign away their rights, and even widows had a difficult time getting a separate share.

24. Interview 2.8, KC, 2/11/92; Interview 1.9, KE, 12/10/91.

25. Interview 3.17, SN, 12/28/92.

26. Interview 2.11, KC, 2/12/92.

27. Interview 2.4, KC, 2/6/92; Interview 3.24, SN, 1/5/93.

28. Interview 3.7, SN, 12/11/92; Interview 2.14, KC, 2/18/92.

29. Interview 2.6, KC, 2/7/92.

30. Interview 3.9, SN, 12/14/92; Interview 3.17, SN, 2/28/92.

31. Chowdhry 1994, 271–72; U. Sharma 1980, 53–55; Wadley 1995, 99. Senior women's power may be eroded with the death of their husbands (Wadley 1995, 99; Jeffery and Jeffery 1996, 245).

32. Interview 3.24, SN, 1/5/93.

33. Interview 2.9, KC, 2/11/92.

34. 36.7 percent women reported parents owning at least five bighas of land, as compared to 53.3 percent women claiming this about in-laws. In 10 percent cases parents owned more than one hundred bighas but only 3.3 percent women reported in-laws doing so; however, 26.7 percent in-laws owned ten to one hundred bighas while 16.7 percent parents did so.

35. Interview 2.5, KC, 2/6/92.

36. Interview 3.8, SN, 12/12/92.

37. Interview 3.19, SN, 12/27/92.

38. White (1993, 129–35) shows Muslim women's disinheritance from family property in Bangladesh.

39. Croll on China (1984); Burman on South Africa (1984); Merry, using African, particularly Zambian examples (1982); E. Moore on Rajasthan, India (1993); Toungara on the Ivory Coast (1994).

40. One needs to be careful about implying that resource distribution in kinship-based systems was inherently more fair, because women were deprived of access to property or power in many such milieus. As White-head asserts (1984a, 185), systems based on kinship do *not* imply relations of equality. However, it can be generally stated that in societies where land was communally owned, family members could get maintenance, and where cash was not the crucial path to resources, women's vulnerability was likely to be much less.

41. Many examples of this are from Africa: Oboler (1982, 13–17); P. Caplan (1984); Westwood (1984, 141–42). Westwood concludes that women can be far more empowered through wages and productive work than looking to property or the household (1984, 155).

42. If Islamic law can be enforced, for instance, women have inalienable legal rights to inheritance even though they are constrained by getting half-shares compared to brothers, a solid legal claim as opposed to usufructuary dependence (Agarwal 1994, 227–28; P. Caplan 1984, 32–33; Starr 1984, 101–103; however, White 1993, 129–35 refutes this notion).

43. Because death duties related to property are substantial in India, premortem gifts to the person likely to live longer than the current property owner—e.g., the younger spouse or a child—are generally a common device to avoid paying those taxes.

44. Interview 2.13, KC, 2/17/92.

45. Interview 3.14, SN, 12/24/92.

46. Interview 2.13, KC, 2/17/92.

47. Interview 3.23, SN, 1/4/93.

48. United Nations. 1985. In *The State of the World's Women 1985*, 4. Nairobi: U.N.

## Chapter 3. Gifts for Alliance

1. Perhaps the foremost proponent of this approach, Marcel Mauss, suggested that gift giving structures the formation of crucial social links (1967, 69–81). Mauss claimed that gifts were neither entirely "spontaneous" nor "disinterested" (1967, 71), but that they facilitated cultural relations deliberately and metonymically.

2. Levi-Strauss ([1949] 1969, 233–34, 466–67); Dumont (1983, 103); Meillassoux (1981, 64, 78). Gayle Rubin contends (1975, 174–76) that women in marriage often function not just as vehicles of transferring property among groups through marriage but as property themselves (though the value of their labor and status differs widely).

3. See Kaplan (1985) for accounts from European history, Watson and Ebrey (1991) for accounts from Chinese history. There is contradictory evidence about the relationship between the rise of capitalism and the significance of dowries: some scholars contend that dowry disappeared with the rise of capitalist relations because individuals could establish an independent fund through wages, and family property was no longer as crucial (Kaplan 1985, 2–6; Nazzari 1991), resulting however in a weakening of women's power within the family and women's dependency on the

male "family" wage; others claim that men's access to wages and entry into capitalist relations have brought about increases in dowry and a lowering of women's status (e.g., Heyer 1992; Kapadia 1993; Moors 1995).

4. The most influential proponents of this approach are Goody and Tambiah (1973), who characterized dowry as the woman's equitable share of property that was given to her at marriage, over which she had some measure of control, and which often served as a starting economic base for the couple. Numerous scholars (Agarwal 1994, 134–40; Bossen 1988, 140; Ebrey 1991, 3–4; Schlegel and Eloul 1988, 301–303; U. Sharma 1994, 351–52) and Tambiah himself (1989, 425–26) question the relevance of this definition in the North Indian context. Tambiah points to evidence such as the difference in dowries between sisters and variations according to the status of the groom. Tambiah's revised concept is that the Indian model of dowry may best be visualized as "double transmission" (not equal) of property through sons and daughters, with the woman's dowry/property share contributing to the joint family unit and coming to the conjugal unit only if joint family resources are divided (1989, 426). Furthermore, such dowry may be viewed as the means by which the groom's family acquires upward socioeconomic mobility.

5. Interview 2.14, KE, 2/24/92.

6. Interview 1.11, KE, 12/13/91.

7. Sprecher and Chandak (1992) and Sharma and Shriram (1979) also found religion, class, and community homogeneity to be most important in their studies of attitudes. In the study by Sprecher and Chandak, caste was considered important by a significant number of respondents, but also deemed irrelevant by a large number (1992, 64). However, it is important to remember that in colloquial use, "caste" may refer to the subcommunity or *jati* rather than broad meta-"caste" or *varna*, i.e., people may focus on jati compatibility as a primary criterion. Subcommunity and ethnicity (rather than caste) rank very high as parameters of choice, although they may be overridden in favor of compatible standards of living or class status (Chanana 1993).

8. The data revealed no significant difference in modes of arranging marriages over time. Among the forty-two weddings for which information on modes of arrangement was reported, 66.6 percent of which had taken place within the last ten years and 33.3 percent between ten and twenty years ago, there was an *exactly identical* proportion of the different paths of arranging weddings: 57.1 percent through relatives or extended kin; 14.3 percent through neighbors; 14.3 percent through friends or acquaintances. The only two reported cases of finding matches through newspapers were

reported to be in the previous decade, but in the decade before that the use of a marriage broker was reported, a function possibly taken over by media sources in contemporary times.

9. Interview 3.13a, SN, 2/24/92; Interview 2.7, KC, 2/7/92. While in these two examples the giving of brides/grooms was unidirectional, indicating the potential for hypergyny, in other cases there was reciprocal exchange of brides and grooms among affines.

10. Interview 2.14, KC, 2/18/92; Interview 2.9, KC, 2/11/92.

11. As kin networks get more and more attenuated with regional and even worldwide migration, other strategies are used to search for endogamous partners. Chanana (1993) found that for middle-class Punjabi families who had migrated to Delhi from Pakistan, friends and business associates had begun to play especially important roles in marriages as community connections became distant. The matrimonial sections of U.S.-based newspapers on India and even cyber services continue to seek matches in terms of narrow age, employment, skin color, gender attribute, and caste/community parameters. An instance: "Hi Netters: I am looking for a good-humored Tamil Iyer girl for a friend of mine who is 28 years old, 5'7", and currently working in the U.K. on an assignment from India. He has a BE in Computer Science and an MBA from IIM Bangalore. The girl should be between 22 and 26 years old and be prepared to travel around the world as his job demands" (India News Network, June 1995). Note that in addition to caste and ethnic restrictions (and the need for "good humor"!), the qualifying age and travel requirement establish the primacy of the man's power and career aspirations.

12. Paul (1986, 188) also found that dowry was less in self-arranged marriages, although not absent as in this one.

13. Sikh place of worship.

14. Interview 2.1, KC, 2/3/92.

15. While it is relatively rare, cases of brothers or other relatives accepting money to give their sisters in marriage have been documented (often the "buyers" are grooms who also have disadvantages in the marriage market, Jeffery and Jeffery 1996, 231–44). In such marriages, women often lose most connections with natal kin and get no natal property, but these marriages are still viewed by them and their families as a preferable, respectable option as compared to the practice of selling women into prostitution.

16. According to Apte, the main "Hindu marriage rites" are "'grasping of hands' (*panigrahana*), 'stepping on the stone' (*asmarohana*), 'circum-

ambulations around the holy fire' (*agniparinanyana*), 'offering of roasted grains' (*lajahoma*) and 'walking together seven steps' (*saptapadi*)" (419).

17. Ceremonies like chunni charhana (most common among Punjabis) and ring ceremony were more prevalent in KC and KE, whereas residents of SN were much more likely to give gifts as tika or tilak. The differences could be attributed both to regional/ethnic customs (there were no Punjabis in SN), as well as relative wealth, most chunni charhana and ring ceremonies being elaborate and expensive affairs.

18. Only 42.9 percent women from KE, 25 percent from KC and 13.3 percent from SN mentioned such occasions, indicating that such receptions were usually undertaken when the groom's family was perceived to be prosperous and were thus a marker of status.

19. Gowna was found only in SN, where most women had married at a prepubertal (or, at most, teen) age and stayed on at their natal home for a few years after the wedding till they were more grown up, unlike in KE and KC where they usually married as adults and moved into the affinal home directly after the wedding. However, the most relevant factors for observance of gowna were ethnicity and rural versus urban residence rather than age at marriage per se. Gowna was most common among rural families at all socioeconomic levels from Bihar, the Uttar Pradesh plains and Rajasthan, but was dying out in cases where the bride was raised in the city and married into an urban family. In the weddings that were being negotiated in SN while I worked there, the brides were usually in their mid to late teens (i.e., they were much younger than brides in the other neighborhoods who were usually married in their early twenties), but were marrying substantially later than their mothers or rural female cousins, and moving directly into the affinal home rather than waiting out puberty in their natal home.

20. Number of ceremonies per wedding were added up here, and synonyms for wedding ceremonies were not counted separately.

21. Interview 1.6, KE, 12/7/91; Interview 1.14, KE, 2/24/92.

22. Interview 3.1, SN, 12/7/92; Interview 3.13a, SN, 12/23/92. There was no significant difference in the number of rural versus urban weddings with more than three ceremonies, viz. between KE/KC weddings (mostly urban) and SN weddings (mostly rural).

23. The cultural borderlines between Punjabi Hindus and Sikhs are very thin, bordering on nonexistent. Many families have members from both "sides," and adhere to religious practices of both faiths.

24. Mehr is the woman's fund of resources, her financial reserve to get her through crises like breakdown of marriage. It may be "prompt," i.e.,

payable after the wedding, or "deferred," i.e., payable after divorce or upon widowhood.

25. Other kinds of prestations include payments from the groom's family to the bride's (and thence to the bride), such as the mehr among Muslims, known as "indirect dowry," and gifts to the groom's relatives from the bride's family, sometimes classed as "groomprice."

26. Billig 1992; Kapadia 1993; V Rao 1993.

27. Kanyadan is literally "the gift of a virgin daughter," and a wedding including this rite is viewed as the most prestigious of the eight kinds of weddings described in ancient Hindu texts (Verghese 1980, 6; Paul 1986, 6).

28. Dumont (1983) pointed out that because Hindu marriages including kanyadan were also ideally "hypergamous" (hypergynous) for women, there was a hierarchy between bride-givers and bride-takers and women were circulated only in one direction, making gifts to the groom and family a compensation and also a payment to acquire higher status. The North Indian practice of kanyadan is typically associated with high payments to grooms' families and patrilineal inheritance.

29. Madan delineates *stridhanam* as "a *substitute* for women's *lack* of rights of inheritance" and in a different modality from inheritance (1975, 237, emphasis mine).

30. The principle of reciprocity is much stronger in South Indian Hindu communities, where cross-kin marriages are prevalent and alienation of the bride after marriage is less of an issue (Srinivas 1984, 8–10; Bradford 1985).

31. Interview 2.1, KC, 2/3/92.

32. Interview 3.13a, SN, 12/23/92.

33. The exception was Shashi, who recalled her daughters' weddings in the 1950s costing between Rs. 50,000 and 70,000 (Interview 2.7, KC, 2/7/92).

34. Interview 2.14, KE, 2/24/92.

35. Interview 2.14, KE, 2/24/92.

36. A tabulation of gifts over time indicated that while the value and quality of goods had increased over the decades, the kinds of gifts had not changed significantly over time. Gifts of clothing or jewelry to the grooms' extended families were reported in 53.5 percent weddings in the last decade, 50 percent of weddings ten to twenty years ago, and 45.5 percent weddings twenty to forty years ago. Even with regard to modern items like TVS, VCRs, or other appliances, which would be expected to increase much

more in recent weddings, they were reportedly given in 17.9 percent wed-dings in the last decade, 14.3 percent weddings ten to twenty years ago, and 9 percent (only one reported case) in weddings twenty to forty years ago. Furniture was reported as a gift in 30.4 percent of weddings in the last decade, and 39.3 percent weddings ten to twenty years ago. Grooms' families had allegedly made gifts of clothing and/or jewelry to the bride in 41 percent of weddings in the last decade, 42.9 percent of weddings ten to twenty years ago, and 45.5 percent of weddings twenty to forty years ago.

37. Information provided here by the respondents is based on their experiences of being part of weddings as the bride's family, the groom's family, or both. Their knowledge may be gained from being brides, moth-ers, or sisters, but they refer to concrete instances from weddings in which they have been closely involved. Actual gifts are counted, not their ideas of what ought to be given.

38. Interview 3.15, SN, 12/25/92.

39. Most studies of North Indian dowries enumerate similar categories of prestations: (a) the bride's personal items, viz. clothing and jewelry; (b) household items, e.g., furniture, vessels, appliances for "setting up the household," often used in the joint household; (c) gifts of clothing and jewelry for the groom and his extended kin, including large cash payments in some cases; and (d) the bride's family's expenses for feeding/entertain-ing the wedding party (Paul 1986: 31–33; L. Caplan 1994: 368; Teja 1993: 61; Hershman 1981: 244–46; Tambiah 1989: 425–26).

40. Many studies of dowry in the urban environment have, however, reported the prevalence of substantial cash gifts, (Teja 1993; Paul 1986).

41. Interview 1.9, KE, 12/10/91.

42. Interview 1.11, KE, 12/13/91.

43. Interview 3.2, SN, 12/8/92.

44. A contrary example is that of the wealthy Kannadiga Lingayats, whose alliances apparently bear no traces of hypergyny, where grooms' families spend lavishly for entertainment while brides' families pay a hefty "groom fee"; Bradford argues that the groom fee in these cases creates an indebtedness that is compensated by the grooms' families' expenses (1985, 293).

45. Bradford 1985; Dumont 1983; Kolenda 1984; Kumari 1989; Paul 1986.

46. In contemporary India, weddings appear to be crucially important as displays of status for both sides (more so among the nouveau riche).

Paul contends that *izzat* (honor/prestige) is demonstrated through a marriage alliance, and that dowry is a "mechanism of actualization" thereof (1986, 187).

47. Interview 1.2, KE, 12/3/91.

48. Bossen (1988) points out the gender-blindness of the very definitions of dowry, bridewealth and brideservice commonly used by anthropologists such as Levi-Strauss, Dumont, and Comaroff, which assume that exchanges take place between groups of men and measure loss of labor and resources from men's perspective, while the benefits or burdens to women remain invisible.

49. Jethmalani 1985; McCoid 1989; Shukla 1987.

50. Basu 1985; Carroll 1991; Palriwala 1989.

51. In M. Sandhu's comparative study (1988), the giving of dowry was not connected to women's work status (i.e., economic independence made no difference). Teja (1993, 97) also found a low association between women's economic independence and favorable attitudes to dowry.

52. However, it is important to remember that many families with no explicit demands at the time of the wedding may later harass brides for inadequate dowry (Kumari 1989).

53. Bhachu shows this in the case of British women of Sikh origin (1993); Teja for employed women in Chandigarh (1993); Paul a selection of families who have migrated to Delhi (1986, 189); Nadagouda et al. married women in Dharwad city (1992); and M. Sandhu (1988) and Teja (1993, 69) a combination of married women who were in and outside paid work.

54. In Teja's study, for example, women claimed "love and affection for the daughter" to be the most important reason for parents to give dowry even when it was not demanded (1993, 79–81).

55. The pleasure in gifts is not necessarily naive. Raheja's analysis of songs indicates that women saw gifts from the natal family as signs of love, but that they were also aware of the "power relations" that framed the gift giving (1995, 51).

56. See Jeffery and Jeffery (1996, 69–70) for other situations where few marriages were not accompanied by dowries, whether there had been demands for dowry or not.

57. Interview 1.14, KE, 2/24/92.

58. Interview 2.6, KC, 2/7/92.

59. Interview 3.17, SN, 12/28/92.

60. Interview 1.9, KE, 12/10/91.

61. Interview 2.14, KC, 2/18/92.

62. Interview 3.22, SN, 1/4/93.

63. Interview 3.30, SN, 1/8/93.

64. The groom's occupational and educational standing and/or his family's wealth are also seen to set the "rate" in other studies; e.g., Kapadia 1993, Billig 1992; Paul 1986, 186. However, the bride's relative attributes also influence the equation (e.g., Ahmed and Naher 1987, 190–91). U. Sharma found that the groom's family's expectations rather than the bride's family's property/wealth set the standard for dowry, further confirming the lack of equivalence between dowry and property (1980, 47–48).

65. Interview 1.9, KE, 12/10/91.

66. Interview 3.5, SN, 12/9/92.

67. Interview 3.13b, SN, 2/24/92.

68. Similarly Jeffery and Jeffery (1996, 128).

69. Interview 3.19, SN, 12/27/92. Moors describes similar ideas about mehr as the sale of women (1995, 108).

70. In Moors's study, dower or mehr/mahr was still regarded as a primary source of women's property. However, women's dower varied substantially by class and educational background, and token dowers were often regarded as modern and tasteful in the urban context. Moreover, Moors found that the content of consumption goods in the dower had grown, and that the money could be used by the women's relatives or become the basis of a conjugal fund rather than being put aside for the woman (1995, 87–148).

71. 42.9 percent respondents from KE, 85.7 percent from KC and 90 percent from SN said that women held on to most of their own jewelry and personal items. The apparently lower percentage from KE does not imply that in-laws kept the women's jewelry in those cases, because responses claiming that in-laws kept the jewelry are no higher from KE than from KC, and are lower than from SN. Rather, several respondents were unresponsive, either because they had not been married or had no clear account of what happened.

72. In Teja's study in Chandigarh, too, 84.8 percent of women individually held on to or were free to use their own jewelry/clothing (1993, 67); U. Sharma also confirms women's control of personal items like clothing and jewelry (1980, 50–52).

73. The total number of daughters'/women's weddings considered here was sixty-seven (fifteen from KE, nineteen from KC, and thirty-three from SN), and the total number of sons' weddings was thirty (nine from KE, seven from KC, and thirteen from SN). Categories of payers are not mutually exclusive.

74. Interview 3.22, SN, 1/4/93.

75. Interview 3.17, SN, 12/28/92.

76. Interview 3.1, SN, 12/7/92.

77. Interview 3.19, SN, 12/27/92.

78. Interview 2.2, KC, 2/4/92.

79. Interview 2.9, KC, 2/11/92.

80. Interview 2.14, KC, 2/18/92.

81. Interview 1.7, KE, 12/9/91; Interview 1.2, KE, 12/3/91.

82. Interview 2.10, KC, 2/12/92.

83. Interview 2.2, KC, 2/4/92.

84. Interview 3.12, SN, 12/22/92.

85. Paul also claims that keeping affines happy and hence ensuring that the daughter stays content is one of the main functions of dowry, alongside its functions as partial transfer of resources to the daughter and showcase of her natal family's status (1986, 33).

## Chapter 4. "Wo Ayee Hak Lene"/"There She Comes to Take Her Rights"

1. See Raheja (1995, 27) for similar ideologies about women taking too much from their natal families.

2. The Urdu *hak* can be translated as "right," both in the sense of legal rights and in the sense of true or correct.

3. A similar tension persists in English in the pun on *right*, and the closeness between *property* and *propriety*, both of which (according to the *Oxford Dictionary of English Etymology*) are derived from the Latin *proprius* meaning "one's own, special, peculiar"; thus, property is that which rightfully belongs to one, but there are certain right/proper paths to get it, and in a parallel sense, propriety or doing the right thing can bring rights to social capital/property.

4. In Moors's sample, brotherless daughters and older widows with adult sons often laid claim to natal and affinal property respectively. Women from wealthy families, the single and elderly, those who got maternal property, and who got premortem gifts from fathers were most likely to receive property (1995, 53–74).

5. In Sethi and Sibia's study of rural Jat women, 87.5 percent women were aware of changes in Indian property law but two-thirds were unfavorably inclined toward women availing of those rights. The only favorable responses to women taking property were from women who had more than a high school education, but even 60 percent of women in that group did not agree that women should take property. Sethi and Sibia attribute this pattern to a "strong force of tradition" (1987, 107–11).

6. Interview 3.21, SN, 12/30/92.

7. Interview 3.28, SN, 1/7/93.

8. Interview 3.22, SN, 1/4/93.

9. Interview 1.11, KE, 12/13/91.

10. Interview 2.14, KE, 2/24/92.

11. Interview 1.10, KE, 12/11/91.

12. From the film *Neel Kamal* (1968) directed by Ram Maheswari. Music director: Ravi; Lyrics: Sahir Ludhyanvi; Singer: Mohammed Rafi. The song originally accompanies scenes of a bride leaving her natal home, but appears as a refrain later in the movie when she begins to suffer at her in-laws' house; that is, the representation of the song in the film marks both the ideology of severance and its inherent pitfalls.

13. See U. Sharma (1980, 137) and Chanana (1993) for a further discussion on the significance of wedding songs. The ideology of the woman's severance from the natal family has been documented in various studies (Sax 1991, 77–81; Raheja and Gold 1994, 83–85; Jacobson 1977, 264–65).

14. Jacobson 1977, 276–77; Sax 1991, 83–98. Raheja and Gold analyze how some Uttar Pradesh women subvert proverbs and songs to critique and resist patriarchal kinship norms (1994, 74–104), pointing to women's depth of love for their natal families and widespread skepticism about their affines.

15. Bharti, a married woman with two brothers, Interview 1.7, KE, 12/9/91.

16. Interview 3.19, SN, 12/27/92.

17. These signed releases sealed the woman's refusal of property even where the brother did not fulfil his part of a specific bargain. See, for example, Shipra's situation described in chapter 2.

18. Hershman narrates that an old Sikh man told him that the brother-sister relationship represented true love, as opposed to the husband-wife relationship, which had to deal with everyday economic matters. However, Hershman also repeats a common jest of the area that brothers had become more carefully attentive to sisters since the laws changed, showing that people were often well aware of the conflicting economic interests of brothers and sisters, and chose to manipulate it using the emotional dimension (1981, 175–91).

19. Interview 1.9, KE, 12/10/91. Rani had one brother and her husband had no sisters, and claimed to have no disputes in their families.

20. Interview 3.28, SN, 1/7/93.

21. Interview 3.17, SN, 12/28/92.

22. Interview 3.13b, SN, 12/24/92; Interview 3.3, SN, 12/8/92.

23. Interview 2.2, KC, 2/4/92; Interview 2.12, KC, 2/17/92; Interview 2.9, KC, 2/11/92.

24. Hershman 1981, 63; U. Sharma 1980, 183. Sharma points that even when women do quarrel, it is usually about their husbands' shares; i.e. their greed can only be second hand.

25. Interview 3.13b, SN, 12/24/92.

26. Raheja (1995, 51) provides an example of a song graphically articulating this fear.

27. Interview 3.11, SN, 12/21/92.

28. Interview 3.20, SN, 12/30/92.

29. Interview 2.2, KC, 2/4/92.

30. Interview 1.2, KE, 12/3/91.

31. In the rural areas, the natal home is literally a much freer and more comfortable place for women, because (even married) daughters do not have to veil themselves or not speak to elders or nonfamily like daughters-in-law. Besides, the load of domestic work is usually negligible while they are visiting, although in some cases daughters specifically come home to help with crops. U. Sharma (1980, 19) also shows the central difference between natal and affinal worlds for women, an opposition not particularly significant for men.

32. Interview 3.13b, SN, 12/24/92.

33. Interview 1.14, KE, 2/24/92.

34. Interview 1.10, KE, 12/11/91; Interview 2.13, KC, 2/17/92.

35. Interview 3.9, SN, 12/14/92.

36. Interview 3.5, SN, 12/9/92.

37. In contrast to claims by scholars such as Harrell and Dickey (1985) that dowry is a different and parallel form of property transfer as compared to inheritance, U. Sharma claims that giving dowry is a convenient way of deflecting the question of inheritance, i.e., dowry is really a form of *dis*inheritance [emphasis mine], (1980, 47–48).

38. Interview 2.10, KC, 2/12/92.

39. Interview 2.13, KC, 2/17/92.

40. Interview 2.4, KC, 2/6/92.

41. Some women had multiple responses.

42. Jeffery and Jeffery (1996, 89–90) record numerous examples of women receiving help from natal families for their children's needs. In fact, cash and goods given by the natal family was cited by women as their "income" (1996, 189).

43. Interview 3.26, 1/6/93.

44. Sons were the major helpers in paying back debts where those were incurred, followed by brothers and daughters (from all the neighborhoods).

45. U. Sharma (1980, 190–92) also points to the importance of neighbors for relatively poor rural families.

46. Interview 1.12, KE, 12/14/91.

47. Interview 2.6, KC, 2/7/92.

48. Interview 2.9, KC, 2/11/92.

49. Interview 2.6, KC, 2/7/92.

50. Interview 3.1, SN, 12/7/92.

51. Interview 1.9, KE, 12/10/91. Interview 1.9, KE, 12/10/91.

52. Interview 2.1, KC, 2/3/92.

53. Five percent of the respondents said that women should try their best to compromise, and 13.3 percent said it was all right to leave if there was great misery or danger, both groups indicating that divorce should be initiated only in extreme circumstances.

54. In U. Sharma's study, women did rely on brothers for help in case of marriage breakdowns, coming back to stay with their natal kin, an important factor in their refusals of property. However, there were no cases of legal divorce (1980, 155–57).

55. Ocko (1991, 332), in his analysis of Chinese newspapers, who also found that property for women was mediated through marriage, calls marriage "social property."

56. Adoption of other blood relatives like nephews, sons-in-law, or nonrelatives within the caste as "sons" is the other primary device for securing property in the Indian context. Well-known political examples, e.g., Lord Dalhousie's "Doctrine of Lapse," which prevented sonless rulers from adopting so that their kingdoms could "lapse" into British domain, show the preference for this practice. Many Bengali folktales end with a sonless king offering the poor but deserving stranger "half the kingdom along with the princess," rather than the princess herself succeeding the king.

57. Mitra (1989) on the Santals.

58. In Hindu *shastric* texts this is framed as the "appointed daughter" or putrikaputra, variously interpreted as "the daughter appointed as son" or "the son of an appointed daughter" (Agarwal 1994, 87).

59. Interview 1.14, KE, 2/24/92.

60. Interview 3.14, SN, 12/24/92.

61. In Hershman's study (1981, 79), it was usually nephews rather than sons-in-law who inherited; U. Sharma (1980, 55) found that brotherless daughters did inherit in line with the new laws, but often tended to sell the property to male cousins at a low price, thus maintaining goodwill with natal kin.

62. Interview 3.9, SN, 12/14/92.

63. Interview 3.17, SN, 12/28/92.

64. Interview 3.13b, SN, 12/24/92.

65. Interview 2.13, KC, 2/17/92.

66. Interview 2.13, KC, 2/17/92.

67. See note 58.

68. Interview 3.15, SN, 12/25/92.

69. Interview 3.18, SN, 12/28/92. Durga's mother's situation is a vivid illustration of a trend recently uncovered by researchers (Chen and Dreze

1992; Gulati 1993), that widows with even minimal property tend to be treated with more care and respect in their families as compared to widespread neglect of widows without property.

70. Interview 3.6, SN, 12/10/92.

71. Interview 2.6, KC, 2/7/92.

72. Interview 3.1, SN, 12/7/92.

73. Interview 1.14, KE, 2/24/92.

74. Interview 3.3, SN, 12/8/92.

75. Interview 3.17, SN, 12/28/92.

76. Interview 3.30, SN, 1/8/93.

77. Interview 2.11, KC, 2/12/92.

78. Wadley's research shows that the most important economic resources for women were land, which they rarely got control over, and sons, through whom they could have a place to live and eat and be protected from the ill treatment of the affines and the natal family (1995, 114). In the present study, a son often though not always took on eldercare.

79. Interview 1.11, KE, 12/13/91; Interview 2.13, KC, 2/17/92.

80. Interview 2.8, KC, 2/11/92.

81. Interview 1.5, KE, 12/5/91.

82. Interview 2.2, KC, 2/4/92.

83. Like the contested Hebrew-to-English translation of the word *virgin* in "Virgin Mary," here too the word *kanya* can mean both "young daughter" and "sexually virgin." In the case of child marriages, the meanings usually converge.

84. In some families this may be done by the maternal uncle and is a sign of the mother's family's participation.

85. As Trautmann puts it, "The idiom of *kanyadan* is the patrilineal idiom of complete dissimilation of the bride from her family of birth and her complete assimilation to that of her husband" (1981, 291).

86. Interestingly, food or drink or visits are acceptable when a grandson, the daughter's son rather than the daughter, is an earning member and the ostensible host.

87. Interview 2.1, KC, 2/3/92.

88. Interview 3.13a, SN, 12/23/92.

89. Interview 3.25, SN, 1/5/93.

90. Interview 3.13b, SN, 12/24/92.

91. In "Ideology," Hall argues that people are not necessarily passive recipients of dominant cultural norms, and posits a range of subjectivities that goes from those in complete identification with dominant ideology to those with varied negotiations to those who are entirely oppositional.

## Chapter 5. Knowing Themselves

1. Women were finally deemed to be "simultaneous heirs" in cases of intestate succession because of provisions in the new Constitution.

2. The extent and meaning of stridhan has been the subject of an ongoing debate in the courts. Some important cases are: Pratibha Rani V. Suraj Kumar AIR 1985 SC 628, Vinod Kumar Sethi V. State of Punjab AIR 1982 P&H 372, Suresh Kumar vs. Saroj Bala AIR 1988 P&H 217.

3. Interview 1.1, KE, 12/3/91.

4. The attitude of banking money as the prime means of savings showed a very small negative correlation with age, i.e., younger women were slightly more likely to trust this form of savings; the correlation coefficient is −0.12, and the P-value 0.3. On the other hand, there was a very small positive correlation between age and citing property as the prime savings mode (a correlation coefficient of 0.157 at a P-value of 0.23), i.e., women's likelihood of citing this increased with age, and a minimal positive correlation between age and naming jewelry as the prime saving (a correlation coefficient of 0.067 at a P-value of 0.61). None of these figures point to strong statistical correlations between age and attitudes toward saving.

5. Interview 3.10, SN, 12/21/92.

6. "Kitties" is the Indian English word for women's revolving credit schemes, where women put in money every month and get the whole "kitty" or total every few months depending on the total number of participants. Getting the money out of turn, for special needs or emergencies, involves a heavy forfeiture. This money is important for large household expenses and women's personal expenses. The gatherings are also significant as socially sanctioned all-women's economic networks, especially now that they have spread from wealthy groups to middle-class households and poor neighborhoods. 12.5 percent women from KC and 3.3 percent from SN said they belonged to such groups.

7. Interview 2.6, KC, 2/7/92.

8. Interview 3.3, SN, 12/8/92.

9. Interview 1.6, KE, 12/7/91.

10. Parminder, a thirty-four-year-old, married woman with no wages or property of her own, Interview 2.3, KC, 2/4/92.

11. Bina, a fifty-two-year-old, married woman who had their residential flat and a shop in her name, Interview 2.1, KE, 2/3/92.

12. Ritu, a thirty-five-year-old, married woman owning office property, Interview 1.11, KE, 12/13/91.

13. Uma, a twenty-seven-year-old, married woman working in a publishing house and planning to buy joint property with her husband, Interview 1.14, KE, 2/24/92.

14. Parveen, with a small income from home-based sewing but no jhuggi of her own, Interview 3.19, SN, 12/27/92.

15. Protima, a victim of physical and psychological abuse such as withholding household expenses, Interview 3.12, SN, 12/22/92.

16. Interview 3.8, SN, 12/12/92.

17. Interview 1.9, KE, 12/10/91.

18. Interview 3.15, SN, 12/25/92.

19. While there appeared to be some positive correlation between age and the attitude that the main problem was lack of equality or respect (the correlation coefficient is 0.217, the P-value 0.095), the results are skewed by the lack of responses from SN in this category. Because women from SN were a younger group, thirty-five or below in all but four cases, their not mentioning this factor makes fewer younger women fall in this category; from the other groups, women from all age categories, including a substantial number of young women, referred to this.

20. Carol Rose (1992) applies game theory to the subject of women and property to argue that perceptions about unequal strength are just as damaging to a social group as a real inequality, because other groups drive bargains with them on the basis of those perceptions and assume concessions on their part.

21. Interview 2.15, KC, 2/21/92.

22. Interview 1.4, KE, 12/4/91; Interview 2.9, KC, 2/11/92.

23. Interview 1.11, KE, 12/13/91; Interview 1.5, KE, 12/5/91; Interview 2.3, KC, 2/4/92.

24. Interview 1.6, KE, 12/7/91.

25. Interview 1.14, KE, 2/24/92.

26. Interview 2.1, KC, 2/3/92.

27. Interview 2.13, KC, 2/17/92.

28. Interview 1.7, KE, 12/9/91.

29. Interview 2.1, KC, 2/3/92.

30. There was a moderate negative correlation between age and the perception that women's main problems were economic survival related (the correlation coefficient is –0.3, the P-value 0.019); i.e., younger women were more likely to make this connection. However, the results are skewed here because most respondents who brought this up were from SN, and hence represented a younger profile. (See note 19.)

31. Interview 3.12, SN, 12/22/92.

32. While activists associated with domestic violence programs have spoken out about the pervasiveness of domestic violence in all classes among Indians (e.g., Passano 1995; Radhakrishnan 1994; Bhattacharjee 1992), little detailed research exists in this area. Some studies on domestic violence do show its prevalence in all socioeconomic classes (Stefanizzi and Terragni 1993; Lupri 1990; Strauss et al. 1988, 144–45), but many others, using data on reported crimes, claim that such violence usually occurs among poorer groups (R. Jain 1992, 12; Roberts 1987; Finkelhor 1982).

33. Interview 2.12, KC, 2/17/92.

34. Interview 2.3, KC, 2/4/92.

35. Interview 1.5, KE, 12/5/91; Interview 3.2, SN, 12/8/92; Interview 3.11, SN, 12/21/92.

36. Interview 3.1, SN, 12/7/92.

37. Interview 2.13, KC, 2/17/92.

38. Bhavnani (1993, 100–101) and Reinharz (1979, 120) iterate a common dictum of feminist methodology that it is crucially important for researchers to work on topics that are of prime concern to their respondents.

39. Interview 1.5, KE, 12/5/91.

40. Interview 3.15, SN, 12/25/92.

41. Interview 3.2, SN, 12/8/92.

42. Interview 3.30, SN, 1/8/93.

43. Interview 2.9, KC, 2/11/92.

44. Interview 2.6, KC, 2/7/92; Interview 2.4, KC, 2/4/92.

45. Interview 3.13b, SN, 12/24/92.

46. Interview 3.3, SN, 12/8/92; Interview 3.21, SN, 12/30/92.

47. In this sample, younger women were slightly more likely to believe that there could be legal solutions to social problems; the correlation coefficient between age and this attitude is –0.23, the P-value 0.08.

48. E.g., Lazarus-Black 1992; Burman 1984; Starr 1984. However, others have argued that legalization may have mixed benefits and may increase women's vulnerability rather than empowering them (Kishwar 1994a; Ncube 1991; Thornton 1991; Mann 1982; Merry 1982).

## Chapter 6. Protecting Property

1. Shah Bano's case involved Muslim women's right to receive postdivorce maintenance under Section 125 of the Criminal Procedure Code (1898), and took on the fundamental issue of whether or not such an allegedly secular right could be claimed regardless of the provisions of religious personal law (AIR 1985 SC 945). Mary Roy highlighted the inequalities of inheritance for Indian Christians by challenging the Travancore Christian Succession Act (1916) under which daughters received a quarter of a son's share of inheritance (AIR 1986 SC 1011).

2. McClendon 1995; Mani 1990a; Nair 1996.

3. Alexander 1994; Manicom 1992; Parashar 1992; Rosen 1978; Kandiyoti 1991.

4. Starr 1984; Alexander 1994; McClendon 1995; Kapur and Cossman 1996.

5. Chakrabarty 1992; Spivak 1988; Chatterjee 1990; Mani 1990; Nair 1996.

6. Analyses of postindependence efforts to reform family law in India are provided by Som (1994), Singh's chapter "Legislative Dialectics: A Study of the Hindu Code Bill" (1989, 47–57); L Sarkar (1976); and most of all, Parashar (1992).

7. As Coontz and Henderson argue regarding Neolithic societies, the rise of a civil state was usually marked by a "subversion of traditional, kinship-based forms of social control" and a diversion of kinship ties to the "private" sphere, while kinship was also contradictorily undermined by

emphasis on conjugal bonds (1986, 150). In contrast to the dynastic blood-baths they describe, the process of establishing a postcolonial state in-volves a more urbane suppression of precolonial kinship-based hegemonies in order to legitimize the powers of the new political elites. However, in cases such as the one under discussion, many kinship-related privileges continue as a reward for allegiance toward the new powers.

8. These are the Hindu Adoptions and Maintenance Act (1956), the Hindu Minority and Guardianship Act (1956), the Hindu Marriage Act (1955), and the Hindu Succession Act (1956). The "Hindu Code" originally presented by the then Law Minister B. R. Ambedkar was far more inter-nally consistent and radical with respect to gender equality than these present laws.

9. See Deshpande (1993) for a reading of shifts in economic and politi-cal ideologies of the Indian nation.

10. The Hindu Law Committee report says most women witnesses thought daughters should get equal shares but were persuaded to accept the idea of a half share, not intimating why such compromise was deemed necessary (Parashar 1992, 124).

11. For example, under the Indian Divorce Act (1869) by which most Christians obtain divorce, men can ask for divorce on the grounds of their wives' adultery, and women can ask for divorce on multiple grounds only, viz. adultery plus bigamy, adultery plus incest, adultery plus cruelty, adul-tery plus desertion, change of religion and bigamy, rape, sodomy, or bes-tiality (Diwan 1991, 107). Among Hindus, however, divorce provisions are governed by the Hindu Marriage Act (1955), by which men and women have access to the same grounds, and are further able to claim divorce on the grounds of cruelty, adultery, bigamy, or desertion by themselves (not coupled with other grounds), plus insanity, change of religion, "irretriev-able breakdown of marriage," and most importantly, mutual consent.

12. E.g., Santhal and Bhumij inheritance cases, pp. 213–16.

13. According to Carroll, the rights of daughters under Muslim law in India are far superior to the "reformed" provisions of the Hindu Succession Act (1956), despite the fact that sisters get a half share as compared to brothers under Muslim law (1991, 798).

14. Among myriad discussions and analyses of this case, some of the most influential texts are the volume edited by Engineer (1987); Pathak and Sunder Rajan's (1989) article analyzing displaced legal subjectivity; and Tahir Mahmood's 1986 interview explaining why the decision was contrary to an Islamic reading. While the Shah Bano case attracted un-precedented public attention and political furor, in part because the judg-

ment contained commentary on the Quranic origins of *iddat* from an apparently Hindu judge, it is only one of several cases in which divorced Muslim women's rights to adequate maintenance have been debated by the Supreme Court, and relief granted by turning to section 125 of the Criminal Procedure Code (1898) in preference to Muslim personal law (*Bai Tahira vs. Ali Hussain Fissaalhi*, AIR 1979 SC 362; *Fuzlunbi vs. K. Khadervali*, AIR 1980 SC 1730; *Zohara Khatoon vs. Mohd. Ibrahim*, AIR 1986 SC 587; *Begum Subanu alias Saira Banu vs. A. M. Abdul Gafoor*, AIR 1987 SC 1103). See Begam (1989) for detailed analyses of these cases.

15. The Muslim Women's Act has, however, been broadly interpreted by some judges who have awarded maintenance beyond the iddat period (Latifi 1991, Vaghela 1988), providing yet another example of the ways in which laws assume a new life in court beyond the legislative intent which gave birth to them.

16. AIR 1986 SC 1011.

17. She was sixty-three, a former stenographer and partially blind, while the lawyer husband tried to file a pauper's petition and persuaded the Catholic Church to consider annulment even though they knew he was adulterous. Though the amount of maintenance given was very low, the Bombay High Court did decree Jacob Aranha's arrest unless he paid his arrears (*Legal News and Views* June 1992, 213).

18. Reported by Suhasini Ali at a plenary speech at the Association for Women in Development Conference in October 1993. Roy (1996) discusses recent attempts by ministers to reestablish the old law because of "inconvenience" caused to Christian males.

19. Vining 1986; J. White 1993; Schlag 1994.

20. Baar 1990; Baxi 1985, Beller 1983; Cassels 1989. Recently, the numerous favorable judgments given to women under the Muslim Women's (Protection of Rights on Divorce) Act (1986) through creative interpretations of the statute (R. Kumar 1993, 4) indicate that regressive laws may be reconfigured through judicial activism.

21. For most Hindus (including Buddhists, Jains, and Sikhs), succession is decided under the Hindu Succession Act (1956), with exceptional rules for some matrilineal communities. Muslim succession is largely decided under the 1937 Shariat Act, and Christian and Parsi succession is governed by the Indian Succession Act (1925, last amended for Parsis in 1991), in addition to numerous succession codes for Christians in various states. The Hindu Succession Act and the Indian Succession Act stand ahead of the other laws in that daughters and sons get equal rights to self-acquired property in cases of intestate succession, but like the other laws,

they are limited in having minimal shares of ancestral/family property for female heirs, and exemptions to equality provisions for agricultural land (Agarwal 1994, 199–236).

22. The *All India Reporter* is the most well known among the journals that publish the texts of important appellate judgments, that is, the prime source of judgments that become case law.

23. These are appellate court cases (High Courts and Supreme Court) that are published and hence become part of case law, effectively becoming "authoritative" sources, determining legal precedents and the construction of legal notions. It is important, however, to remember that the majority of cases, whether unpublished appellate cases or lower court cases, are largely inaccessible to judges, lawyers, or scholars, and are not considered here.

24. AIR 1988 Bombay 348.

25. AIR 1988 Kerala 133.

26. *Karta / Kartha*: the titular head, usually senior male member of the Hindu joint family, and manager of the coparcenary property with discretion to sell or acquire property in the family's best interest (Diwan 1991, 339–42). Women cannot be karthas "in accordance with the texts of Hindu law" (Diwan 1991, 340), a vivid example of contemporary questions of equality closed by reference to alleged ancient authority.

27. AIR 1988 Kerala 315.

28. AIR 1988 Andhra Pradesh 250.

29. AIR 1991 Calcutta 166.

30. AIR 1990 Supreme Court 1742.

31. See discussion of the putrikaputra and inheritance for brotherless daughters in chapter 4, pp. 143–45.

32. AIR 1989 Karnataka 63.

33. AIR 1988 Karnataka 139.

34. AIR 1990 Orissa 155.

35. AIR 1988 Andhra Pradesh 309.

36. AIR 1989 Allahabad 75.

37. AIR 1988 Calcutta 196; AIR 1988 Punjab and Haryana 198; AIR 1990 Supreme Court 1888.

38. See Kapur and Cossman (1996, 128) for cases discussing marriage as a process of "transplantation for women."

39. AIR 1990 Delhi 59.

40. AIR 1991 Kerala 175.

41. AIR 1988 Patna 129.

42. See note 31.

43. AIR 1991 Patna 138.

44. Apffel-Marglin 1995; Barker 1989; Bayly 1989; More 1995; Mosse 1994.

45. See, for example, Collier's discussion of recent cases (1995).

## Chapter 7. Conclusion

1. Erickson, 1993; Mann 1991; Basch 1986; Klapisch-Zuber 1985; Crummey 1982.

2. Kishwar 1994a; Schuler and Kadirgamar-Rajasingham 1992; Naitao 1990.

# Bibliography

Abu-Lughod, Lila. 1993. "The Romance of Resistance: Tracing Transformations of Power Through Bedouin Women" in *Women's Studies: Essential
Readings*, ed. Stevi Jackson et al., 102–103. New York: New York University Press.

Adas, Michael. 1991. "South Asian Resistance in Comparative Perspective."
In *Contesting Power: Resistance and Everyday Social Relations in South
Asia,* eds. Douglas Haynes and Gyan Prakash, 290–305. Berkeley: Uni-
versity of California Press.

Afshar, Haleh, ed. 1987. *Women, State and Ideology: Studies from Africa
and Asia.* Hampshire: Macmillan.

Agarwal, Bina. 1994. *A Field of One's Own: Gender and Land Rights in South
Asia.* Cambridge: Cambridge University Press.

Ahmed, Rahnuma, and Milu Shamsun Naher. 1987. *Brides and the Demand
System in Bangladesh.* Dhaka: Center for Social Studies.

Ahmed, Sara. 1995. "Deconstruction and Law's Other: Toward a Feminist
Theory of Embodied Legal Rights." *Social and Legal Studies* 4: 55–73.

Ahmed-Ghosh, Huma.1991. "From Ivory Towers to Mud Huts: Trials and
Acceptance of a Fieldworker." In *From the Female Eye: Accounts of Women
Fieldworkers Studying Their Own Communities*, ed. M. N. Panini, Women
In Development Series, Series Editor T. Scarlett Epstein, 11–19. New
Delhi: Hindusthan.

Alcoff, L. 1988. "The Identity Crisis in Feminist Theory." *Signs* 13.3: 405–36.

Alexander, M. Jacqui. 1997. "Erotic Autonomy as a Politics of Decolonization:
An Anatomy of Feminist and State Practice in the Bahamas Tourist
Economy." In *Feminist Genealogies, Colonial Legacies, Democratic Fu-
tures,* eds. M. Jacqui Alexander and Chandra Talpade Mohanty. New York:
Routledge.

———. 1994. "Not Just (Any) Body Can Be a Citizen: The Politics of Law,
Sexuality and Postcoloniality in Trinidad, Tobago and the Bahamas." *Feminist Review* 48: 5–23.

Althusser, Louis. 1971. *Lenin and Philosophy and Other Essays.* New York:
New Left.

Anderson, Benedict. 1983. *Imagined Communities: Reflections on the Origin and Spread of Nationalism*. London: Verso.

Anderson, Kathryn, Susan Armitage, Dana Jack, and Judith Wittner. 1990. "Beginning Where We Are: Feminist Methodology in Oral History." In *Feminist Research Methods: Exemplary Readings in the Social Sciences*. Ed. Joyce McCarl Nielsen, 94–112. Boulder: Westview.

Apffel-Marglin, Frederique. 1995. "Of Pirs and Pandits: Tradition and Hindu-Muslim Cultural Commonalities in Orissa." *Manushi* 91: 17–26.

Apte, Usha. 1982. *Vedic Hindu and Tribal Marriage: A Study in Culture Change*. Hyderabad: AWARE.

Baar, Carl. 1990. "Social Action Litigation in India: The Operation and Limitations of the World's Most Active Judiciary." *Policy Studies Journal* 19.1: 140–50.

Bakshi, P. M. 1990. "Domicile of Married Women." *Lawyers Collective* May 1990: 26–27.

————. 1988. "Wife's House and Husband's Rights." *Lawyers Collective* January 1988: 1–2.

Balakrishnan, Revathi. 1986. *Families in an Indian Urban Labor Colony: Case Studies in Family Resource Management*. East Lansing: Office of WID, Michigan State University Working Paper #112.

Balasubrahmanyan, Vimal. 1990. *In Search of Justice: Women, Law, Landmark Judgements and Media*. Bombay: Research Centre for Women's Studies, SNDT University.

Banerjee, Nirmala. 1991. *Indian Women in a Changing Industrial Scenario*. New Delhi: Sage.

————. 1989. "Trends in Women's Employment 1971–1981: Some Macro-Level Observations." *Economic and Political Weekly* 24: WS 10–22.

Bapat, Meera, and Nigel Crook. 1992. "Struggle and Survival of Poor Metropolitan Households: A Longitudinal Study in Pune, 1976 to 1978." *Economic and Political Weekly*. 27: 1141–47.

Bapat, Meera, and Sheela Patel. 1993. "Shelter, Women and Development: Beating a Path towards Women's Participation." *Economic and Political Weekly*. 28: 465–72.

Bardhan, Kalpana. 1994. "Social Classes and Gender in India: The Structure of Difference in the Condition of Women." In *Gender and Political Economy: Explorations of South Asian Systems*, ed. Alice Clark, 144–78. New Delhi: Oxford University Press.

Barker, Eileen. 1989. "Christian Ashrams: A New Religious Movement in Contemporary India." *Contemporary Sociology* 18.4: 597–98.

Basch, Norma. 1986. "The Emerging Legal History of Women in the United States: Property, Divorce and the Constitution" *Signs* 12.1: 97–117.

————. 1982. *In the Eyes of the Law: Women, Property and Marriage in Nineteenth-Century New York*. Ithaca: Cornell University Press.

Basu, Rumki. 1985. " 'Dowry' and 'Right To Property'." *Mainstream* April 13: 54–55.

Baxi, Upendra. 1985. *Courage, Craft and Contention: The Indian Supreme Court in the Eighties*. Bombay: Tripathi.

Bayly, Susan. 1989. *Muslims and Christians in South Indian Society 1700– 1900*. Cambridge: Cambridge University Press.

Begam, Sherafennisa. 1989. "Maintenance and Muslim Women: Religious Orthodoxy v. Judicial Activism." *Cochin University Law Review* 13: 279– 308.

Bell, Vikki. 1993. *Interrogating Incest: Feminism, Foucault and the Law*. London: Routledge.

Beller, Gerald E. 1983. "Benevolent Illusions in a Developing Society: The Assertion of Supreme Court Authority in Democratic India." *The Western Political Quarterly* 36: 513–32.

Bhachu, Parminder. 1993. "Identities Constructed and Reconstructed: Representations of Indian Women in Britain." In *Migrant Women: Crossing Boundaries and Changing Identities*, ed. Gina Buijs, 99–117. Oxford: Berg.

Bhattacharjee, Anannya. 1992. "The Habit of Ex-Nomination: Nation, Woman and the Indian Immigrant Bourgeoisie." *Public Culture* 5.1: 19–44.

Bhavnani, Kum-Kum. 1993. "Tracing the Contours: Feminist Research and Feminist Objectivity." *Women's Studies International Forum* 16.2: 95–104.

Billig, Michael S. 1992. "The Marriage Squeeze and the Rise of Groomprice in India's Kerala State." *Journal of Comparative Family Studies* 23.2: 197–216.

Bose, Ashish. 1991. *Demographic Diversity of India: 1991 Census State and District Level Data*. Delhi: BR Publishing.

Bossen, Laurel. 1988. "Toward a Theory of Marriage: The Economic Anthropology of Marriage Transactions." *Ethnology* 27.2: 127–44.

Bourdieu, Pierre. 1977. *Outline of a Theory of Practice*. Cambridge: Cambridge University Press.

Bradford, Nicholas. 1985. "From Bridewealth to Groom-Fee: Transformed Marriage Customs and Socioeconomic Polarization amongst Lingayats." *Contributions to Indian Sociology* 19.2: 269–302.

Brettell, Caroline B. 1991. "Kinship and Contract: Property Transmissions and Family Relations in Northwestern Portugal." *Comparative Studies in Society and History* 33.3: 443–65.

Burman, Sandra. 1984. "Divorce and the Disadvantaged: African Women in Urban South Africa." In *Women And Property—Women As Property*, ed. Renee Hirschon, 117–39. London: Croom Helm.

Caplan, Lionel. 1994. "Bridegroom Price in Urban India: Caste, Class and 'Dowry Evil' Among Christians in Madras" In *Family, Kinship and Marriage in India*, ed. Patricia Uberoi, 357–82. Delhi: Oxford University Press.

Caplan, Patricia. 1984. "Cognatic Descent, Islamic Law and Women's Property on the East African Coast" In *Women and Property—Women As Property*, ed. Renee Hirschon, 23–43. London: Croom Helm.

Carroll, Lucy. 1991. "Daughter's Right of Inheritance in India: A Perspective on the Problem of Dowry." *Modern Asian Studies* 25.4: 791–809.

———. 1986. "Rejoinder" To Tahir Mahmood's 'The Grandeur Of Womanhood In Islam'." *Islamic and Comparative Law Quarterly* 6.4: 294–308.

Cassels, J. 1989. "Judicial Activism and Public Interest Litigation in India: Attempting the Impossible?" *American Journal of Comparative Law* 37: 495–519.

Census of India 1991. Series 28: Delhi, General Economic Tables and Social and Cultural Tables. Delhi: Census Operations.

Centre for the Study of Developing Societies. 1974. *Tensions Due to Rapid Growth and Inappropriate Structures: A Case Study of Civic Amenities in Delhi*. Delhi: CSDS.

Chakrabarty, Dipesh. 1992. "Provincializing Europe: Postcoloniality and the Critique of History." *Cultural Studies* 6.3: 337–57.

Chakravarti, Uma. 1993. "Conceptualizing Brahmanical Patriarchy in Early India: Gender, Caste, Class and State." *Economic and Political Weekly* 28: 579–85.

———. 1990. "Whatever Happened to the Vedic *Dasi*? Orientalism, Nationalism and a Script for the Past." In *Recasting Women: Essays In Indian Colonial History*, ed. Kumkum Sangari and Sudesh Vaid, 27–87. New Brunswick: Rutgers University Press.

Chanana, Karuna. 1993. "Partition and Family Strategies: Gender-Education Linkages Among Punjabi Women in Delhi." *Economic and Political Weekly* 28: WS25–34.

"Change in Definition of Dowry Sought: Seminar on Women and Law." 1991. *Janta* 13 January: 31–32.

Chasin, Barbara H. 1990. *Land Reform and Women's Work in a Kerala Village*. East Lansing: Michigan State University.

Chatterjee, Partha. 1990. "The Nationalist Resolution of the Women's Question." In *Recasting Women: Essays In Indian Colonial History*, ed. Kumkum Sangari and Sudesh Vaid, 233–53. New Brunswick: Rutgers University Press.

———. 1989. "Colonialism, Nationalism, and Colonialized Women: The Contest in India." *American Ethnologist* 16.4: 622–33.

Chen, Marty, and Jean Dreze. 1992. "Widows and Health in Rural North India." *Economic and Political Weekly* 27: WS 81–93.

Chhachhi, Amrita. 1991. "Forced Identities: The State, Communalism, Fundamentalism and Women in India" In *Women, Islam and the State,* ed. Deniz Kandiyoti, 144–75. Philadelphia: Temple University Press.

———. 1989. "The State, Religious Fundamentalism and Women: Trends in South Asia." *Economic And Political Weekly* 24: 567–78.

Chowdhry, Prem. 1994. *The Veiled Women: Shifting Gender Equations in Rural Haryana 1880–1990*. Delhi: Oxford University Press.

Clad, James. 1990. "Grave Judgments: Delays Stretching into Decades Bedevil the Legal System." *Far Eastern Economic Review* July 12 : 18–19.

Clark, Alice. 1994. "Analyzing the Reproduction of Human Beings and Social Formations, with Indian Regional Examples Over the Last Century." In *Gender and Political Economy: Explorations of South Asian Systems*, ed. Alice Clark, 115–45. New Delhi: Oxford University Press.

Collier, Richard. 1995. "'Waiting Till Father Gets Home': The Reconstruction of Fatherhood in Family Law." *Social and Legal Studies* 4: 5–30.

Coltrane, Scott. 1992. "The Micropolitics of Gender in Non-Industrial Societies." *Gender and Society* 6.1: 86–107.

Comaroff, J. L., ed. 1980. *The Meaning of Marriage Payments*. London: Academic.

Committee on the Status of Women in India. 1975. *Towards Equality: Report of the Committee on the Status of Women in India*. New Delhi: Govt. of India, Ministry of Education and Social Welfare, Department of Social Welfare.

*Compendium of Statistics and Indicators on the Situation of Women 1986*. 1988. New York: UN.

Coontz, Stephanie, and Peta Henderson, eds. 1986. *Women's Work, Men's Property: The Origins of Gender and Class*. London: Verso.

Cottrell, Allin. 1984. *Social Classes in Marxist Theory*. London: Routledge.

Crenshaw, Kimberle. 1989. "Demarginalizing the Intersection of Race and Sex: A Black Feminist Critique of Antidiscrimination Doctrine, Feminist Theory and Antiracist Politics." *The University of Chicago Law Forum*. 139: 139–67.

Croll, Elisabeth. 1984. "The Exchange of Women and Property: Marriage in Post-Revolutionary China." In *Women and Property—Women As Property*, ed. Renee Hirschon, 44–61. London: Croom Helm.

Crompton, Rosemary. 1993. *Class and Stratification: An Introduction to Current Debates*. Cambridge,UK: Polity Press.

Crummey, Donald. 1982. "Women, Property and Litigation Among the Bagemder Amhara, 1750s to 1850s." In *African Women and the Law: Historical Perspectives*, ed. Margaret Jean Hay and Marcia Wright, 19–32. Boston: Boston University Papers on Africa VII.

Cunningham, Clark D. 1992. "Symposium. The Lawyer As Translator, Representation As Text: Towards an Ethnography of the Legal Discourse." *Cornell Law Review* 77:1298–1387.

Dalton, Clare. 1987–1988. "Where We Stand: Observations on the Situation of Legal Feminist Thought." *Berkeley Women's Law Journal* 3.1: 1–13.

Dandekar, Kumudini. 1993. "The Aged, Their Problems and Social Intervention in Maharashtra." *Economic and Political Weekly*. 28: 1188–95.

Das, Veena. 1996. "Sexual Violence, Discursive Formations and the State." *Economic and Political Weekly* 31.35–37: 2411–23.

Datta, V. N. 1986. "Panjabi Refugees and the Urban Development of Greater Delhi." In *Delhi Through the Ages*, ed. R. Frykenberg, 442–60. Delhi: Oxford University Press.

Delphy, Christine. 1984. "The Main Enemy." In *Close to Home*, by Christine Delphy, 57–77. Amherst: the University of Massachusetts Press.

Delphy, Christine, and Diana Leonard. 1986. "Class Analysis, Gender Analysis and the Family." In *Gender and Stratification*, ed. Rosemary Crompton and Michael Mann, 57–73. Cambridge, UK: Polity.

Desai, Neera, and Maithreyee Krishnaraj. 1990. *Women and Society in India*. New Delhi: Ajanta.

Deshpande, Satish. 1993. "Imagined Economies: Styles of Nation Building in Twentieth-Century India." *Journal of Arts and Ideas* 25–26: 5–36.

Devasia, Leelamma, and V. V. Devasia. 1990. *Women In India: Equality, Social Justice and Development*. New Delhi: Indian Social Institute.

Dhagamwar, Vasudha. 1989. *Towards the Uniform Civil Code*. Delhi: Indian Law Institute.

Dhruvarajan, Vanaja. 1990. "Religious Ideology, Hindu Women and Development in India." *Journal of Social Issues* 46.3: 57–69.

Dietrich, Gabriele. 1986. "The Women's Movement and Religion." *Economic and Political Weekly* 21: 157–60.

Diwan, Paras. 1991. *Family Law*. Allahabad: Allahabad Law Agency.

———. 1978. "Daughter's Right to Inheritance and Fragmentation of Holdings." *Supreme Court Cases* II of 1978: 15–27.

Driver, Edwin D., and Aloo E. Driver. 1987. *Social Class in Urban India: Essays on Cognitions and Structures*. Leiden: E. J. Brill.

Dube, Leela, and Rajni Palriwala. 1990. *Structures and Strategies: Women, Work and Family*. New Delhi: Sage.

Dumont, Louis. 1983. *Affinity As a Value: Marriage Alliance in South India, with Comparative Essays on Australia*. Chicago: University of Chicago Press.

Eagleton, Terry. 1991. *Ideology: An Introduction*. London: Verso.

Ebrey, Patricia Buckley. 1991. "Introduction." In *Marriage and Inequality in Chinese Society*, ed. Rubie S. Watson and Patricia Buckley Ebrey, 1–24. Berkeley: University of California Press.

Eisenstein, Zillah R. 1989. *The Female Body and the Law*. Berkeley: University of California Press.

Engel, David M., and Frank W. Munger. 1996. "Rights, Remembrance and the Reconciliation of Difference." *Law and Society Review* 30.1: 7–54.

Engels, Friedrich. 1985. *The Origin of the Family, Private Property and the State*. New York: Viking.

Engineer, Asghar Ali, ed. 1987. *The Shah Bano Controversy*. Hyderabad: Orient Longman.

Erickson, Amy Louise. 1993. *Women and Property in Early Modern England*. London: Routledge.

Feliciano, Myrna S. 1994. "Law, Gender and the Family in the Phillipines." *Law and Society Review* 28.3: 525–37.

Fernandes, Walter. 1990. *Women's Status in the Delhi Slums: Urbanisation, Economic Forces and Voluntary Organisations*. New Delhi: Indian Social Institute.

Finkelhor, D. 1982. "Sexual Abuse: A Sociological Perspective." *Child Abuse and Neglect* 6: 94–102.

Finley, Lucinda M. 1993. "Breaking Women's Silence in Law: The Dilemma of the Gendered Nature of Legal Reasoning." In *Feminist Legal Theory: Foundations*, ed. D. Kelly Weisberg, 571–81. Philadelphia: Temple University Press.

Fortmann, Louise, and Nontokozo Nabane. 1992. *The Fruits of Their Labours: Gender, Property and Trees in Mhondoro District*. Harare: Center for Applied Social Sciences Occasional Paper Series.

Foucault, Michel. 1980. *Power/Knowledge: Selected Interviews and Other Writings 1972–1977*. Ed. Colin Gordon. Trans. Colin Gordon et al. New York: Pantheon.

Frug, Mary Joe. 1992. *Postmodern Legal Feminism*. New York: Routledge.

Fruzzetti, Lina. 1994 (1982). *The Gift of a Virgin*. Delhi: Oxford University Press.

Fruzzetti, Lina, and Akos Ostor. 1990. *Culture and Change Along the Blue Nile: Courts, Markets and Strategies for Development*. Boulder, Colo.: Westview.

Galanter, Marc. 1989. *Law and Society in Modern India*. Delhi: Oxford University Press.

Ganai, N. A. 1988. "Familial Rights of Muslim Women under Customary Law in Kashmir: Myth and Reality." *Cochin University Law Review* 12: 359–90.

Gates, Margaret. 1977. "Homemakers into Widows and Divorcees: Can the Law Provide Economic Protection?" In *Women into Wives: The Legal and Economic Impact of Marriage*, ed. Jane Roberts Chapman and Margaret Gates, 215–32. London: Sage.

Giddens, Anthony. 1973. *The Class Structure of the Advanced Societies*. London: Hutchinson.

Gill, Kulwant. 1986. *Hindu Women's Right to Property in India*. New Delhi: Deep.

Gill, Lesley. 1994. *Precarious Dependencies: Gender, Class and Domestic Service in Bolivia*. New York: Columbia University Press.

Gledhill, Christine. 1988. "Pleasurable Negotiations." In *Female Spectators: Looking at Film and Television*, ed. E. Deidre Pribram, 64–89. London: Verso.

Glendon, Mary Ann. 1980. "Modern Marriage Law and Its Underlying Assumptions: The New Marriage And The New Property." *Indian Socio-Legal Journal* 6: 113–29.

Goldthorpe, John H. 1983. "Women and Class Analysis: In Defence of the Conventional View." *Sociology*, 17: 465–88.

Goody, Jack, and S. J. Tambiah. 1973. *Bridewealth and Dowry*. Cambridge: Cambridge University Press.

Gottell, Lise. 1995. "Litigating Feminist 'Truth': An Antifoundational Critique" *Social and Legal Studies* 4: 99–131.

Gramsci, Antonio. 1971. *Selections from the Prison Notebooks of Antonio Gramsci*. Ed. and Trans. by Quintin Hoare and Geoffrey Nowell Smith. New York: International.

Grolier CD Encyclopaedia. 1993. "New Delhi." Grolier Electronic Publishing Inc. [CD Rom].

Guha, Ramachandra. 1989. *The Unquiet Woods: Ecological Change and Peasant Resistance in the Himalaya*. Delhi: Oxford University Press.

Guha, Ranajit, and Gayatri Chakrabarty Spivak, ed. 1988. *Selected Subaltern Studies*. New York: Oxford University Press.

Gulati, Mitu, and Leela Gulati. 1993. "Remnants of Matriliny: Widows of Two Kerala Villages." *Manushi* 76: 32–34.

Gupta, Shriniwas. 1985. "Supreme Court on Stridhan." *Kerala Law Times*: 61–64.

Gurney, Joan Neff. 1985. "Not One of the Guys: The Female Researcher in a Male-Dominated Setting." *Qualitative Sociology* 8.1: 42–62.

Guru, Gopal. 1992. "Shetkari Sanghtana and the Pursuit of 'Laxmi Mukti'." *Economic and Political Weekly*. 27: 1463–65.

Haksar, Nandita. n.d. "Women and Public Interest Litigation: A Decade of Struggle." *Samya Shakti* 37–44.

Hale, Sondra. 1991. "Feminist Method, Process, and Self-Criticism: Interviewing Sudanese Women." In *Women's Words: The Feminist Practice of Oral History*, Sherna Berger Gluck and Daphne Patai, 121–36. New York: Routledge.

Hale, Sylvia. 1989. "Status of Women in India." *Pacific Affairs* 62.3: 364–81.

Hall, Stuart. 1987. *Cultural Studies: An Introduction*. London: Macmillan.

Haque, T., and G. Parthasarathy. 1992. "Land Reform and Rural Development: Highlights of a National Seminar." *Economic and Political Weekly*. 27: 395–97.

Harrell, Stevan, and Sara A. Dickey. 1985. "Dowry Systems in Complex Societies." *Ethnology* 24.2: 105–20.

Harris, Cheryl I. 1993. "Whiteness As Property." *Harvard Law Review* 106: 1709–91.

Hawkesworth, M. 1989. "Knowers, Knowing, Known: Feminist Theory and Claims of Truth." *Signs* 13.3: 533–57.

Hay, Margaret Jean, and Marcia Wright. 1982. *African Women and the Law: Historical Perspectives*. Boston: Boston University Papers on Africa, VII.

Haynes, Douglas, and Gyan Prakash. 1991. "Introduction: The Entanglement of Power and Resistance." In *Contesting Power: Resistance and Ev-*

*eryday Social Relations in South Asia,* ed. Douglas Haynes and Gyan Prakash, 1–22. Berkeley: University of California Press.

Hennessy, Rosemary. 1993. *Materialist Feminism and the Politics of Discourse.* New York: Routledge.

Herlihy, David. 1985. *Medieval Households.* Cambridge: Harvard University Press.

Hershman, Paul. 1981. *Punjabi Kinship and Marriage.* Delhi: Hindustan.

Heyer, Judith. 1992. "The Role of Dowries and Daughters' Marriages in the Accumulation and Distribution of Capital in a South Indian Community." *Journal of International Development* 4.4: 419–36.

Hirschon, Renee, ed. 1984. *Women and Property—Women As Property.* London: Croom Helm.

Holcombe, Lee. 1983. *Wives and Property: Reform of the Married Women's Property Law in Nineteenth-Century England.* Toronto: University of Toronto Press.

Honigmann, John J. 1982. "Sampling in Ethnographic Fieldwork." In *Field Research: A Sourcebook and Field Manual*, ed. Robert G. Burgess, 79–90. London: Allen.

Howell, Martha C. 1987. "Marriage, Property and Patriarchy: Recent Contributions to a Literature." *Feminist Studies* 13.1: 203–23.

Jacobson, Doranne. 1977. "Flexibility in Central Indian Kinship and Residence." In *The New Wind: Changing Identities in South Asia*, ed. Kenneth David, 262–83. The Hague: Mouton.

Jaeyulu, K. P. 1986. "Divergent Judicial Opinion on Property of a Female Hindu." *Supreme Court Journal* II of 1986: 21–16.

Jain, Ranjana. 1992. *Family Violence in India.* New Delhi: Radiant.

Jain, Shobhita. 1996. "Property as Negotiation: Some Aspects of Kinship and Gender in North India." *Indian Journal of Gender Studies* 3.1: 1–22.

Jameson, Frederic. 1995. "Marx's *Purloined Letter.*" *New Left Review.* 209: 75–107.

Jeffery, Patricia, and Roger Jeffery. 1996. *'Don't Marry Me to a Plowman': Women's Everyday Lives in Rural North India.* Boulder, Colo.: Westview.

———. 1994. "Killing My Heart's Desire: Education and Female Autonomy in Rural North India." In *Women As Subjects: South Asian Histories*, ed. Nita Kumar, 125–71. Charlottesville: University Press of Virginia.

Jeffrey, Robin. 1993. *Politics, Women and Well-Being: How Kerala Became "A Model."* Delhi: Oxford University Press.

Jethmalani, Rani. 1987. "Religion Politics and Law: Why Men Do Not Burn—The Politics and Pathology of Sati." *Supreme Court Bar Association Seminar.* New Delhi, October 17.

———. 1985. "Dowry and the Law: Subversion of Human Rights." In *Social Action Through Law*, ed. P. K. Gandhi, 114–26. New Delhi: Concept.

Jorgensen, Danny L. 1990. *Participant Observation: A Methodology for Human Studies.* Newbury Park: Sage.

Joshi, Ravinder. 1990. "Kanya Daan: Ban This Practice." *Lawyers Collective* August 1990: 10.

Joshi, S. C. 1994. *Migration to a Metropolis*. Jaipur: R.B.S.A.

Kalkar, Govind. 1985. *Women and Structural Violence in India*. New Delhi: Centre for Women's Development Studies.

Kandiyoti, Deniz, ed. 1991. *Women, Islam and the State*. Philadelphia: Temple University Press.

Kannabiran, Vasanth, and Kalpana Kannabiran. 1991. "Caste and Gender: Understanding the Dynamics of Power and Violence." *Economic and Political Weekly* 26: 2130–33.

Kapadia, Karin. 1995. *Siva and Her Sisters: Gender, Caste and Class in Rural South India*. Boulder, Colo.: Westview.

———. 1993. "Marrying Money: Changing Preference and Practice in a Tamil Marriage." *Contributions to Indian Sociology: New Series* 27.1: 25–51.

Kaplan, Marion A, ed. 1985. *The Marriage Bargain: Women and Dowries in European History, Women and History #10*. New York: Haworth.

Kapur, Ratna, and Brenda Cossman. 1996. *Subversive Sites: Feminist Engagements with Law in India*. New Delhi: Sage.

Karlekar, Malavika. 1982. *Poverty and Women's Work: A Study of Sweeper Women in Delhi*. New Delhi: Vikas.

Kirp, David L., Mark G. Yudof, and Marlene Strong Franks. 1986. *Gender Justice*. Chicago: University of Chicago Press.

Kishwar, Madhu. 1994a. "A Code for Self-Monitoring: Some Thoughts on Activism." *Manushi* 85: 5–17.

———. 1994b. "Public Interest Litigation: One Step Forward, Two Steps Backwards." *Manushi* 81: 11–23.

———. 1989a. "Dowry and Inheritance Rights." *Economic and Political Weekly* 24: 587–88.

———. 1989b. "Towards More Just Norms for Marriage: Continuing the Dowry Debate." *Manushi* 53: 2–9.

———. 1987. "Toiling without Rights: Ho Women of Singhbhum." *Economic and Political Weekly* 22: 95–101, 149–55, 194–200.

Kishwar, Madhu, and Ruth Vanita, eds. 1990. "Inheritance Rights for Women: A Response to Some Commonly Expressed Fears." *Manushi* 57: 3–15.

———. 1984. *In Search of Answers: Indian Women's Voices from Manushi*. London: Zed.

Klapisch-Zuber, Christiane. 1985. *Women, Family and Ritual in Renaissance Italy*. Trans. Lydia G. Cochrane. Chicago: University of Chicago Press.

Kolenda, Pauline. 1984. "Woman as Tribute, Woman as Flower: Images of 'Woman' in Weddings in North and South India." *American Ethnologist* 11: 98–117.

Kozlowski, Gregory C. "Muslim Women and the Control of Property in North India." In *Women in Colonial India: Essays on Survival, Work and The State*, ed. J. Krishnamurty, 114–32. Delhi: Oxford University Press.

Kumar, Nita, ed. 1994. *Women as Subjects: South Asian Histories.* Charlottesville: University Press of Virginia.

Kumar, Radha. 1993. *The History of Doing: An Illustrated Account of Movements for Women's Rights and Feminism in India 1800–1990.* London: Verso.

Kumari, Ranjana. 1989. *Brides Are Not for Burning: Dowry Victims In India.* New Delhi: Radiant.

Lateef, Shahida. 1990. *Muslim Women In India: Political and Private Realities 1890s–1980s.* New Delhi: Kali.

Latifi, Danial. 1991. "Women, Family Law And Social Change" *Lawyers Collective* January 1991: 26–29.

Lazarus-Black, Mindie. 1992. "Bastardy, Gender Hierarchy and the State: The Politics of Family Law Reform in Antigua and Barbuda." *Law And Society Review* 26.4: 863–99.

———. 1991. "Why Women Take Men to Magistrate's Court: Caribbean Kinship Ideology and Law." *Ethnology* 30: 119–33.

Levi-Strauss, Claude. 1969 (1949). *The Elementary Structures of Kinship.* Trans. J. H. Bell et al. Boston: Beacon.

Liddle, Joanna, and Rama Joshi. 1986. *Daughters of Independence: Gender, Caste and Class in India.* New Delhi: Kali.

Lieten, G. K. 1992. "Literacy in Post-Land Reform Village." *Economic and Political Weekly.* 27: 103–109.

Lupri, Eugen. 1990. "Harmony and Aggression: The Dialectics of Conjugal Violence." *Kolner Zeitschrift fur Soziologie und Sozialpsychologie* 42.3: 474–501.

Mackinnon, Catherine. 1987. *Feminism Unmodified: Discourses on Life and Law.* Cambridge: Harvard University Press.

Madan, T. N. 1975. "Structural Implications of Marriage in North India: Wife-givers and Wife-takers among the Pandits of Kashmir." *Contributions to Indian Sociology (n.s.)* 9: 217–43.

Magu, Poonam. 1996. "The Hindu Succession Act—Has It Really Helped Women?" *Legal News and Views* 10.8: 1–3.

Maher, Vanessa. 1974. *Women and Property in Morocco: Their Changing Relation to the Process of Social Stratification in the Middle Atlas.* London: Cambridge University Press.

Mahila Dakshata Samiti. 1988. *Report of Seminar on Amendment to the Prohibition of Dowry Act and Protection of Abandoned Women and Children.* Mahila Dakshata Samiti.

Mahmood, Tahir. 1986. "The Grandeur of Womanhood in Islam." *Islamic and Comparative Law Quarterly* 6.1: 1–26.

———. 1982. "Matrimonial Laws in Goa, Daman and Diu: Need for Legislative Action." *Islamic and Comparative Law Quarterly* 2.2: 93–100.

Majumdar, Tapan K. 1988. "The Urban Poor and Social Change: A Study of Squatter Settlements in Delhi." In *The Indian City: Poverty, Ecology and Urban Development*, ed. Alfred de Souza, 29–60. New Delhi: Manohar.

Majury, Diana. 1991. "Strategizing in Equality." In *At the Boundaries of Law: Feminism and Legal Theory*, ed. Martha Albertson Fineman and Nancy Sweet Thomadsen, 320–38. New York: Routledge.

Mani, Lata. 1990a. "Contentious Traditions: The Debate on Sati in Colonial India." In *Recasting Women: Essays in Indian Colonial History*, ed. Kumkum Sangari and Sudesh Vaid, 88–126. New Brunswick: Rutgers University Press.

———. 1990b. "Multiple Mediations: Feminist Scholarship in the Age of Multinational Reception." *Feminist Review* 36: 24–41.

Manicom, Linzi. 1992. "Ruling Relations: Rethinking State and Gender in South African History." *Journal of African History*. 33: 441–65.

Mann, Kristin. 1991. "Women, Landed Property, and the Accumulation of Wealth in Early Colonial Lagos." *Signs* 16.4: 682.

———. 1982. "Women's Rights in Law and Practice: Marriage and Dispute Settlement in Early Colonial Lagos." In *African Women and the Law: Historical Perspectives*, ed. Margaret Jean Hay and Marcia Wright, 151–71. Boston: Boston University Papers on Africa VII.

Marx, Karl. [1894] 1977. *Capital: A Critique of Political Economy*. Trans. Ben Fowkes. New York: Vintage.

Mathew, P. M. 1992. "Women's Industrial Employment in India." In *Class, State and Development in India*, ed. Berch Berberoglu, 207–40. New Delhi: Sage.

Mauss, Marcel. 1967. *The Gift: Forms and Functions of Exchange in Archaic Societies*. Trans. Ian Cunnison. New York: Norton.

McCauliff, C. M. A. 1992. "The Medieval Origin of the Doctrine of Estates in Land: Substantive Property Law, Family Considerations and the Interest of Women." *Tulane Law Review* 66.4: 919–1013.

McClendon, Thomas V. 1995. "Tradition and Domestic Struggle in the Courtroom: Customary Law and the Control of Women in Segregation-Era Natal." *The International Journal of African Historical Studies* 28.3: 527–60.

McCoid, Catherine Hodge. 1989. "Dowry Deaths in India: A Materialist Analysis." *Women in International Development Michigan State University Working Paper # 188*. East Lansing: Michigan State University.

McCreery, John L. 1976. "Women's Property Rights and Dowry in China and South Asia." *Ethnology* 15.2: 163–74.

McRobbie, Angela. 1984. "Dance and Social Fantasy." In *Gender and Generation*, ed. Angela McRobbie and Mica Nava, 130–61. Hampshire: Macmillan.

Meillassoux, Claude. 1981. *Maidens, Meal and Money*. Cambridge: Cambridge University Press.

Merry, Sally Engle. 1995. "Resistance and the Cultural Power of Law." *Law and Society Review* 29.1: 11–26.

———. 1986. "Everyday Understandings of the Law in Working-Class America." *American Ethnologist* 13: 253–70.

———. 1982. "The Articulation of Legal Spheres." In *African Women and the Law: Historical Perspectives*, ed. Margaret Jean Hay and Marcia Wright, 68–89. Boston: Boston University Papers on Africa VII.

Metcalf, Alida C. 1990. "Women And Means: Women and Family Property in Colonial Brazil." *Journal of Social History* 24.2: 277–98.

Minister, Kristina. 1991. "A Feminist Frame for the Oral History Interview." In *Women's Words: The Feminist Practice of Oral History*, ed. Sherna Berger Gluck and Daphne Patai, 27–41. New York: Routledge.

Minow, Martha. 1991. "From Class Action to Miss Saigon: The Concept of Representation in Law." *Cleveland State Law Report* 39: 269–300.

Mitra, Manoshi. 1989. "Women In Santhal Society: Women As Property; Women and Property." *Samya Shakti* 4/5: 213–27.

Mody, Nawaz. 1987. "The Press in India: The Shah Bano Judgement and Its Aftermath." *Asian Survey* 27.8: 935–53.

Mohammed, Noor. 1984. "Battered Wives: A Study of Socially and Economically Backward People of Slum Areas" *Indian Journal of Criminology* 12.2: 102–107.

Mohanty, Chandra T. 1991. "Under Western Eyes: Feminist Scholarship and Colonial Discourses." In *Third World Women and the Politics of Feminism*, ed. Chandra T. Mohanty, Ann Russo, and Lourdes Torres, 51–80. Bloomington: Indiana University Press.

Moore, Erin P. 1993. "Gender, Power and Legal Pluralism." *American Ethnologist* 20: 522–42.

Moore, Sally Falk. 1992. "Treating Law As Knowledge: Telling Colonial Officers What to Say to Africans about Running Their Own Native Courts." *Law and Society Review* 26.1: 11–47.

Moors, Annelies. 1995. *Women, Property and Islam: Palestinian Experiences, 1920–1990.* Cambridge: Cambridge University Press.

More, J. B. P. 1995. "Christian-Muslim Influence on Pondicherry, South India." *Islam and Christian-Muslim Relations* 6.1: 63–78.

Morris, Anne, and Susan Nott. 1995. *All My Worldly Goods: A Feminist Perspective on the Legal Regulation of Wealth.* Dartmouth: Aldershot.

Mosse, David. 1994. "Idioms of Subordination and Styles of Protest among Christian and Hindu Harijan Castes in Tamil Nadu." *Contributions to Indian Sociology* (new series) 28.1: 67–106.

Mullatti, Leela. 1995. "Families in India: Beliefs and Realities." *Journal of Comparative Family Studies.* 26.1: 11–25.

Nadagouda, Sharada G. et al. 1992. "Influence of Socioeconomic Factors on the Employed Hindu Woman's Attitude towards Dowry." *Indian Journal of Social Work* 53.4: 679–88.

Nair, Janaki. 1996. *Women and Law in Colonial India.* New Delhi: Kali.

Naitao, Wu. 1990. "Disseminating the Law among Citizens." *Beijing Review* July 30: 21–24.

Narayan, Kirin. 1993. "Refractions of the Field at Home: American Representations of Hindu Holy Men in the Nineteenth and Twentieth Centuries." *Cultural Anthropology* 8.4: 476–509.

*National Perspective Plan for Women, 1988–2000.* 1988. New Delhi: Department of Women and Children.

Nazzari, Muriel. 1991. *Disappearance of the Dowry: Women, Families and Social Change in Sao Paolo, Brazil (1600–1900).* Stanford: Stanford University Press.

Ncube, Welshman. 1991. "Dealing with Inequities in Customary Law: Action, Reaction and Social Change in Zimbabwe." *International Journal of Law and the Family* 5.1: 58–79.

Newman, Katherine S. 1981. "Women and Law: Land Tenure in Africa." In *Women and World Change: Equality Issues in Development*, ed. Naomi Black and Ann Baker Cottrell, 120–38. London: Sage.

Ngwafor, Ephraim. 1990. "Cameroon: Property Rights for Women—A Bold Step in the Wrong Direction?" *Journal of Family Law* 29.2: 297–302.

Nongbri, Tiplut. 1988. "Gender and the Khasi Family Structure: Some Implications of the Meghalaya Succession To Self-Acquired Property Act, 1984." *Sociological Bulletin* 37.1–2: 71–82.

Oakley, Ann. 1981. "Interviewing Women: A Contradiction in Terms." In *Doing Feminist Research*, ed. Helen Roberts, 30–61. Boston: Routledge.

Oboler, Regina Smith. 1982. "Women, Men, Property and Change in Nandi District, Kenya." Ph.D. Dissertation. Temple University.

Ocko, Jonathan K. 1991. "Women, Property and Law in the People's Republic of China." In *Marriage and Inequality in Chinese Society*, ed. Rubie S. Watson and Patricia Buckley Ebrey, 313–46. Berkeley: University of California Press.

O'Hanlon, Rosalind. 1989. "Cultures of Rule, Communities of Resistance: Gender, Discourse and Tradition in Recent South Asian Historiographies." *Social Analysis* 25: 94–114.

Okin, Susan Moller. 1989. *Justice, Gender and the Family.* New York: Basic.

Oldenburg, Veena Talwar. 1991. "Lifestyle as Resistance: The Case of the Courtesans of Lucknow." In *Contesting Power: Resistance and Everyday Social Relations in South Asia,* eds. Douglas Haynes and Gyan Prakash, 23–61. Berkeley: University of California Press.

Omvedt, Gail. 1992. "Capitalist Agriculture and Rural Classes in India." In *Class, State and Development in India*, ed. Berch Berberoglu, 82–138. New Delhi: Sage.

O'Neill, Onora. 1990. "Justice, Gender and International Boundaries." *British Journal of Political Science* 20: 439–59.

Palriwala, Rajni. 1989. "Reaffirming the Anti-Dowry Struggle." *Economic and Political Weekly* 24: 942–44.

Parashar, Archana. 1992. *Women and Family Law Reform in India: Uniform Civil Code and Gender Equality*. New Delhi: Sage.

Parsons, Talcott. 1954. *Essays in Sociological Theory*. Glencoe, Ill.: Free Press.

Passano, Paige. 1995. "Interview: Taking Care of One's Own: A Conversation with Shamita Das Dasgupta." *Manushi* 89: 17–26.

Patai, Daphne. 1991. "U.S. Academics and Third World Women: Is Ethical Research Possible?" In *Women's Words: The Feminist Practice of Oral History*, ed. Sherna Berger Gluck and Daphne Patai, 137–53. New York: Routledge.

Patel, Vibhuti. 1989. "National Conference on Women, Religion and Family Laws in India." *The Indian Journal Of Social Work* 50.1: 125.

Pathak, Zakia, and Rajeswari Sunder Rajan. 1989. "Shahbano." *Signs*. 14: 558–82.

Patnaik, Prabhat. 1992. "A Perspective on the Recent Phase of India's Economic Development." In *Class, State and Development in India*, ed. Berch Berberoglu, 185–206. New Delhi: Sage.

Paul, Madan C. 1986. *Dowry and Position of Women in India: A Study of Delhi Metropolis*. New Delhi: Inter-India.

Pina-Cabral, Joao de. 1984. "Female Power and the Inequality of Wealth and Motherhood in Northwestern Portugal." In *Women and Property— Women As Property*, ed. Renee Hirschon, 75–91. London: Croom Helm.

Pugh, Cedric. 1991. "Housing and Land Policies in Delhi." *Journal of Urban Affairs*. 13.3: 367–82.

Radhakrishnan, Mita. 1994. "Feminism, Family and Social Change: Myths and Models." *Social Action* 44.4: 34–51.

Radway, Janice A. 1984. *Reading the Romance: Women, Patriarchy and Popular Literature*. Chapel Hill: University of North Carolina Press.

Raheja, Gloria Goodwin. 1995. " 'Crying When She's Born, and Crying When She Goes Away': Marriage and the Idiom of the Gift in Pahansu Song Performance" In *From the Margins of Hindu Marriage: Essays on Gender, Religion and Culture,* ed. Lindsey Harlan and Paul B. Courtright, 19–52. New York: Oxford University Press.

———. 1994. "Women's Speech Genres, Kinship and Contradiction." In *Women As Subjects: South Asian Histories*, ed. Nita Kumar, 49–80. Charlottesville: University Press of Virginia.

Raheja, Gloria Goodwin, and Ann Grodzins Gold. 1994. *Listen to the Heron's Words: Reimagining Gender and Kinship in North India*. Berkeley: University of California Press.

Rai, Shirin M. 1995. "Women Negotiating Boundaries: Gender, Law and the Indian State." *Social and Legal Studies* 4: 391–410.

Ram, Kalpana. 1991. "Moving in From the Margins: Gender as the Center of Cultural Contestation of Power Relations in South India." In *Intersexions: Gender/Class/Culture/Ethnicity*, ed. Gill Bottomley, Marie de Lepervanche, and Jeannie Martin, 1–13. Sydney: Allen and Unwin.

Ramamurthy, Priti. 1994. "Patriarchy and the Process of Agricultural Intensification in South India." In *Gender and Political Economy: Explorations of South Asian Systems*, ed. Alice Clark, 179–214. New Delhi: Oxford University Press.

Ramu, G. N. 1989. *Women, Work and Marriage in Urban India: A Study of Dual and Single Earner Couples*. New Delhi: Sage.

Rao, K. Ranga, and M. S. A. Rao. 1991. "Cities, Slums and Urban Development: A Case Study of a Slum in Vijayawada." In *A Reader in Urban Sociology*, ed. M. S. A. Rao, Chandrashekar Bhat, and Laxmi Narayan Kadekar, 314–34. Hyderabad: Orient Longman.

Rao, Vijayendra. 1993. "Dowry 'Inflation' in Rural India: A Statistical Investigation." *Population Studies* 47.2: 283–93.

Reinharz, Shulamit. 1979. *On Becoming a Social Scientist*. San Francisco: Jossey-Bass.

Roberts, Albert R. 1987. "Psychosocial Characteristics of Batterers: A Study of 234 Men Charged with Domestic Violence." *Journal of Family Violence* 2.1: 81–93.

Robertson, Claire. 1997. *Trouble Showed the Way: Women, Men and Trade in the Nairobi Area, 1890–1990*. Bloomingtron: Indiana University Press.

———. 1984. *Sharing the Same Bowl*. Bloomington: Indiana University Press.

Robertson, Claire, and Iris Berger, eds. 1986. *Women and Class in Africa*. New York: Africana.

Rodman, William L. 1985. "A Law unto Themselves: Legal Innovation in Ambae, Vanuatu." *American Ethnologist* 12: 603–24.

Rose, Carol M. 1992. "Women and Property: Gaining and Losing Ground." *Virginia Law Review* 78.2: 421–59.

Rosen, Lawrence. 1978. "Law and Social Change in the New Nations." *Comparative Studies in Society and History* 20.1: 3–28.

Roy, Mary. 1996. "Reader's Forum: Ants in the Pants." *Manushi* 92–93: 5.

Rubin, Gayle. 1975. "The Traffic in Women: Notes on the 'Political Economy' of Sex." In *Towards an Anthropology of Women*, ed. R. Reiter, 157–219. New York: Monthly Review.

Rudmin, Floyd Webster. 1992. "Cross-Cultural Correlates of the Ownership of Private Property." *Social Science Research* 21.1: 5–83.

Salmon, Marylynn. 1986. *Women and the Law of Property in Early America*. Chapel Hill: University of North Carolina Press.

Sanchez-Eppler, Benigno. 1992. "Telling Anthropology: Zora Neale Hurston and Gilberto Freyre Disciplined in Their Field-Home-Work." *American Literary History* 4.3: 464–88.

Sandhu, M. K. 1988. "A Study of Dowry among Working and Non-Working Women." *Indian Journal of Social Work* 49.2: 155–64.

Sandhu, Ranvinder Singh. 1987. "Not All Slums Are Alike: A Comparison of Squatter Housing in Delhi and Amritsar." *Environment and Behavior*. 19.3: 398–406.

Sangari, Kumkum. 1993. "Consent, Agency and Rhetorics of Incitement." *Economic and Political Weekly* 28.18: 867–82.

Sanghera, Jyoti, and Nirlep Malhana. 1984. "Women and Property: Implications for Organization." Paper Presented at Second National Conference on Women's Studies, Kerala University, Trivandrum, India, April 1984.

Sarkar, Lotika. 1976. "Jawaharlal Nehru and the Hindu Code Bill." In *Indian Women: From Purdah to Modernity*, 87–98. New Delhi: Vikas.

Sarkar, Tanika. 1993. "Rhetoric Against Age of Consent: Resisting Colonial Reason and Death of a Child-Wife." *Economic and Political Weekly* 28: 1867–78.

Saroja K., and S. M. Chandrika. 1991. "Income and Dowry: Some Revealing Connections." *Indian Journal of Social Work* 52.2: 205–13.

Sathe, S. P. 1992. "Sexism in Law and Justice." *Indian Journal of Social Work* 53.3: 475–83.

Sax, William S. 1991. *Mountain Goddess: Gender and Politics in a Himalayan Pilgrimage*. New York: Oxford University Press.

Scaglion, Richard. 1990. "Legal Adaptation in a Papua New Guinea Village Court." *Ethnology* 29: 17–33.

Scales, Ann C. 1986. "The Emergence of Feminist Jurisprudence: An Essay." *The Yale Law Journal* 95: 1373–1403.

Schlag, Pierre. 1994. "The Problem of the Subject." In *Postmodernism and Law,* ed. Dennis Patterson. New York: New York University Press.

Schlegel, Alice, and Rohn Eloul. 1988. "Marriage Transactions: Labor, Property, Status." *American Anthropologist* 90.2: 291–309.

Schuler, Margaret, ed. 1986. *Empowerment and the Law: Strategies of Third World Women*. Washington, D.C.: OEF International.

Schuler, Margaret, and Shakuntala Kadirgamar-Rajasingham, ed. 1992. *Legal Literacy: A Tool for Women's Empowerment*. Washington, D.C.: OEF International.

Schuler, Sidney. 1987. *The Other Side of Polyandry: Property, Stratification and Nonmarriage in the Nepal Himalayas*. Boulder, Colo.: Westview.

Scott, James C. 1990. *Domination and the Arts of Resistance: Hidden Transcripts*. New Haven, Colo.: Yale University Press.

———. 1986. "Everyday Forms of Peasant Resistance." In *Everyday Forms of Peasant Resistance in South-East Asia,* eds. James C. Scott and Benedict J. Tria Kerkvliet, 5–35. London: Frank Cass.

Sethi, Raj Mohini, and Kiran Sibia. 1987. "Women and Hindu Personal Laws: A Sociolegal Analysis." *Journal of Sociological Studies* 6: 101–13.

Shanley, Mary Lyndon. 1989. *Feminism, Marriage and the Law in Victorian England, 1850–1895*. Princeton, N.J.: Princeton University Press.

———. 1986. "Suffrage, Protective Labor Legislation, and Married Women's Property Laws in England." *Signs* 12.1: 62–77.

Sharma, Abha, and Rajlakshmi Shriram. 1979. "Opinions of Married Couples Regarding the Selection of Marriage Partner: A Study of Couples Residing in Baroda." *Sociological Bulletin* 28.1–2: 71–82.

Sharma, Neena. 1985. *Political Socialization and Its Impact on Attitudinal Change towards Social and Political System: A Case Study of Harijan Women of Delhi*. Delhi: Inter-India Publications.

Sharma, Ursula. 1994. "Dowry in North India: Its Consequences for Women." In *Family, Kinship and Marriage in India*, ed. Patricia Uberoi, 341–56. Delhi: Oxford University Press.

———. 1980. *Women, Work and Property in Northwest India*. London: Tavistock.

Shastri, Madhu. 1990. *Status of Hindu Women: A Study of Legislative Trends and Judicial Behavior*. Jaipur: RBSA.

Shields, Vickie Rutledge, and Brenda Dervin. 1993. "Sense-Making in Feminist Social Science Research: A Call to Enlarge the Methodological Options of Feminist Studies" *Women's Studies International Forum* 16.1: 65–81.

Shukla, Sonal. 1987. "Dowry in Bombay: Some Observations." *Vikasini*: 64–80.

Singh, Indu Prakash. 1989. *Women, Law and Social Change in India*. New Delhi: Radiant.

Singha, Radhika. 1996. "Making the Domestic More Domestic: Criminal Law and the 'Head of the Household,' 1772–1843." *The Indian Economic and Social History Review* 33.3: 309–43.

Sivaramayya, B. 1983. "Law, Status of Women and Social Change." *Journal of Indian Law Institute* 25.2: 270–88.

———. 1971. "Women's Rights of Inheritance and Fragmentation of Agricultural Landholdings: Some Observations." *Supreme Court Journal* II of 1971: 6–9.

Smart, Carol. 1995. *Law, Crime and Sexuality: Essays in Feminism*. London: Sage.

———. 1989. *Feminism and the Power of Law*. London: Routledge.

———. 1984. *The Ties That Bind: Law, Marriage and the Reproduction of Patriarchal Relations*. London: Routledge.

Snow, David A., Robert D. Benford, and Leon Anderson. 1986. "Fieldwork Roles and Informational Yield: A Comparison of Alternative Settings and Roles." *Urban Life* 14.4: 377–408.

Som, Reba. 1994. "Jawaharlal Nehru and the Nehru Code: A Victory of Symbol over Substance?" *Modern Asian Studies* 28: 165–94.

Spaulding, Jay. 1982. "The Misfortunes of Some—The Advantages of Others: Land Sales by Women in Sinnar." In *African Women and the Law: Historical Perspectives*, ed. Margaret Jean Hay and Marcia Wright, 3–18. Boston: Boston University Papers on Africa VII.

Spivak, Gayatri Chakravorty. 1988. "Can the Subaltern Speak?" In *Marxism and the Interpretation of Culture*, ed. Cary Nelson and Lawrence Grossberg, 271–316. Urbana: University of Illinois Press.

Sprecher, Susan, and Rachita Chandak. 1992. "Attitudes about Arranged Marriages and Dating among Men and Women from India." *Free Inquiry in Creative Sociology* 20.1: 59–69.

Srinivas, M. N. 1984. *Some Reflections on Dowry*. Delhi: Oxford University Press.

Stacey, Judith. 1991. "Can There Be a Feminist Ethnography?" In *Women's Words: The Feminist Practice of Oral History*, ed. Sherna Berger Gluck and Daphne Patai, 111–19. New York: Routledge.

Starr, June. 1984. "The Legal and Social Transformation of Rural Women in Aegean Turkey." In *Women and Property—Women As Property*, ed. Renee Hirschon, 92–116. London: Croom Helm.

Starr, June, and Jane F. Collier, eds. 1989. *History and Power in the Study of Law: New Directions in Legal Anthropology*. Ithaca, N.Y.: Cornell University Press.

Staves, Susan. 1990. *Married Women's Separate Property in England, 1660–1833*. Cambridge: Harvard University Press.

Stefanizzi, Sonia, and Laura Terragni. 1993. "Marital Violence in Milan: The Results of an Empirical Research Project." *Sociologia del Dritto* 20.3: 45–68.

Stein, Dorothy. 1988. "Burning Widows, Burning Brides: The Perils of Daughterhood in India." *Pacific Affairs* 61.3: 465–85.

Strauss, Murray A., Richard J. Gelles, and Suzanne K. Steinmetz. 1988. *Behind Closed Doors: Violence in the American Family*. Newbury Park: Sage.

Szelenyi, Szonja. 1992. "Economic Subsystems and the Occupational Structure: A Comparison of Hungary and the United States." *Sociological Forum*. 7: 563–85.

Tambiah, Stanley J. 1989. "Bridewealth and Dowry Revisited: The Position of Women in Sub-Saharan Africa and North India." *Current Anthropology* 30.4: 413–35.

Tapper, Nancy. 1991. *Bartered Brides: Politics, Gender and Marriage in an Afghan Tribal Society*. Cambridge: Cambridge University Press.

Teja, Mohinderjit Kaur. 1993. *Dowry: A Study in Attitudes and Practices*. New Delhi: Inter-India.

Thorbek, Susanne. 1994. *Gender and Slum Culture in Urban Asia*. Trans. Brian Fredsfod. London: Zed.

Thorne, Barrie. 1983. "Political Activist as Participant Observer: Conflicts of Commitment in a Study of the Draft Resistance Movement of the 1960s." *Contemporary Field Research: A Collection of Readings*, ed. Robert M. Emerson, 216–34. Boston: Little.

Thornton, Margaret. 1991. "Feminism and the Contradictions of Law Reform." *International Journal of the Sociology of Law* 19.4: 453–74.

Tiffany, Sharon W. 1983. "Customary Land Disputes, Courts and African Models in the Solomon Islands." *Oceania* 53: 277–90.

Toungara, Jeanne Maddox. 1994. "Inventing the African Family: Gender and Family Law Reform in Cote d'Ivoire." *Journal of Social History* 28: 37–61.

Trautmann, Thomas R. 1981. *Dravidian Kinship.* Cambridge: Cambridge University Press.

Tripathi, Shrish Mani. 1987. "The Supreme Court for Indians: Spotlight on Public Interest Litigation." *Journal of Sociological Studies* 6: 141–61.

Uberoi, Patricia, ed. 1996. "Hindu Marriage Law and the Judicial Construction of Sexuality." In *Feminist Terrains in Legal Domains,* ed. Ratna Kapur, 184–209. New Delhi: Kali.

———. 1994. *Family, Kinship and Marriage in India.* Delhi: Oxford University Press.

United Nations. 1985. *The State of the World's Women 1985,* World Conference to Review and Appraise the Achievements of the United Nations Decade for Women, Nairobi, Kenya, July 15–26, 1985.

U.N. Committee on Elimination of Discrimination against Women: Report of the Ninth Session. 1990. New York: United Nations.

U.N. Economic and Social Commission for Asia and the Pacific: Guidelines on Upgrading the Legal Status Of Women. 1989. New York: United Nations.

Upadhya, Carol Boyack. 1990. "Dowry and Women's Property in Coastal Andhra Pradesh." *Contributions to Indian Sociology* 24.1: 29–59.

Vaghela, Ramesh P. 1988. "Muslim Women's Act: A Misinterpreted Law." *Lex Et Juris* 3.2: 22–25, 43.

Van Willingen, John, and V. C. Channa. 1991. "Law, Custom and Crimes against Women: The Problem of Dowry Death in India." *Human Organization* 50.4: 369–77.

Vatuk, Sylvia. 1975. "Gifts and Affines in North India." *Contributions to Indian Sociology, n.s.* 9: 155–96.

Verghese, Jamila. 1980. *Her Gold and Her Body.* Ghaziabad: Vikas.

Vlassof, Carol. 1990. "The Value of Sons in an Indian Village: How Widows See It." *Population Studies* 44.1: 5–20.

Vining, Joseph. 1986. *The Authoritative and the Authoritarian.* Chicago: University of Chicago Press.

Viswanathan, Susan. 1989. "Marriage, Birth and Death: Property Rights and Domestic Relationships of the Orthodox/Jacobite Christians of Kerala." *Economic and Political Weekly* 24: 1341–46.

Wadley, Susan S. 1995. "No Longer a Wife: Widows in Rural North India" In *From the Margins of Hindu Marriage: Essays on Gender, Religion and Culture,* ed. Lindsey Harlan and Paul B. Courtright, 92–115. New York: Oxford University Press.

Walby, Sylvia. 1986. "Gender, Class and Stratification: Towards a New Approach." In *Gender and Stratification*, ed. Rosemary Crompton and Michael Mann, 23–39. Cambridge, UK: Polity.

Watson, Rubie S. 1991. "Marriage and Gender Inequality." In *Marriage and Inequality in Chinese Society*, ed. Rubie S. Watson and Patricia Buckley Ebrey, 347–68. Berkeley: University of California Press.

West, Jackie. 1978. "Women, Sex and Class." In *Feminism and Materialism: Women and Modes of Production*, ed. Annette Kuhn and Annemarie Wolpe, 220–53. London: Routledge.

West, Robin. 1993. "Jurisprudence and Gender." In *Feminist Legal Theory: Foundations*, ed. D. Kelly Weisberg, 75–98. Philadelphia: Temple University Press.

Westwood, Sallie. 1984. "'Fear Woman': Property and Modes of Production in Urban Ghana." In *Women and Property—Women As Property*, ed. Renee Hirschon, 140–57. London: Croom Helm.

White, James Boyd. 1990. *Justice As Translation: An Essay in Cultural and Legal Criticism*. Chicago: University of Chicago Press.

White, Lucie E. 1990. "Subordination, Rhetorical Survival Skills, and Sunday Shoes: Notes on the Hearing of Mrs. G." *Buffalo Law Review* 38.1:1–58.

White, Sarah C. 1993. *Arguing with the Crocodile: Gender and Class in Bangladesh*. London: Zed.

Whitehead, Ann. 1984a. "Women and Men; Kinship and Property: Some General Issues." In *Women and Property—Women As Property*, ed. Renee Hirschon, 176–92. London: Croom Helm.

———. 1984b. "'I'm Hungry, Mum: The Politics of Domestic Budgeting." In *of Marriage and the Market: Women's Subordination Internationally and Its Lessons*, ed. Kate Young, Carol Wolkowitz, and Roslyn McCullagh, 93–116. London: Routledge.

Williams, Patricia. 1991. *The Alchemy of Race and Rights: Diary of a Law Professor*. Cambridge: Harvard University Press.

Woolf, Virginia. 1929. *A Room of One's Own*. New York: Harcourt, Brace and Company.

*World Development Report 1994: Infrastructure for Development*. 1994. Washington, D.C.: Published for World Bank by Oxford University Press.

Wynter, Pauline. 1990. "Property, Women Fishers and Struggle for Women's Rights in Mozambique." *Sage* 7.1: 33.

Yngvesson, Barbara. 1990. "Contextualizing the Court: Comments on the Cultural Study of Litigation." *Law and Society Review* 24.2: 467–77.

Zetkin, Klara. 1984. *Selected Writings*. Ed. Philip S. Foner. New York: International.

# Index

302 INDEX